THE FOOLISHNESS OF GOD

THE FOOLISHNESS OF GOD

is wiser than men

Kenneth R. Adams

CHRISTIAN LITERATURE CRUSADE
Fort Washington, Pennsylvania 19034

CHRISTIAN LITERATURE CRUSADE
Fort Washington, Pennsylvania 19034

CANADA
Elgin, Ontario K0G 1 E0

GREAT BRITAIN
The Dean, Alresford, Hampshire

AUSTRALIA
P.O. Box 91, Pennant Hills, N.S.W. 2120

DEDICATION

Dedicated to my personal "Seven Sisters":
Georgina Emma—my godly, selfless mother
Gladys, Doris and Marjorie—caring sisters
Bessie Jane—beloved wife and wise encourager
Margaret and Janet—vivacious daughters who brighten and
broaden Mom and Dad's outlook on life.

MY SINCERE THANKS...

To Kathleen Whittle for the many hours given, typing the original manuscript, handling all the changes and corrections, and producing the final copy for typesetting. Even with the aid of your word processor it has been a big task.

To Leslie Coley of CLC U.K., John Davey and Percy Page of CLC Canada, Bob Gerry, John Whittle and Ron Zuck of CLC U.S.A., Norman Grubb of WEC, and Pat Gower, one of CLC's many "helps"—for all your untiring assistance in bringing the record to completion.

To my wonderful co-worker and beloved wife Bessie, for your chapter-by-chapter review, wise guidance and enthusiastic encouragement day by day.

To all the CLC family, past and present, who have made this story possible by your obedience to the Captain.

Christ—Books that Bless—Submitting to the Fellowship—
Only One Culture—Still Learning

SECTION III   A TREE...BEARS FRUIT IN HIS SEASON
—Psalm 1:3

Impact—The Life Counts—Sharing Together Enthusiastically—Encouraging Results—The Secret—In the Service of
the King Together

FOREWORD

What joy I have in writing the foreword to this record of the Christian Literature Crusade by its human founder, Ken Adams. I was with Bessie and Ken forty-one years ago in that room in Colchester when the Lord gave the vision of starting this Crusade—just these two young people in the midst of World War II in that small garrison town in eastern England. Now we compare it with its worldwide spread of today!

My chief joy is that this is a story not of a movement but of a man, and then men, to which the title can boldly be given of "The foolishness of God," adding the remainder of that saying of Paul's—"which is wiser than men!" For this has always been God's way throughout history—the work of God through the men of God. "There was a man sent from God..."; "Come now, I will send thee"; "Here am I, send me." Sometimes, as now, He works through a youth whom the Spirit has caught hold of in his early days, like Joseph or Daniel, and indeed the Savior Himself. I personally saw that young couple with their worldwide literature vision starting out in one small room with a borrowed £100 worth of books that pointed to Christ; Ken himself trundling all their earthly possessions in a handcart from this one room to their first shop; and the magnificent office of this "Crusade" being a table nailed to the wall to give it support! All this happened in days of war when government restrictions severely limited opening bookstores or publishing books.

I am so thankful that from those first days they were not only "obedient to the heavenly vision," but also to the ways of God laid down in the Scriptures for the provision of all material supplies: "Take no thought, saying, What shall we eat? or, What shall we drink?...but seek ye first the kingdom of God and His righteousness [His right ways], and all these things shall be added unto you." As they started out by conforming to that principle of earthly provision, indeed with many privations and in cramped quarters, so they and the whole company of Crusaders, now increasing to nearly six hundred in forty-six countries with an annual turnover of millions of dollars, walk this same way of faith and sacrifice. You will read the story told in Ken's own personal terms of what we can only call miracle after miracle in country after country. It is like reading another section of the Acts of the Apostles, a thousand miles from a dry account of mere book distribution.

Two other facts are a special joy to me. One is that faith is evidenced by good works, and God's people should be the best at their practical jobs in the world. Ken himself rapidly acquired expertise in the ramifications of book salesmanship. Then he saw to it that the enlarging staff was also trained in the same efficiency while maintaining a personal witness to the Savior to whom the books point, sometimes leading customers to Christ.

My other special personal joy is that Ken and the CLC started its life linked with the Worldwide Evangelization Crusade (to which I have belonged for my lifetime). Thus they were soaked in the principles of faith, fellowship, and sacrifice of its founder C.T. Studd, even while moving on—as we always aimed that it should—to become its own Christian Literature Crusade. Because of these close bonds with the WEC, there has been forged a link of special fellowship between the two.

So as the story unfolds, you will see the outflowing rivers of the Spirit through the numerous fellow-Crusaders, the vine of the Lord's planting with its branches spread widely over the wall— international, interracial, neither male nor female, a glorious present-day witness to that "foolishness of God which is wiser than men."

I had the privilege of writing the first story of the developing Crusade, called *Leap of Faith*. Now with Ken's fully expanded and vividly personal record of its whole history (always in cooperation with the whole Body of Christ in all its outreaches), we can watch as area after area sends its call "Come over and help us," and as occupied countries greatly enlarge their literature distribution. Truly our CLC, by each new venture of faith and expansion, will continue to be CLC Unlimited!

Norman Grubb
Fort Washington, Pennsylvania 19034

A PERSONAL NOTE OF EXPLANATION

The story you are about to read has been long in unfolding, as you will discover—nearly sixty years! Looking forward, it would have seemed an eternity to my boyish mind. Looking back, it is a mere sixty seconds—in the light of eternity!

I have revelled in the writing. How good God has been to me—to us, Bessie and me. Never once since the day we met did we dream of all that was ahead. Of course, we have touched the highlights only, but every specific detail, leading to each mountain top, has been just as exciting.

I hope we will have succeeded in making you "feel" this excitement. On the other hand, be prepared for some surprises—and some shocks!

The heart of the story is people. Not just the two Adamses, for over the years eight or nine hundred have linked arms and hearts with us. Together we have shared in the adventures, fulfilling a role "for such a time as this," to help get vital Christian literature to the ever-increasing literate world.

Yes, serving the literate WORLD. Does that surprise you? Multiplied thousands know of CLC (Christian Literature Crusade), having read books distributed or published by us. They have visited one or more of our 150 bookcenters or ordered books through the mail, never realizing that this Christian business enterprise is essentially a missionary society—a CRUSADE, with the book as the tool, the "weapon of our warfare."

And that's where you may be in for a shock! CLC is a missionary society with a difference. We are nonconformists, in principle, in practice and in methods, and yet—at least *we* think—the results are convincing!

We also have touched on just a few of the gracious dealings

of the Lord in our own lives—the prunings, the moldings, and the remoldings. Without them the book might not have been written. And there are more chapters to come! This is an on-going story. Indeed, even during the writing some changes in the text had to be made to keep the record as factual and up-to-date as possible. New developments are even now taking place.

Our hope is that God will use this book to encourage you and spur you on to personally prove that "greater is He that is in you, than he that is in the world." He is "the same yesterday, today and forever"; the same trustworthy One, living His life through each member of the family.

Ken and Bessie Adams
314 Wesley Avenue
Ocean City, N.J. 08226
September, 1981

SECTION I

SOIL FOR THE GREEN SHOOT
Mark 4:30-31

And he said, To what shall we liken the kingdom of God? Or with what comparison shall we compare it? It is like a grain of mustard seed, which, when it is sown in the earth, is less than all the seeds that are in the earth.

Mark 4:30, 31

1

NURTURED AND ADMONISHED

The usually boisterous English Channel was exceptionally calm on that moonlit evening in July 1934. It was an encouraging start to my first venture from the shores of my native England. Earlier in the year I had been in touch with missionaries from Spain who had suggested I should consider visiting them during their workers' annual get-together. The two-week conference was to be held in Marin in the northwest corner of Spain.

To prepare for this adventure I had purchased a used Royal Enfield motorcycle. And apart from this journey across the Channel, I would do the whole trip by road. The overnight Channel crossing was uneventful, and after a hearty breakfast I set out for the city of Rouen, carefully following the explicit instructions prepared for me by the British Automobile Association.

There were some testing experiences along the way. For instance, when the intake valve broke I spent some frustrating hours trying to explain the problem to a none-too-patient French mechanic, waiting for the repair to be completed and then bargaining about the price! Yet, altogether the journey was without serious problem. Indeed it grew more exciting as the miles slipped by. Crossing the Pyrenees Mountains with their hairpin bends was a challenge to a nineteen-year-old motor bike enthusiast—but we made it, to the surprise and relief of some of the older members of the missionary band gathered at the Spanish conference.

Although the ten days with this group were inspiring, for me the outstanding incident occurred when one of the younger missionaries asked if I would transport him to a village about twenty-five miles away. We arrived safely and parked the motor bike in the village plaza. But the missionary requested that I not accompany him on his visit to the family, who were showing a growing interest in spiritual things. He felt that my presence, as a stranger and without the Spanish language, would defeat the purpose of the visit. Instead he, wisely, left me with a handful of gospel tracts in Spanish. I had a very eventful hour communicating with these new friends, not by word of mouth—except the odd greeting or two—but by the printed page.

Those silent messengers would continue to communicate long after we were back at base. Now I felt I had done at least one piece of genuine missionary service, passing along some living literature to searching minds and hearts.

The significance of this one incident was to fall into place later in the constant unfolding of God's total plan for my life.

It all started, of course, nineteen years earlier when on October 11, 1914 I appeared on the scene, the fifth and last child born to Alfred and Georgina Adams. Apparently I was not a robust boy. My brother, their first born, had died when he was only eleven months old and my mother must have wondered if her only other son was also to be short-lived. The doctor diagnosed tuberculosis and my mother was advised to move from the fogs of London to the seaside resort of Westcliff-on-Sea where the tides of the North Sea, as they enter the mouth of the River Thames, recede more than a mile, leaving health-giving ozones to impregnate the atmosphere and administer health to people like me.

This was not the only problem causing concern in our household. Just what the basic domestic trouble was I never learned, but apparently my father volunteered his services to help in World War I. A number of years were spent on the island of Malta; so he was away from home all the war years. Indeed, I only remember meeting him twice, once at about age five, when we were visiting my grandmother in Tottenham, north

London. It was not until I was nearly ten years of age that we met again. Apparently a serious attempt at reconciliation was made between my parents but, unfortunately, it did not succeed, and I was to be robbed of the help and guidance of a father in my formative years.

I never saw him again, but my mother rose to the challenge. She became mother and father, breadwinner and spiritual head. Her confidence had been a personal daily faith in the God of her fathers. Grandpa Heinkle was of German ancestry. He knew how to *stand and withstand,* and as a result of his bold witness for Jesus Christ was ostracized by his family. Obviously much of his strength of character had been passed on to his daughter, and the four of us children were the ever grateful benefactors. Ultimately each of us entered full-time Christian service. Gladys, after years of faithful service in North Africa and France, is now with the Lord. Doris, Marjorie and myself are still on the firing line.

My cherished memories are of my mother's love, protection and advice; of the many times I was able to confide in her and depend on her; of the tasks she performed so untiringly to make me a better boy and man. Undoubtedly the most valued possession in the world is someone who cares. I had that in my dear mother. As the years unfolded I constantly strove to aim high in appreciation of her love for I wanted her to be as proud of me as I am of her.

I believe the most fruitful part of her training and example was her love and enthusiasm for her Lord and for the work of His kingdom and His church around the world. She was so hospitable to the Lord's servants that our house never seemed to be empty of visiting preachers and missionaries, especially over weekends. A lasting memory of my early years was a three-day visit to the Westminster Central Hall in London to share in the Annual Missionary Convention of the group to which we belonged at that time, the Plymouth Brethren. The place was filled to overflowing with more than 5,000 people and I can remember sitting high in one of the balconies peering down to the faraway speaker on the main platform. A pair of binoculars would have helped to bring the speakers into better focus! I hung on every word as one after another shared the stories of the battle and blessing, failures and fruit of missionary endeavors in country after country.

Because of my poor health and consequently limited education, not starting school until I was almost eight years old, I became an avid reader. *Pilgrim's Progress* was one of the first books I tackled. It was the forerunner of many more books recounting progress. Biographies were my main diet. I was fascinated by the way each person made headway step by step, and when those steps were clearly ordered by the Lord then meaningful lives developed. The two sizeable volumes of Hudson Taylor's life and his far-reaching ministry into inland China left indelible impressions. The first volume, *The Growth of a Soul,* was even more meaningful to me than the second volume, *The Growth of a Work.* I began to see in my limited way that the growth and maturing of the spirit was more important than the growth and development of the work. Indeed it almost seemed as though the growth of any work of God would be dependent upon the measure of spiritual growth.

So, with all this influence of a godly mother, a Christian home, and volumes of Christian literature, it was not surprising that at an early age I had my personal encounter with Jesus Christ—and to the measure I understood it, it was to be a lifetime contract. The thrust of the evening gospel message which the Lord used was, "Is your name written in the Lamb's Book of Life?" Charles Hickman was by no means a children's preacher, but that night the Holy Spirit was able to get through to an eight-year-old lad in no uncertain way. The question was simple enough, and I had no difficulty in answering it: "No, my name is not written in the Lamb's Book of Life."

My very willingness to answer was indicative of a desire to change the status quo. That night by my bedside I thanked the Lord Jesus for the sacrifice He had willingly made for me, and I asked Him to write my name in His book. I told Him my name was Kenneth Raymond Adams. I wanted there to be no confusion when the records were searched at a later date!

Along with that conversion experience two other things happened in quick succession. That same night before my prayer was concluded, I told the Lord, "From now on, You can count on me!" The fact that He had readily written my name in His Book of Life and made me the immediate possessor of His marvelous gift of eternal life meant, on my part, that I considered I was automatically enrolling in His army for service. This was a moment of serious and irrevocable commitment, both on the Lord's part and on mine.

Just minutes after this dual transaction was completed, I put action to my words. My sister, Marjorie, twenty-one months my senior, was told what had transpired in those last few minutes and she, too, met the Lord Jesus as her personal Saviour and life partner then and there in her bedroom. Next, we had to share the good news with Mother and sister Doris downstairs. That was a joyful evening at our home and in the courts of heaven, to be sure!

The next day there was a third understanding of what had transpired the night before. Sitting at my desk in school the thought came to me, "Ken, now that you are a Christian because of what happened last night, you won't be able to cheat any more!" Frankly, I was not aware I was in the cheating business, but what was coming home to me quite clearly was that not only had my sins been forgiven and not only had I enlisted in the army of the Lord, but that this new relationship meant a new law of uprightness was now operative and was to make itself apparent in every walk of life. God was now my Father. Jesus Christ was the Lord and Captain of my life. I had now set my feet firmly and resolutely on the highway of our God called "the way of holiness."

From now on I could and would live the expectant life. My Captain would certainly issue orders and it would be my duty to respond promptly.

Nothing dramatic happened. It was just steady progress. Two

years after this experience I was baptized, believing this to be a further step of obedience and a public affirmation of the new life I was now enjoying. It was beginning to work just as Paul said it would: "I live; yet not I, but Christ lives in me; and the life which I now live in the flesh, I live by the faith of the Son of God." It was getting exciting, this life of daily expectation, and I was to learn much more!

Through home and church activities—Sunday School, youth gatherings, and the main services—through fellowship and sharing with young people of similar convictions, and through my own personal reading and studying of God's Word and good books, I was growing stronger each day. I slowly understood and experienced this principle of living "by the faith of the Son of God" as it began to operate through my own little personality. By the age of twelve I preached my first sermon—well, not exactly mine, for if I remember correctly it was at one of the midweek meetings, and my talk was taken almost completely from one of Andrew Murray's books on prayer! Frankly, I do not believe the message got across very well, but it was a beginning! From then on more opportunities came to share my faith, not only in church activities but on street corners, and during the summer months on the main promenade at Southend-on-Sea.

2

IMPLANTED DESIRES

At fourteen a drastic change in lifestyle took place. I left school in early June of 1929 and spent the rest of the month job hunting. My ambition was to become "a city gentleman," so I scanned the London newspapers and soon had several interviews lined up by the time I was ready to take the forty-five mile train journey to the Big City. I returned home with two jobs at which I was to start the following Monday morning!

Of course, I shared the good news with Mother. "How do you plan to work at two jobs in different locations at the same time?" was her reaction. Logical reasoning to be sure, although I had missed it in the excitement of the prospect of working in London. As I considered the matter, I soon found that another principle of this new life in Christ was to be obeyed. One job would pay almost 15 per cent more than the other, but I would have to work one hour longer each day. This meant that I could not get home in time to continue attending most of the activities at my church during the week—the prayer meeting on Tuesdays, the Bible study on Thursdays and especially the midweek youth service on Wednesdays in which I helped. So the issue was clear. Would I go for the higher wage and possible quicker promotion, or the lower wage which would enable me to keep involved in my Christian activities?

The Captain's word was clear—"Put Me first." Take the job with lesser pay and maintain your spiritual commitments. More than five years later this same principle was to become a pivotal turning point in my whole future.

My dear mother's life motto was becoming a basic guideline

for me also. The words skillfully etched in old English lettering by a cousin and set in an attractive frame hung in a prominent place in our home—"That in all things He might have the preeminence." It was not just a motto on a wall but a way of life for a godly woman.

I shall ever be grateful for the spiritual enrichment I received during my teen years. The Word of God was becoming very real, and I read it through for the first time during my two hour-long train journeys each day. Books were becoming increasingly important to me, too. Study books assisted me in my personal digging into God's Word. I also continued to read biographies.

I did not realize any particular significance at the time, but the job which I had taken was located within walking distance of St. Paul's Cathedral, and on the opposite side of the Cathedral was Paternoster Row which, in those days, was a focal point for evangelical publishers and bookstores. Many days I would spend at least half of my lunch hour browsing and buying. When I found a particularly exciting book I would share the good news with the young people back home. Indeed, it wasn't long before I actually carried a small supply of books in my home as a sort of book agent. Then when someone expressed a desire to have a copy I was able to make one immediately available.

Along with taking in there was abundant opportunity for giving out. Doors opened for speaking in country churches and on Saturdays there were the street meetings at a strategic corner on High Street, Southend-on-Sea. From Easter to the end of October the weekends were spent on the main promenade, for Southend was the nearest seaside resort to London and holiday makers poured in by the thousands, especially over the long weekends when Monday was a national holiday. On those occasions it was a very full weekend for our youth group, preaching the good news five times—Saturday and Sunday evenings, and morning, afternoon and evening on the Monday.

Those were great days. Literally several hundred people would gather around to listen to these young people sharing their faith. As each meeting came to a close a little gospel booklet such as *God's Way of Salvation* or *Safety, Certainty and Enjoyment* or *The Reason Why* was offered to any who were interested. We kept our eye on those who had taken booklets and talked with them as soon as the meeting was finished. Many times we had the joy of leading people to a personal knowledge of Jesus Christ as Saviour and Lord.

Other activities developed. Saturday afternoons we would cycle out to nearby villages and meet in the village square or at some other suitable gathering place. On other occasions we went to a nearby Gypsy encampment. As we grew in experience more opportunities opened up. We began Sunday after-church rallies in a central public hall. The place was filled to overflowing with more than five hundred people each week and many decisions were registered. The news of this spread, and similar opportunities opened up as far away as the university city of Cambridge.

During these years some of the older young people were responding to God's call to full-time Christian service, both in the homeland and overseas. My oldest sister, Gladys, had already begun her missionary service in North Africa. One of my Sunday School teachers, Harold Wildish, set out for missionary service in Brazil, penetrating deep into tribal areas of the upper Amazon River. Later he was to spend many fruitful years in the islands of the West Indies. Godfrey Robinson left for Spurgeon's College and later became an outstanding Baptist minister. Jack and Margaret Hume, who had been leaders in the youth activities, left for distant shores and established a vital ministry in New Zealand. Others maintained their business careers but kept their sharp cutting-edge for God.

Now at nineteen I, too, was anticipating some further personal direction from my Captain.

3

FURTHER TRAINING

The trip to Spain had made an indelible impression on me
and I enjoyed sharing the experiences of my visit and the challenge of missionary outreach in Spain as opportunities opened
up. Strangely, though, I felt no leading to any specific involvement in overseas missionary service. It was my growing interest
in Christian literature which was coming into sharper focus. I
believed that a Christian bookstore could help me continue my
personal witness to those needing to find God and that books
would also strengthen the spiritual life of those who had already
found Him. Thus, toward the end of 1934 I left my London job
and prepared to open a Christian bookshop in my hometown.

Once again I found my dear mother keenly interested in the
proposition and ready to help with some finances which I believe
came from borrowing on an insurance policy. So, just in time to
catch the Christmas business, a small lock-up shop was opened.
After Christmas we moved to a better location at 585 London
Road, Westcliff-on-Sea, where we not only had the shop but
living quarters above. The months of 1935 proved to be a year of
struggle with this new venture, but it was also a year of spiritual
expansion.

My missionary interests were growing. Three groups headed
the list—the China Inland Mission, Regions Beyond Missionary
Union, and the Worldwide Evangelization Crusade. The WEC
was in the throes of a big faith undertaking, building a new
headquarters complex in Upper Norwood, south London.
Young people like Ena Bush and John Lewis, who lived in the
same general area, would come into my shop and bubble over

(especially Ena!) with excitement about this fascinating faith venture.

Remarkably, each new candidate had a particular trade and arrived at the Crusade's London base just when his services were needed—masons, plumbers, electricians, welders, etc. Funds, too, were "prayed in," often arriving just in time to keep the bills paid as the work progressed. The building inspector said he had never seen such enthusiasm and such thorough workmanship before!

I was fascinated by these running commentaries!

As my first full year of business came to a close, it seemed the time had come for me to add to my stock some non-religious lines to help bring in more customers and more money. I was considering a third move and had already looked over possible premises in a much better location. Then the Captain's voice was heard again. I must admit I had not been particularly prayerful about this anticipated enlargement, although I was motivated by the conviction that success in business would mean I could channel more money into God's work and particularly into the world-wide missionary outreach.

That sounded plausible enough, and I know that I was genuine in my intention, but it was not God's way for me.

He didn't want to run *my* business for me! And so His word was clear: "I want you out of your personal business enterprise and into the program I have foreordained for you. Your next step is Bible School—the Faith Mission Bible College in Edinburgh, Scotland."

Naturally I again turned to my human counselor, Mother. After all, she was vitally interested in this literature ministry and it was her financial help which had made it possible. What would she say to this sudden change of direction?

I can still remember that Sunday evening vividly. Sitting around a cozy fire in the living room above the bookstore, I shared these thoughts of what seemed to be the new direction the Captain was giving. Her conclusion was so typical: "Son, if this is what God wants for you, then that is what you must do."

There was no thought of herself, even though I was the only male member of the family and in the last few years had carried increasing responsibility for some of our family matters. Yet unhesitatingly it was again "that *in all things* He must have the pre-eminence."

Now, what about the disposition of the business? What about the funds that would be needed for Bible School?

These and other questions seemed to have no immediate answer. Yet the attitude was the same—if this is what God is asking then He will have His own provision ready just as each need arises. How true her words proved to be! How far-reaching was the decision now being made!

An indication of the Lord's deliverance was not long in coming. A friend of the family in his early seventies heard about this plan to close the bookshop and returned in a few days to share his idea. He would buy our stock. He knew of a shop available in another location which would still serve the general area and he also knew of a young man, John Whittle, who could run the shop. Soon the transfer of the business and payment of all outstanding bills was completed. We were so glad that this bookstore ministry would be maintained.

At the same time I was in touch with the Faith Mission College and indicated on my application papers that my two years with them were primarily for training in readiness for anticipated missionary service in Spain. Soon after Easter, 1936, all arrangements had been completed and I was on my way to Edinburgh, Scotland. Actually in those days the training program was quite a bit different from today! Just nine months were spent in the lecture rooms and with the books, the other fifteen months were spent in practical outworking of what we had learned from the Word.

During the summer several students were teamed up and spent a couple of months in evangelism. My first summer was in the north of England at Newbiggin-by-the-Sea where we had daily open air services on the beach for both children and adults. The second summer, four of us were assigned to a tent campaign in the southeast of Scotland. Later this was to prove very significant for me.

During both these summer assignments we saw people finding the Lord and Christians being built up in the faith. In the autumn Tom Morgan and I were sent to northeast Scotland in the County of Angus. For the first month we were in a village called Friockheim, about twenty-five miles from Dundee. We were on loan to the Angus Christian Union and the Secretary warned us that this village was *the hardest place in the county.* We were to go from door to door with tracts and booklets and see what we could do on a one-to-one basis to introduce needy hearts to Jesus Christ.

I was back with literature again!

By the end of the first week every home had been visited and literature had been placed in those homes. Then we went around the village a second time the following week and received a slightly warmer reception. The children and young people particularly were intrigued by these two "Pilgrims"—the official title of Faith Mission workers. We soon felt that the young people were to be the key to cracking open this *hard* situation, so we spent time with them on Saturdays on their ball field and began to win their confidence. Next, we rented a local village hall and gathered the young people under the sound of the gospel. We then went for the adults and soon had nearly one hundred coming out night after night to hear the gospel. Praise God many lives were touched.

My final assignment was on the west coast of Scotland in the Kintyre Peninsula and some of the outer islands. Bill Black, an Irish lad, was my fellow worker this time. We started out in the village of Auchmithy and then went to Campbeltown at the southern end of the peninsula. Here the campaign was to last two weeks, but God's blessing was so evident that we continued for another two weeks. Some of the older residents told us that never had there been such crowds to a religious meeting since the days of Moody!

Once again literature played a significant part. We arrived on the west coast of Scotland with hundreds of books. By the time we returned to Edinburgh everything had been sold, much to the surprise of Miss Manwarring, the Faith Mission book manager, who had never seen anything like this happen before in all her years, so she told us!

4

PRICED ABOVE RUBIES

The days of training in Scotland became history. However. my next move was uncertain for during the two years of training General Francisco Franco had come into power in Spain and the considerable liberty which missionaries and local workers had enjoyed for five years came to an abrupt end. I was advised that I should not apply for a visa at this time but should postpone any thought of missionary service in Spain. Disappointed, I applied to the North Africa Mission and was accepted.

Then, the Captain's voice was heard again.

Scripture tells us that when we turn to the right or to the left the Captain's voice will be heard saying, "This is the way, walk in it." I heard His voice, for apparently I was turning in the wrong direction when thinking of North Africa. But on which path should I be walking? Especially when several doors of opportunity opened within a matter of weeks! The Faith Mission wanted me to stay with them. One of my colleagues, Andrew Workman, had returned to Northern Ireland. God was blessing his ministry and he asked me to join him. Then Cornwall, in the southwest of England, came into the picture.

I had met Major and Mrs. Flint during our tent campaign days in Scotland, and they now shared the news with me that God had been blessing in revival in some of the Methodist chapels in the Falmouth-Penzance area of the county. Would I come and share the Word with the many new converts? The witness came that this was God's way as the next step. Just what He had in mind I had no idea, but I was relying on His promise that He would speak should I turn to the right or to the left.

There was no correcting voice, so in May, 1938 I climbed into my dilapidated Austin 7 car and headed west. It was great to meet the Flints again and to learn of all that the Holy Spirit had been doing over recent months in this part of the country. I was also fascinated by the countryside and the rugged coastlines with their intriguing inlets, harbors and beaches, for this was my first visit to the west country.

The very first meeting which had been arranged the day after I arrived was in the picturesque village of Porthleven. Mrs. Flint drove me around and showed me some of the sights. They took my breath away. So by the time we arrived at the church for my talk to the united women's group I was in a romantic mood. In expressing my fascination for their lovely village I told the ladies that it would be a delightful place for one's honeymoon! That wasn't quite prophetic but close to it!

On our return to the Flint's sprawling estate perched on the side of the rocky cliffs of St. Kevern, I found that another guest was to spend a few days in this delightful spot. Just weeks before, she and the family had suffered the loss of her much loved father, and so Bessie Miners had been invited to spend some quiet restful days for spiritual, emotional and physical renewing at the Flint's home.

Her father had been a great influence in this young lady's life, for Ned Miners was a fearless and successful fisherman and an outstanding Christian. He had a great heart of compassion and would give away his last shilling to any who needed help. He was also a fearless preacher, sharing his faith with an eloquence which commanded attention and compelled an affirmative response from his hearers. And daughter Bessie was invariably at his side as she grew older. They would walk for miles through the Cornish lanes to Methodist chapels to which Edward Miners had been assigned as a leading Methodist lay preacher. During these walks the conversation was always on the living Lord; so, in a sense, Bessie Miners had a personal tutor in the things of the Spirit and a dynamic example of practical and applied Christianity. It was strange that in spite of this she did not make her personal commitment until she was sixteen years of age, and it was another eight years before she made a total commitment and handed her life over without reserve to her lovely Lord Jesus.

Soon after this second encounter she left business and joined a group known as the Friends Evangelistic Band, beginning her full-time Christian service in the villages of England. But this was soon to be tested, and after only a matter of weeks she was back home with a bout of severe food or water poisoning. This persisted on and off for a number of years, although she was able to continue her service with the village mission until early 1938.

Now her beloved father was failing in health, and she was to see this robust man stricken with cancer and by Easter of that year succumb to this frightening disease. Even in the closing months of his life, Edward Miners stayed by his daughter's side, for revival meetings were in full swing and scores of people were finding Jesus as their personal Saviour. In one village a truck driver came under such conviction of sin, even though he did not attend any of the revival services, that he pulled his truck to the side of the road, climbed over the hedge, and got right with God in the open field. In another village a confirmed drunkard was soundly converted and his life was so changed that the village policeman said, "This young lady is doing me out of a job!"

I was blessed as day after day Major and Mrs. Flint and Miss Miners recounted more of the wonderful things God had been doing...and Bessie Miners, I learned, had been one of the main instruments whom God was using in these revival stirrings which had been and still were taking place in this part of the country. Most evenings the four of us were together in local churches, and I had the privilege of opening the Word to many of these recent converts, as well as to the old-timers in the faith who were now growing stronger in the things of the Lord.

I was in my twenty-fourth year and up to now had not been overly serious with any of the fine young ladies who had crossed my path, but things changed rapidly in Cornwall. Before many weeks had passed I found another reason why my Captain had led me this way out of the maze of other open doors. I was captivated by the charisma of Christ in this young woman. Here surely was the Lord's gracious answer to this second most important life decision that most of us are called upon to make. Our love for each other deepened rapidly.

Opportunities for church services and street meetings were plentiful. Bessie had already responded to several invitations for future evangelistic campaigns. The autumn months right up to Christmas were filled. As we were already beginning to work together in public, it seemed wise that in the best interest of a Christian testimony we should get into harness together. Therefore on September 14, 1938, the knot was tied as Bessie Miners became Mrs. Kenneth Adams.

It was a full church. Many had come from far and near. They had known and been blessed by Bessie's ministry, and they wanted to share with us in this happy occasion. But because some in the gathering did not know Jesus Christ in a personal way, immediately after the ceremony and before signing the official register, I went to the platform and gave my testimony, basing my remarks on the "I will" that the Lord Jesus was waiting to hear from every heart. This made headlines in the West Britain newspaper: Bridegroom preaches at his wedding!

We spent our three week honeymoon motoring up the west side of England and into Scotland to fellowship with some of the friends of my campaigning days in the Campbeltown and the Kintyre Peninsula area, and then continued over to the east coast and down to London, stopping along the way to visit other friends and relations, and then went back to Cornwall to begin the ministry of evangelism in the village churches. It all seemed so exciting and so full of intriguing prospects.

But the Captain had something else to say.

The campaigns in Cornwall were encouraging and fruitful and yet, strangely enough, other invitations did not materialize, so by early 1939 we left Cornwall and headed for London and the east coast of England. While Bessie had not had formal Bible School training, she had served for a number of years with a home mission known as the Friends Evangelistic Band. It was not a Quaker group in spite of its name, although the founders, Mr. and Mrs. George Fox, were Quakers. The main thrust of this group was to reopen closed chapels (a lot of them Methodist chapels), and reinstate a vital Christian testimony in the village. The workers lived in very primitive conditions, often in horse-drawn gypsy caravans (no fancy names like house trailer or mobile homes in those days!). It was a faith mission and the workers had to trust the Lord personally for their daily needs. Therefore, Bessie already had wide experience in down-to-earth, day-by-day faith while watching God provide for personal needs in many different ways.

We decided to contact Mr. Fox and share our situation with him.

Just at this time, while we were wondering what our Captain had for us—and there had been no clear, direct word from Him—a letter was received from the Secretary of the Plymouth City Mission in Devon. We were asked to consider superintending this work. The terms were quite attractive. There would be a steady income, a furnished home, and an annual vacation with pay! Naturally we laid this letter before the Lord. We agreed to pray about the matter separately and then after a few days compare notes.

By now Mr. Fox had also made a proposition. Because of our experience in evangelism, he felt we could be useful in the FEB ministry. In his judgment, some of the little village meeting-places were ready for a time of reaping. He would gladly recommend to the local FEB missioner that we be invited to conduct a gospel campaign.

We were staying in London at the time with close friends, Harold and Ethel Hogbin, who have remained very much with us in spirit over the years. We shared with them both possibilities, the opportunity in Plymouth and the invitation from George Fox. Their conclusion was that the Plymouth City Mission proposition was much more attractive and seemed to them the logical step we should take. Bessie and I again prayed and waited, and finally we felt constrained to accept the proposition Mr. Fox had made, even though we knew that there would be no regular pay packet. It was a challenge to the life of faith and it was His way for us. We shared our conviction with the Hogbins and in no way did they try to dissuade us, believing God had made His mind clear to us. They sent us on our way with a generous gift, a Godspeed, and the assurance of their continued prayer fellowship.

It was early spring and we found a small cottage in the village of Scunthorpe in Norfolk. This became our base for the evangelistic campaigns which we would conduct in fellowship with the workers of the Friends Evangelistic Band. When summer came, we were assigned one of the rickety gypsy caravans and were supplied with a tent which would seat about 150 people. This began a new experience for us, operating on our own, under canvas, and going out into the highways and byways to get the children, young people and adults to come and hear the good news we were so anxious to share with them. It meant a lot of hard work going from door to door in the village and also getting out into the surrounding countryside where the farmers lived, off the main roads. The Lord encouraged us as we saw young people and adults filling the tent night after night.

One thing troubled us.

In our visitation we discovered that others had been there before us. The people were very warmhearted and readily opened their doors, for they recognized us as the missioners from the tent. Even their children were telling them of the good things that were going on. Invariably they would tell us about these other missioners, who had lots of books and magazines which they tried to sell on their house visits. They seemed to be well-versed in the Bible, we were told, and could quote many scriptures. They also talked about coming events and what the future held.

We knew these "other missioners" as Jehovah's Witnesses, who were promoting a gospel which was not the true gospel. Theirs was a message that did not have Jesus Christ as the one and only hope for broken and sin-sick humanity. We tried to warn the people, and at the same time we prayed, for our hearts were troubled as we realized the energetic, zealous effort which was being put into this door-to-door visitation by these people. Knowing books as I did, I was concerned that so little was being done by evangelical Christians to spread the truth of the gospel through the printed page.

Could this concern be a sort of troubling of the waters by our divine Captain? We certainly began to see that we, too, should make books available at our campaigns and in our house-visiting.

August came. This was the main holiday month in Britain —especially for families, as children in the elementary schools had only a five-week vacation, beginning late July and ending early September. The leadership of the FEB usually held a summer convention using a much larger tent, and this year they chose the central village of Walsingham, just fifteen miles from where we lived. We suggested to Mr. Fox and to one of his senior colleagues, Rev. George Banks, that this would be an opportune time to have a good book display.

They agreed and asked me to organize the book program. It went very well and the leadership was impressed. So were we. The thought came to us, wouldn't it be wonderful if the FEB developed a literature arm so that supplies of good Christian books could be sent to their missioners in the villages and they, in turn, could see that these books were made available to the people? We said nothing but just continued to pray. On one point we agreed: we had no intention of becoming involved. This was just an idea which, of course, others would have to put into operation. Yet as time passed, the conviction began to grow that perhaps we might have a small part in getting the program going. At least we got to the place of partial willingness to become involved in a limited way.

So we left it, and agreed that any initiative would have to come from the mission leadership. If they approached us we would be willing to discuss the subject with them.

5

GOD WORKS IN AN EMBATTLED BRITAIN

No sooner had we arrived at this conclusion than a letter marked "Confidential" arrived! I looked at Bessie and said, "I think I know what this is about." So did she. Sure enough, it was a request from Mr. Fox asking us to establish a literature ministry which could serve the FEB village workers.

The Lord had already prepared our hearts and so we replied in the affirmative, but with a very definite proviso. We were willing to help get the program started and would take one year out of our evangelistic ministry, during which time the FEB would find other personnel to continue the literature work and release us to return to our evangelistic campaigns.

Where would the money come from to begin this venture? George Banks, who was the Principal of the small Bible School which the FEB operated in Kelvedon about fifteen miles west of Colchester, said there was some money in a building fund which could be made available, with the understanding that it would be repaid within a year or two. The amount was £100 (approximately $500).

By late August rumors of war were in the air, so switching to a less public ministry might be wise. Holding tent campaigns and having large meetings could be frowned upon, we reasoned. Sunday, September 3, 1939 dawned bright and sunny, and yet something ominous was in the air. At 11:15 that morning Prime Minister Chamberlain talked to the people over national radio. His opening statement stunned the nation, "We are at war with Germany."

Now what would happen? God's work would surely be tested

and certainly any new ideas would have to wait for brighter days. I must admit we panicked a little. A tent campaign near Reading in Berkshire was cancelled, much to the disappointment of those who had organized it. Perhaps we were wrong. It could have been a golden opportunity for reaping, with so many people troubled and perplexed by this war news. On the other hand, it could have been God's way of leading us into the literature ministry, for later on Winston Churchill was to release books from any government restrictions, although paper shortages greatly limited production.

After a couple of weeks of vacation in Cornwall, we returned to Colchester to discuss these plans with Mr. Fox and Mr. Banks. Strangely it seems that they, too, had panicked a little and had already moved the mission office to the Foxes' home. This meant that the previous location was empty and could be made available for the literature ministry. Even though the premises were not in a shopping area and the ground floor was not available, we jumped at the opportunity. The other two floors could be made suitable for a bookroom and for living quarters. Because the main function of this new literature ministry would be sending stock to the mission workers out in the villages, the location was not a serious problem.

Now we had our work cut out. Shelves, tables, counters, displays and storage cupboards must either be built or purchased. Basic house furniture must be obtained. Stock for this new enterprise must be purchased and publicity prepared to let local people know that a Christian bookcenter was soon to be opened. I must here record that we were deeply indebted to the publishers in London. Without any questions asked, they supplied the stock we ordered and gave us generous credit terms. After several journeys between Colchester and London in our little car, all was ready and on October 27, 1939 the first Christian bookcenter in the city of Colchester was opened for business. We printed 10,000 handbills announcing the new Christian bookroom and circulated these far and wide. Being so close to the Christmas season, we had hoped to get off to a good start, but it was all uphill right from the beginning. Never once during our eight months in this location did the weekly sales get into two figures!

Along with the bookroom we were now actively engaged in getting parcels of literature out to the country areas for the beginnings of a door-to-door literature ministry. We revamped a little gospel magazine called *Caravan News*, turning it into a tabloid newspaper format and sending them out by the hundreds to the village missionaries.

We also got into the publishing business, producing tens of thousands of a little fifty-page booklet entitled *The Lord Reigneth*. Later, following the great Dunkirk evacuation, we produced another booklet called *Dunkirk*, recording the story of God's miracle of keeping the normally turbulent North Sea almost rippleless for days, enabling every available ship, boat and small craft to bring tens of thousands of soldiers back to Britain safely. God used these booklets in quite remarkable ways.

Then our Captain spoke again. This time, specifically to Bessie.

Colchester is the second largest military town in England and the streets were swarming with young men in battle uniform. Many would be in town for just a matter of weeks before being assigned to one of the battle areas in Europe. How many of them were ready to face the ordeal and pay the ultimate price? It was certain that thousands would never return to see their homeland again. Surely these young people needed to hear God's good news of personal salvation. But who was telling them?

Seeing an evangelistic opportunity, we rented the Friends' meeting house in the center of town and began regular Sunday evening gospel services. By this time we had met a number of keen Christians from several parts of the world—Australia, U.S.A., and Canada—as well as British servicemen and civilians. We worked together as a team. The young fellows would be out on the street corners inviting men in for a time of singing and refreshments. It didn't take long to get the place full, and Sunday after Sunday we had the opportunity of telling these young soldiers the good news of God's love. At the end of each service we offered literature, which was accepted readily. During refreshments and social conversation we had opportunity to talk with those who had indicated an interest and every week had the privilege of leading many to a personal acceptance of Jesus Christ as their Saviour.

In June, 1940, we moved the bookroom to a better location in a shopping area just a few doors from the main bus depot. Now, we had a good ground-floor shop and could make an attractive window display. There were living quarters above and even a basement for storage and packing to help us cope with the growing mail-order department. The very first week in this new location we reached double figures, selling over £11-worth ($50) of vital Christian literature! By Christmas things were really prospering and we just missed hitting the £100 mark in one week! The shop was not big, so we added another room behind the shop for the Christmas display.

Because of the war, we had given no serious thought to our time schedule. With the Lord's evident blessing on both the literature ministry and the evangelistic outreach among the soldiers as well as weekly opportunities in local churches, we were becoming increasingly sure that for the present we were right on track and need not be overly concerned about our future. We also knew our Captain would speak again when necessary.

Then a puzzling thing happened in the early days of 1941. Soon after the beginning of this literature venture, Mr. Fox had written us to clarify the relationship between ourselves and the mission. The letter stated that while the FEB was more than happy to enjoy the benefits of the literature ministry, it was not to be considered an actual department of the organization but rather a personal effort of Ken and Bessie Adams, with priority being given to serving the FEB missioners with their literature needs. This idea had not registered strongly with us. Perhaps we were too caught up with the excitement of seeing the literature getting out. Something was now actually being done to counter the flood of Jehovah's Witness literature.

For some reason the FEB Board felt it necessary to restate this position and even to carry it further. They requested that the £100 loan be repaid as soon as convenient, at which time the bookshop and its related ministries would become the sole responsibility of Ken and Bessie Adams. We complied and within a few weeks sent off the check for £100 and found ourselves with a Christian bookshop on our hands. What was happening? Had God tricked us into this? Hadn't I told Him that having given up business once—for Him—I had no desire and no intention of getting back into personal business again?

Frankly, we were quite puzzled. We were not at all sure we should remain in the Christian bookshop ministry, and yet we were very convinced of the widespread influence of the Christian bookshop in Colchester, particularly in these troublous war days. Just what was our Captain indicating? We had no idea of all that hung upon this momentous decision.

SECTION II

THE TENDER BRANCH WILL NOT CEASE
Job 14:7

For there is hope for a tree, if it be cut down, that it will sprout again, and that its tender branch will not cease.

Job 14:7

6

A BABY IS BORN

As indicated earlier, we had maintained a keen interest in missionary work and several magazines were part of our regular reading. Spain was very much on my heart, and Bessie's interest for years had centered in the Far East, particularly Japan, Korea and China.

I think it was the March issue of *World Conquest,* the monthly magazine of the Worldwide Evangelization Crusade, which stirred our imagination. We learned that the WEC was planning a major advance and this intrigued us. After all, Great Britain was a nation at war. With increasing government restrictions, how could any group be seriously planning a major advance? Along with the article explaining these goals was a map of the British Isles indicating the twelve areas in which the WEC planned to establish what they were calling Regional Headquarters.

This was to be a faith venture. It would call for personnel for each of these advances. Personnel responding to this call would have to pray in the funds to cover the rent and utilities of their center. They would have to see the Lord provide for their food, for entertaining, for personal and family needs and for all the travel costs in connection with the development of the regional ministry. A tall order to be sure, and yet there was a strong, confident note in the article that this plan was of the Lord, and therefore His provision would be forthcoming.

Our hearts warmed to this confident faith. The more we talked about it the more we felt that the Lord might have something in this for us. Perhaps we could be the WEC representatives for our area, called East Anglia, which was made up of the three counties of Essex, Suffolk and Norfolk.

But then, what about the bookshop? Had the Lord purposely put it into our hands? Were we now responsible for the future of this literature work? We surely needed a word from our Captain.

A few days later we learned from one of our local friends that Mr. John Whittle was to be in Colchester to arrange meetings for Mr. Norman Grubb, the General Secretary of the Worldwide Evangelization Crusade. John Whittle was, you will remember, the young man who took over my first bookshop in Westcliff-on-Sea back in 1936 when I left for Bible College. We had met only once since then, and I was intrigued to learn that as a result of his contact with the book ministry, particularly through reading Eva Stuart Watt's book *Floods on Dry Ground,* he had been led to contact the WEC and was now its Public Relations Director. As soon as we knew that John was coming to Colchester, we asked our friends with whom he would be staying to be sure to tell him that we wanted to see him. This would be an ideal opportunity for us to discuss the feasibility of any link we might have with the WEC in connection with this new regional outreach. At the meal table mention was made of our request, and John told us afterwards that as soon as our name was mentioned the Lord indicated to him, "This is your couple for East Anglia!"

John wasted no time in coming to see us, and we wasted no time in getting down to the reason for our desire to see him. We told him we were quite interested in this new regional outreach of the WEC; we were also willing to offer our services to the Crusade—but we had a problem. We then told him the story of "our" bookshop, but he had no word of advice to give us regarding it even though he recognized the value of its Christian witness and the exciting ministry of the soldiers' work. We parted with the promise that we would pray for each other and especially for our possible involvement in this new regional outreach. John also assured us that when Norman Grubb came for his meetings, he would arrange for us to get together.

The day came when Norman Grubb, Leslie Sutton, John

Whittle, and Ken and Bessie Adams sat together in the room behind the bookshop which was again serving as our living room, following its use as a second showroom during the Christmas rush. Well, we again told our story, finishing with "But we have a problem, the bookshop." We had no liberty to close it; we were willing to consider selling it, or to employ someone to carry the main responsibility, which would free us to travel throughout East Anglia in the interest of the WEC. Without hesitation Norman Grubb responded, "Close it? Indeed not! We should have bookshops like this all across the country—a chain of Christian bookshops, sort of 'spiritual Woolworths'!" It witnessed immediately to our hearts. This was the Captain's voice to us in no uncertain terms.

The first priority then was to see the Lord provide personnel who could handle the bookstore and its related ministries to release the Adamses for their itinerant ministry. And so to one faith venture was added another—and all because of an impromptu meeting of the minds—the mind of Christ coming through five members of His body. For us, this was indeed a refreshing breath right from the very heart of God, and we responded to it without hesitation.

For the next few days we seemed to be walking on air. Suddenly, not only was the bookshop to remain but it was to become the first of a chain of bookstores throughout the country, and what was even more exciting, it was to be linked with a missionary society.

Finally, we descended from the mountain top and began to face the realities of what all this would entail. As we prayed and thought and dreamed, the vision kept enlarging. We could see not only a chain of bookshops with their spiritual ministry across the British Isles, but a chain of bookstores throughout the English-speaking world—in the U.S.A., Canada, Australia, New Zealand, South Africa, and even in other countries where English was widely used. And more, we could even be a service agency for the literature needs of missionary societies and the national church around the world. We had been doing this very thing in a limited way for the Friends Evangelistic Band. Now, the whole world was in our vision.

Mr. Grubb lost no time in implementing some of the ideas which we had discussed. On his way back to London he stopped in Chelmsford for two meetings and met Mr. and Mrs. Fred Whybrow, who were the local WEC representatives. During a meal he shared with them this new faith literature vision, ending with the statement, "We must now see the Lord raise up personnel, first to release the Adamses for the deputation ministry, and then others to enable more bookcenters to be opened."

That night in their home the Whybrows discussed what Norman Grubb had told them about this anticipated new literature development. For some time they had been wondering if the Lord might have a place of full-time service for them, and what they had now heard set them thinking. Mr. Grubb was quite unaware of this when he was so enthusiastically sharing with them. So the Whybrows decided to visit the Adamses in Colchester and find out what all this was really about. They seemed impressed, and we all agreed to give the matter definite prayer. Bessie and I were quite excited: things seemed to be falling into place in quick succession, much faster than we had dared to believe possible.

By now Mr. Grubb had shared things with some of his staff in London and he was finding a number of them had considerable misgivings. The idea of Christian bookshops throughout the country was no problem, but should they be linked with the WEC? The mission was going through a rather difficult period, and some felt that people might suspect the workability of the life of faith if WEC were to open business branches selling books. Then, too, what about the personnel and the life of faith? WEC home workers were not receiving any wage or allowance from Crusade funds, but surely these people in this literature business would expect to draw a minimum wage from the operation.

We met Mr. Grubb again, and he shared these things with us, although he made no attempt to press us into changing our ways, for he knew that we were taking £1($5) per week from the till to

meet our basic food needs. To live the life of faith was no problem to either of us, for this is what we had been doing for the last
several years, but was this to be the way for those who would join
us in this new literature vision? Obviously a foundation principle
of this not-yet-born work was at stake.

We met again with the Whybrows to share what Norman
Grubb had told us, for during our first visit we had told them
they would be free to take the £1 each week as we were currently
doing. We would not continue to take anything, because we
expected to be traveling quite a lot and would trust the Lord to
provide our needs separately from the bookstore. We sensed a
definite warming toward joining us in this new literature venture,
but now there was this thought of living by faith. The four of us
agreed to give this new idea further careful thought and prayer
before making any decision.

A few weeks later we met again and found that we were
unanimous in believing that the Lord was leading the four of us
to trust Him solely for our personal needs, whether serving in the
shop or out on deputation. Both were alike to Him. Our God
was not limited to providing for just certain types of ministry. On
this visit the Whybrows also indicated that the Lord had clearly
shown them that they were to join us, and they would do their
best to run the bookshop—freeing us for the deputation ministry
for the WEC in East Anglia.

It was agreed that the Whybrows could join us in May and
they would now begin working toward that goal. This meant that
we would need to find a house, because we could not all live
together in the limited space above the bookshop. Through
another series of miracles a large house was found with adequate
living quarters plus a nice big room for meetings. For it was our
intention to develop, as quickly as possible, a regular prayer
meeting, both for the WEC and for this new literature work
which seemed to be in the making. The interesting thing about
this particular house was that it had been where Mr. and Mrs.
George Fox of the Friends Evangelistic Band had lived for many
years. It had changed hands when the Foxes centralized the FEB

ministry in the Bible School premises in Kelvedon. Dr. Bolton, a keen Christian, had become the next tenant, but was now needing to move so he graciously persuaded the landlord to allow us to become the new tenants. So in mid-May, 1941, the Whybrows and the Adamses set up house together at 1 Balkerne Gardens, Colchester.

Just what the Lord had in mind we really did not know, for as yet there was no actual organization. The Colchester bookshop was just known as The Bible Depot. But there were growing signs that something new and different was in the making.

Over the next six months three more workers joined us. Meanwhile several visits were made by Mr. Whybrow and myself to London to meet with Norman Grubb and others, to slowly hammer out some basic fundamental principles and establish anticipated goals for this new thing which had been conceived by none other than the Spirit of God back in late February. What were some of these principles?

One was faith.

Some years later we were to learn of The Four Pillars of WEC, but in this gestatory period of the coming literature work, no attempt was made to duplicate these pillars. They would have to be given of God for this new organization which was in the making but yet to appear. The very structure of the work and, in a sense, the application of faith to it, might not be identical with that of the WEC. God would show. This literature work would be seen as a business enterprise—we would be buying and selling Christian merchandise. True, it would have a strong evangelistic thrust as was evident by the soldiers' work in Colchester. Nonetheless, it would appear as a Christian business to the uninformed. Realistically, could we hope to develop such a work by faith? Would friends, relations, churches, support those who served in a Christian literature ministry? For a giveaway program, especially if it included the Scriptures, yes, maybe. But selling the merchandise, that was open to question. I remember during our prosperous Christmas in Colchester one of the local pastors commenting, "You have a gold mine here!"

In spite of all this, we were growingly convinced that God's way for us in these beginning days was this way of faith, expecting the Lord to provide the day-to-day needs. After forty years we do not regret this decision. Indeed, we know that much of the expansion over the years has been made possible because of this very principle in daily operation.

Another principle was sacrifice.

We felt we were honored and privileged to forego a weekly pay packet. We gladly chose to live simply, thus releasing as much money as possible for the expansion of the ministry. This was true, not only for the workers but also for the work. I remember when we set up the offices above the Colchester bookshop, we made do with odd tables and chairs rather than spending "unnecessary" money buying fancy furnishings. The table which Mr. Whybrow used when he later became the bookkeeper and treasurer of the organization was so uncertain on its legs that we nailed it to the wall! We salvaged every piece of wrapping paper and string, every cardboard carton which brought our stock from the publishers, so that we could reuse it in our own mail-order program. Not an unnecessary penny was spent. This same principle was gladly accepted on a personal level, too.

I remember mentioning to Bessie once that I believed the Lord was going to entrust us with a lot of money, not for us personally, but for His work. After all, this bookshop wasn't ours in the truest sense of the word. We hadn't put our money into it so what right did we have to claim it as ours? No, it was the Lord's bookshop. I recalled the day when the Captain had said to me, "Ken, I do not intend to run your business." Now, it was growingly evident that we were being given the privilege of running our Captain's business! He was and still is the sole Owner and Proprietor, and even though the work has greatly prospered since those early struggling days we have continued—gladly—to live the simple life (I like that word better than calling it the sacrificial life).

On the day he wrote the first check for £1,000 to one of our suppliers, I can remember Mr. Whybrow sharing with us, with a chuckle, that he did not have enough personal money to get his hair cut so his good wife did the job for him!

Another matter was hammered out which we might call a policy rather than a principle. As the Lord brought new people to us—and we would certainly need many if we were going to reach our goals—it was agreed that the candidates would spend some time in the WEC headquarters for preparation and orientation. These workers would then be transferred to the literature ministry. Because God was showing us that literature was a specialized type of ministry, and because we believed God was going to privilege us to be a service agency to other missionary societies, it was agreed that this literature work would not become known as the literature, or the publishing, arm of the Worldwide Evangelization Crusade. It would be established as autonomous right from its inception but linked in fellowship with the WEC. It would have its own governing body and it would be financially independent with its own bookkeeping system and annual audit. Of course, WEC would be ready to give advice and even practical help on occasion.

This introduced the principle of fellowship.

For the past ten years the WEC had been developing a democratic type of government. It had done away with an outside Board of Directors, believing that the way for them was that the work should be governed under the direction of the Holy Spirit by the people actually doing the work. Rather than board meetings, there would be staff meetings made up in the main of mission personnel who had been in the Crusade at least two years. We agreed that this new autonomous literature work would follow the same administrative policy.

Fellowship, for us, would also extend to all branches of the church. This did not mean that we would be in total agreement with the teaching of each group; neither did it mean that each worker would have to surrender personal beliefs and convictions on the lesser aspects of Biblical revelation; but we would not let these doctrinal differences hinder us from a willingness to serve all denominations in respect to their literature needs. This did not mean, either, that we would be ready to supply anything which was asked for. Our position was to be uncompromisingly evangelical and the literature we would stock would have to conform to our Statement of Faith.

Later this fellowship policy was to lead us into a strongly interracial position recognizing God's people of any nationality as one in the Body of Christ and, therefore, eligible for service in our mission. Our Captain is no respecter of persons.

The full impact of this interracial fellowship principle was to be tested for me personally in an unexpected way.

There were other lesser matters, but the one remaining essential was to find a name for this coming literature organization. The title we chose was Evangelical Publishing House. Just a year or so later it would be changed to Christian Literature Crusade because the earlier name by no means indicated the complete ministry which the Lord had for His literature organization. But He was very patient with us and allowed us to start off with this limited title. For us, at the time, it did seem to adequately cover our objectives—a chain of Christian bookshops in the English-reading world.

With these major and general matters fairly well settled after six months of concentrated study, discussion and prayer, the Christian literature organization under the title of Evangelical Publishing House was born on November 1, 1941. At this time the name did not need to be registered with any government department, but on that day it was my happy privilege to go to our local bank and change the bank account name from The Bible Depot, Proprietor, Kenneth R. Adams, to the Evangelical Publishing House, with myself and Fred Whybrow as the two signatories to operate the account. We did not, of course, register with the bank the name of the true Proprietor, but to us and to the rest of our small team of workers we fully and gladly recognized His name to be the Lord Jesus Christ.

7

GOD'S WAYS UNFOLD

We look back with satisfaction knowing that there has been no human founder of this literature work, which for thirty-eight of its forty years has been known around the world as the Christian Literature Crusade. It is true that Ken and Bessie Adams were the only two workers when things began in October 1939, but now in 1941, almost two years to the day, there were others to shoulder the load. We had entered the year alone, frustrated and bewildered, puzzled by the turn of events, and frankly wondering just what the future held.

We were tempted to quit.

The inner urge to an evangelistic and preaching career was very real, but, thankfully, we did hold steady in the darkness. Now we know that dark tunnels have a light at the end. And that light is, in fact, the beginning of a new day with new experiences of enlargement and growth. We were to witness this a number of times in the years ahead, but this experience of early 1941 would stand us in good stead—for, in one sense, it stands alone as perhaps the most important experience for us personally, and for the story we are now recording. Indeed, a mis-move in those first months of 1941 could have spelled disaster and meant that there would be no story to record.

Now that the literature work was actually born, just how was it to be handled? What actions, if any, would be necessary to see its purpose unfold? Mr. Grubb was again God's instrument in these beginning days. He is a great enthusiast, and once an idea has gripped him and he is clearly convinced that it is of God, there is no stopping him! The news of this new EPH (Evangelical

Publishing House) must be shared, and what better way than to put an article in the Crusade's *World Conquest* magazine. I think it was the October issue of 1941 when that article appeared.

When we read it we wondered. It seemed that the whole idea had been expanded, at least in Mr. Grubb's mind, far beyond anything we had talked about during our months of deliberations and certainly far beyond our vision. Just where he got the figure from I don't know—or do I?—but he boldly stated that the goal of this young literature work was to open two hundred of these "spiritual Woolworths" up and down the country!

It alarmed us.

Our hands were full enough trying to keep one budding Christian bookshop afloat. How in the world could we tackle another twenty, let alone two hundred! In his article he had also highlighted some of the other activities still going on in Colchester, particularly the soldiers' work. Well, there was nothing we could do about it. After all, the article was written, the magazine was now in circulation, and Christmas was upon us—so we had our hands full for the present.

This article was to stir other people's imagination, and before six months had passed we were to see some striking evidences of God's purposes unfolding. Several inquiries from prospective workers reached us within the next few months, and then came a long distance telephone call from the city of Leicester, about one hundred miles north of London. Alfred Finney, a successful businessman, was on the line, and he had a proposition. It is worth sharing some of the details, because it is an example of the unique way our Captain was handling His EPH/CLC literature enterprise. We were to see this sort of thing in one form or another many times in the future.

Mr. Finney was a keen WEC supporter and an active Christian in his community. Leicester was another key city in the overall war effort. Here many young men were being trained to become officers to serve in some theatre of the war. As part of his personal effort to reach these cadets with the gospel, Mr. Finney had ordered from the WEC copies of a booklet entitled *A New*

Life for You! by Bill Pethybridge. The booklets arrived safely and he was about to throw away the wrappings when his eye caught an article about a Christian literature work among soldiers in Colchester. For protection in the mail the booklets had been wrapped in back issues of the *World Conquest* magazine, and now Mr. Finney was reading an intriguing story written by Mr. Grubb eight or nine months earlier!

He was captivated.

Surely something similar could be done in Leicester, he mused, and in less than no time he had found some premises on the main London Road which could well serve the dual purpose of literature and evangelism.

This was the news he shared with me on the telephone and he urged that I come up as quickly as possible to look over the proposition—a Christian bookshop on the ground floor and plenty of room upstairs to develop a ministry among the cadets. He had no idea of how successful it would be, so he generously offered us the bookshop rent free for the first year.

But another problem appeared on the horizon.

Not long after Norman Grubb's article about the two hundred shops throughout Britain, the newspapers announced that the government was restricting the opening of any new shops or businesses. The war was the first priority. Nothing must be allowed to distract the nation from its avowed intent to win the war, so declared Winston Churchill. There was one loophole. Application could be made to the Board of Trade and a permit would be granted if the proposed business was, in their judgment, justified.

Now what were we to do? There could be no turning back, for we were convinced that what we were planning was of the Lord, so without delay we applied for permission to open the Christian bookshop in Leicester. There was much rejoicing when, several weeks later, our telephone in Colchester rang and the Secretary of the Board of Trade in Leicester gave us the good news that permission had been granted. I do not know what she thought of our response when we spontaneously shouted, "Hallelujah! Praise the Lord!"

No sooner was the Leicester shop opened when we received a request from Mr. Harry Miller in Chatham, Kent. Chatham is located on the River Medway and is a training and recruiting center for the navy. Harry Miller was convinced that a Christian bookshop was needed and with his letter he sent a generous gift to help make it possible. Good premises at 118 High Street, Chatham were obtained and in early 1943 bookshop number three was opened under the managership of Alec and Hilda Thwaites.

By the time the war ended six bookshops had been opened, five in England and one in Dundee, Scotland. Apart from the Colchester shop the other five needed permits. Four of them had been granted on the first application. We were turned down twice for the other one, but we persisted and on the third time won the day!

8

THE MAIN BASE ESTABLISHED

The question of guidance had never been a real problem to us, either in our personal life or in the development of the work. Now that the CLC had become a reality, the vision continued to enlarge, mainly through other people. There seemed to be "Alfred Finneys" and "Harry Millers" all over the place. We had not studied the map of the British Isles and pinpointed cities which should become targets of faith. Rather it was becoming a pattern that some local person would take the initiative and approach us requesting that we help bring a literature center into the area. Sometimes we were asked to take over an existing work, as was the case in the town of Ipswich. On our part it was a matter of just seeking the Lord for His go-ahead, and with this granted we took the next step. The next three centers opened because each town had its concerned individual at the heart of things.

Then in 1944 there was an exception to this growing pattern.

We were now receiving letters from overseas expressing an interest in this new literature ministry and indicating that something similar should be done in their country. Earl Frid of Canada was inspired by our example in Britain, which he had read about in the *World Conquest* magazine, and he was already negotiating about taking over a small bookcenter in a suburb of Toronto, Ontario. Similar word came from Australia. Conrad Lieber caught the vision through the same article and planned to come to Britain to learn more about the program and to get some basic training.

All this stirred our imagination, and in our fellowship gatherings we began to talk about the probability that one day we would have to establish our main base in London. After all, if we really meant business in seeing a chain of Christian bookcenters throughout the English-reading world, then this could hardly be done from a provincial town like Colchester. The hub of the publishing world in Britain was London, and we would need to be in touch with all the Christian publishing companies in the Big City.

It was only a far-off dream and no attempt was made to set any target date, although it was something which we sincerely believed would come about. For the present, the idea was very much on the back burner—until one of my periodic visits to London.

I had a little extra time before my train would leave for Colchester so decided to walk instead of take the bus. As I walked up Ludgate Hill on my way to Liverpool Street Station I noticed several empty buildings and the thought struck me that it would be a good idea to find out what sort of rent we would face when the time would come for our move to the city. No doubt, quite astronomical. Without any further thought I made a note of the address of the real estate agent. This was prominently displayed on the "To Let" sign outside the three dilapidated buildings—35, 37 and 39 Ludgate Hill, almost in the exact center of the one square mile which is actually the City of London.

The address was none other than Liverpool Street, so I hastened my stride, thinking perhaps the office would still be open. To my dismay when I arrived, there was no office. Hitler had demolished the building with his bombs and incendiaries during the London blitz. There was, however, the address of the firm's new location in the west end of the city. With this in my possession I caught my train and mulled over things during my journey back to Colchester.

That evening I shared with Mr. Whybrow and the rest of our small team. (By the way, the Whybrows mentioned earlier in this book were in their late forties, whereas the rest of us were in our twenties or early thirties. In those days in Britain you didn't

call your elders by their first names. Yet, in a developing fellowship where we were aiming to demonstrate a oneness in the Body
of Christ, the "Mr." and "Mrs." were too formal. To solve our problem we dubbed the Whybrows "Pa and Ma"! I do not know if
that made them feel too elderly, but at least it gave the rest of us a
sort of balanced familiarity and all through the years this dear
couple has been known among us as Pa and Ma Whybrow—or
to shorten it, "Pa and Ma Why.")

The next day Pa and I prepared a letter and sent it off to the
estate agent in London. Their reply came by return mail. We
were agreeably surprised at the rental figure. It was quite a bit
lower than we had expected. There were unexpired leases on
number 37 and number 39, and this meant that the rent would
not be increased for seven or eight years. Wonderful. We were
quite excited, although we could not say categorically that the
Lord was now leading us to go to London. But again, as was our
custom, we would just follow step by step. We would expect His
voice if we were not on course, veering to the right or to the left.

Within a few days Pa Whybrow and I headed for London to
look over these properties. Number 37 was in fair condition. It
had been a showroom and offices for the Gestetner Corporation.
Number 39 was a mess and in our judgment had suffered more
damage from the bombing, but it was more spacious. It had been
a china and glassware shop and I could mentally recall it from
my pre-war days when I worked close by. The second floor had
also been a showroom and there was plenty of mahogany shelv-
ing on both floors. The other four floors had been used as offices
and there was also a full basement. In spite of the layers of dust
and debris we were attracted to Number 39. The other building
didn't seem big enough for all we envisioned! On sharing the
news with our team in Colchester, it was agreed that we should
write, expressing our interest and asking for full details.

With this information in hand we called in a Christian surveyor and asked for his appraisal. He was most discouraging.
Indeed, he strongly advised us to forget the whole idea and look
for something elsewhere. In his judgment it would prove very

costly to put the building into good repair although apparently the owners, the Prudential Insurance Company, were willing to do some of this, such as replacing the plate glass windows, getting the elevator operating, and repairing other obvious war damage.

The big snag was that the London Fire Department was insisting that all older buildings in the city be equipped with an enclosed concrete stairway. Our surveyor informed us that this cost would have to be borne by the incoming tenants. In spite of his negative advice, we felt we should approach the owners and tell them we were interested, but only on the understanding that they would completely renovate the building and install the enclosed stairway should this be called for—at their expense.

The answer came with little delay: "Sorry, we cannot comply with your demands." So the matter was closed and for us the episode was over. We made no further attempt to search for other properties in London.

Approximately nine months went by. Then a letter arrived from the Prudential Insurance Company reminding us of our previous inquiry about 39 Ludgate Hill and asking if we had found other premises or were we still interested. Our reply was brief and to the point. Yes, we are still interested but only on the terms outlined in our previous letter. Within a couple of weeks their answer came. They were willing to prepare a contract on our terms!

We again contacted our surveyor and he couldn't believe what his eyes were reading when we showed him the letter. He also felt this was evidence enough of the probable leading of the Lord and that we should carry the matter further. So we instructed him to proceed, and the result was a miracle. The surveyor's carefully prepared document presented 365 separate items for complete renovation of the building, both inside and outside. It also included the previous request covering any demand from the London Fire Department regarding the stairway. To the surprise and delight of all of us the insurance company agreed to the total proposition without changing one clause! We signed a fourteen-year lease, taking into account the years still under the old contract. Once again we had witnessed the hand of our miracle-working God.

Our first inquiry had been made in late 1944 when the country was still at war, and by late summer 1946 all was ready for occupancy. Since some things, such as repairing the elevator and replacing the plate glass windows, were not done because of limited supplies, the landlord generously adjusted the rent downward until everything was completed some years later.

We were to witness many more miracles. It was amazing how the London publishers rallied around us. We estimated that we would need a minimum of an extra £10,000 ($50,000) of stock to adequately fill the two showrooms, and we were given generous long-term credit to help us through these growing experiences. With the move to London, Colchester became just one of the branch shops. All but one couple took up residence in south London, where again we were to witness the Lord's miracle providing adequate housing.

Several things happened in quick succession during 1946 and 1947 to confirm the rightness of the move to London. World War II was now history, although armies of occupation were to remain in Europe and Japan for several years. This brought a new challenge, a new opportunity, and a completion of the basic overall vision and purpose for which CLC had been brought into existence.

With the growing conviction that one day our ministry would reach more than the English-speaking world, we established a foreign department, the main function of which was to research what literature was currently available. We started off with the European languages. Because Switzerland had remained neutral in the war and was still actively producing books, Phil Booth could gather copies of Christian literature in German, French, Italian and other European languages. These books, usually two or three of each title, were the beginning of a multi-language reference library.

Now that the war was over and CLC was reasonably well

established at its London base, requests for Christian literature, particularly in German, and some in French and Italian, were coming in quick succession. Keen Christians in the army of occupation saw Christian books as a unique tool. Restrictions were being lifted so service personnel could now move more freely among the general populace, and they were being invited into local homes. For these alert Christian young people this presented a golden opportunity. They were not able to converse too well because of their limited knowledge of the language, but if they could obtain tracts, booklets, and books, this would be wonderful. They could give books as a small token of their appreciation for the hospitality they were enjoying and these would surely help meet the spiritual vacuum evident in these early postwar days. After all, the young people of Germany had been led astray by a book. Hitler's *Mein Kampf* had outlined his goals and strategy convincingly, and the response from Germany's youth was enthusiastic. Now, the task of spiritual rehabilitation could begin through books.

Week after week requests poured in, both through the mail and especially from young soldiers on leave who were determined to take back good supplies of Christian literature.

I had been invited to speak at a Saturday night youth rally in Chatham. Because I had been introduced by the M.C. of the evening as being connected with the Christian Literature Crusade, I used the first few minutes of my time to outline some of our goals, making particular reference to our hope to publish and distribute books in many different languages. This good brother took special note of my opening remarks, and after the evening was through he asked me what books we had in German. I had to enlighten him. What I had shared was a goal, an objective, a hope; nothing had yet been produced.

He was crestfallen. I can hear him yet pouring out his heart, for as chaplain of the prisoner-of-war camps in southeast England, he was desperately in need of Christian literature in German. He couldn't even obtain Bibles and New Testaments; none were available, not even from the Bible Society.

I mentioned that while CLC had not started publishing, we did know of about two dozen titles, including the Scriptures, which were available from Switzerland. His face lit up. He was immediately alert. These books must be made available to him without delay. He could use hundreds of copies, and God would bless the printed word to bring new hope and personal salvation to many of the frustrated prisoners he contacted every day.

The full story has been told elsewhere* but we set to work immediately to obtain supplies. Once again we watched miracle after miracle unfold as the way was cleared to allow us to import from Switzerland. This opened the way for yet another advance, which again came to our attention because of concerned people. An influential Christian officer challenged us to open Christian bookcenters in Germany. He would handle procedural red tape and knew of some Christian businessmen who could make premises available.

Calls were also coming from elsewhere. John Davey, WEC missionary to the small island of Dominica in the West Indies, knew of this young literature work from correspondence with Norman Grubb, and he was sure something should be done in Dominica. After all, this was an English-reading area of the world!

I must admit this was something which had been overlooked. We had been thinking in terms of the larger, more advanced countries, forgetting that many smaller countries also have English as their major language. John was ready to take action if CLC London would send adequate supplies, for he had no money to buy the initial stock. London agreed and so John set about looking for premises. Once again the timing of the Lord was evident, for the people in the shop downstairs (the Daveys lived above the store) were vacating. This was an answer to prayer, for this was a rum shop and the odors were not all that pleasing to the upstairs tenants! Negotiations were completed and CLC took over this shop just as the merchandise from London was arriving. John got busy making shelves and display counters, and within a short time the work was started. CLC had raised its standard in yet another country.

Leap of Faith by Norman Grubb, published by CLC.

9

FOCUS ON OTHER CONTINENTS

The news from North America continued to be encouraging. Not only had a small beginning been made in Toronto, but a bookroom located on the fourth floor of a downtown office building in Rochester, New York, on the south shore of Lake Ontario, had been taken over by the young work in Canada. Now, CLC had a toehold in yet another country, our fifth—the United States of America.

In October, 1947 the WEC had planned a sort of mini-international conference in Chicago, and they had written, kindly suggesting that I should attend this conference.

Their reasons were convincing. The John Daveys would be there, which would give me an opportunity to discuss the young work in Dominica. I would also have the opportunity to meet Earl Frid and the other workers in the budding North American CLC. A personal visit would give those on that side of the Atlantic a much clearer picture of the goals and hopes of CLC. Also, Norman Grubb would be going, and as he knew the beginnings of CLC in Britain, he could help clarify the picture for North America. So, on October 10, 1947 Norman Grubb and I boarded the Cunard liner *Queen Mary*. Early next morning we sailed out of Southampton and five days later arrived in New York, immediately entraining for Chicago.

Two results touching CLC came out of the Chicago conference. The John Daveys agreed to consider the possibility of transferring from WEC to CLC upon their return to Dominica after furlough. John would spearhead the advance into other Caribbean Islands, for he felt this area was ripe for an aggressive Christian literature program.

The second outcome was an urgent request that I return to North America as soon as possible for two years, to help establish the work on the CLC principles, methods, and goals. This witnessed to my own heart and I agreed to present the proposition to the British CLC upon my return to England in April, 1948. I spent the next five months in North America traveling west through Canada, then down to Los Angeles, back to Chicago, further east to Philadelphia and then on to New York, to board Cunard's *Queen Elizabeth* for my journey across the Atlantic. I left North America greatly encouraged. The people right across the continent had received me warmly and caught the vision of the young CLC and its growing world outreach with enthusiasm.

Six weeks later I crossed the Atlantic for the third time. On this journey my wife Bessie and our two young daughters, Margaret and Janet, accompanied me. As British subjects we decided to make our base in Toronto, Canada, although giving the majority of our time to the United States. During these two years the little bookshop in suburban Toronto was moved to 550 Yonge Street, the bookroom in Rochester was moved to a ground floor store on Main Street, and we took over an existing store in Raleigh, North Carolina.

During my previous six months in North America things had continued to develop in Britain. Negotiations were in progress regarding bookcenters in Birmingham and in Aberdeen, Scotland. They were also expanding overseas, and CLC had been able to respond to the call for bookcenters in Germany. The first was opened in Lubeck, another in Oldenburg, and a third in Hamburg.

This was our biggest overseas advance to date, and we had seen the Lord's financial provision in a remarkable way. I remember well the particular prayer meeting when this whole subject was thoroughly discussed. The Lord gave us the figure of £1,000 ($5,000) as the sum we should ask Him for. The conviction was also strong among us—indeed was unanimous—that we should move ahead without delay. To all of us this was the

Captain's instruction, and with confidence we would count on Him to honor His promise and provide the wherewithal to fulfill His will.

On the strength of this we went to our knees, but the note in our prayer changed quickly from asking to praising. We just thanked Him for the funds He was going to supply and even had the audacity to tell the Lord the date by which we expected the £1,000! Sizeable orders were sent off to Switzerland for stock and other actions were taken, freely spending the money which was not yet visible! We were tested, but faith never wavered. A few small gifts came in but nothing near the figure we were expecting.

Then, it happened.

Word came from the bank just a day or two before the month ended telling us that an anonymous gift of £1,000 ($5,000) had been placed in our account earmarked for our work in Germany! What rejoicing in our ranks! We were to spend many more large sums on the developing work in Germany, and every time a new need arose we saw the Lord's faithful provision.

While all this was going on, Africa appeared on the horizon. Herb and Marion Congo, WEC missionaries on their way for furlough in Canada, stopped off in London. They, too, had read about this young CLC. They, too, came to share a burden. Liberia's national language was English. All education and commerce in the capital city of Monrovia was conducted in English. Monrovia must have a Christian bookcenter. Would CLC act? They also put action to their appeal. They were willing to help get a bookstore started upon their return to Liberia on the understanding that CLC would send reinforcements as quickly as possible to carry on the program.

Before the decade of the forties ended, CLC was to enter one more city in one more country on one more continent—Montevideo, Uruguay, South America. This time we witnessed a lesson on the flexibility of the Holy Spirit.

Our Captain made it clear that our work was not to be based on or controlled by the logic of human wisdom. Rules and guidelines are necessary, but they must never become the "law of the

Medes and Persians." God will do His work His way—always.

Several times I had stayed in the lovely home of Bertram and Margaret Jones in Northampton, England, and they were always keen to know the latest developments. Margaret was a child of missionary parents and had spent most of her first twelve years in Spain. Bertram was a partner in a family shoe business, and now in their late forties business was prospering and they were enjoying the comforts of their home. But God's work and God's will were uppermost in their minds and hearts. Because they personally knew the value of Christian literature and saw its potential as a tool in the ongoing missionary program, they offered their services to CLC for work in South America. Their application papers were processed and accepted so they went to London for their orientation and preparation for mission service.

CLC Britain's hands were full. The national program was expanding, the work in Germany was demanding, and keeping supplies moving to Dominica was as much as they could handle. They decided that if CLC North America was ready to begin work in South America, they would gladly send the Joneses to Canada for any further training. Then North America would have to be fully responsible for their support and the financing of any work started in South America.

Fair enough! The Joneses were ready to accept the proposition and so was the Canadian CLC staff. How to implement it was another matter!

At first glance it was a pretty reckless enterprise: two people, well past middle life, one of them without the Spanish language and neither of them experienced in running a Christian bookcenter or literature program. With just a willingness to go and an expectation that God would be their wisdom each step of the way, this couple set sail into the unknown. CLC had not put a blank check in their hands nor opened a bank account for them in Montevideo from which they could draw ample supplies. They just had the promises of their God—adequate enough by any measure. They were fully prepared to prove the workability of "having nothing, yet possessing all things."

There were the usual ups and downs and tests of faith, but through it all, a bookcenter was opened in Montevideo and a small publishing effort in Spanish was started. The work was strengthened with the coming of Gladys Brownlee who spoke Spanish, having worked in Colombia for some years. Soon a local young lady, Esther Naylor, joined the team. God used this older couple as the pioneers and then brought younger people along to continue the work and to spread it from Montevideo into the Argentine and Chile.

Now in 1981, thirty-three years later, the work in Uruguay continues. Indeed, it has become one of our most stable and productive ministries in South America. We are thankful that we followed the flexibility of the Spirit, the wisdom of our God and not the logic of our limited understanding.

This experience was to stand us in good stead for it happened again in 1949.

10

LAND OF THE RISING SUN

Japan, the Land of the Rising Sun, was just beginning to revive from the shattered ruins of its towns and cities. Sixty per cent of the capital, Tokyo, lay in shambles. Hiroshima and Nagasaki were still reeling from the devastation of the A-bombs. Japan's new leader, Douglas MacArthur, was not a divine emperor but a foreign general. That was in the Divine ordering, for MacArthur was a man of unswerving principle and deep Christian conviction. He was God's man in God's place at God's time, and with two bold decisions he set the stage for an unprecedented new day for the people of that broken nation. In assuring the Japanese that he was there not as a conqueror but as a fellow man dedicated to restoration, he informed them in one of his public speeches that *you cannot have a democracy without Christianity*. In the hope of making the latter become a reality, he called upon the churches of the West to "send an army of missionaries" to Japan as quickly as possible. After years of being open a mere crack, suddenly the door swung wide open for the entry of the publishers of the good news.

Just as we had seen great opportunities in post-war Germany, our hearts were now sensitive to Japan's potential for the gospel. We knew the Japanese were great readers, so a Christian literature ministry should make a significant contribution to "publishing good tidings" in the Orient. In the light of General MacArthur's appeal, we were giving the matter much prayerful consideration, although we did not plan to take any specific action. Bessie and I were in North America on a two-year assignment to help get the work on its feet; perhaps after that, something could be considered.

On one of my trips to Chicago I visited Kenneth Taylor, then Director of Moody Press. Among other things, we discussed this new challenge regarding Japan. We agreed that literature should be one of the key ways of spreading the gospel throughout the country, but neither of us had any facts as to just what was currently available or how the opportunity should be tackled. He assured me that Moody would be keenly interested in any facts that I might glean and would stand ready to help in any way possible.

I left Ken's office stirred in spirit and wondering what CLC could or should be doing. In less than twenty-four hours the answer came. Go yourself and look the situation over.

But wait a minute!

We had only been in North America about ten months and our program was full. What would our British colleagues say if I took off for Japan? Still the inner witness was clear—go immediately to Japan. Yes, this was the Captain's voice. We must obey at any cost and not be swayed by the logical reasonings of the human mind. The Holy Spirit was again indicating, as He had regarding Uruguay, *who* is actually in charge of CLC.

Things fell into place quickly. I was able to obtain a sailing from San Francisco. The foreign missions department of the Church of the Nazarene agreed to allow Dr. Eckel, their representative in Japan, to sponsor my visit. (This was a requirement at that time.) Funds for the journey were provided and by mid-March, 1949 I was on my way to the west coast.

A month later I began my two-week journey across the Pacific. There were thirty missionaries among the several hundred passengers. Most of them were first termers heading to different countries of the Far East. We had good fellowship and good opportunities for ministry including conducting Sunday services on board.

But I will never forget Easter Sunday.

We had decided to have a sunrise service on deck. It was windy and rainy but we found a reasonably sheltered area and tried to make the best of a rather disappointing Easter Sunday weather-wise. As the service proceeded a beautiful thing happened. God came to meet us.

Suddenly there was a break in the overcast sky and the sun shone! A few minutes later there appeared the brightest, most complete and colorful rainbow I have ever seen. It was as though God was saying to this intrepid band of beginners, myself among them, "I am your Covenant-keeping God. Trust Me. Count on Me always!" The rest of that sunrise service was alive and enthusiastic, I can assure you.

I spent over two months in Japan. The missionaries were warm and cordial, especially the few senior workers who had served in Japan prior to the war. They supplied me with the facts and figures I was looking for, and the picture was not bright.

Halfway through my stay I set up a two-day conference. About twenty-five gathered, representing sixteen missions. This was basically all of the missions at work in Japan at that time. Most of the missionaries were new to the country, still grappling with the language, which can take as many as five years to master! I had previously circulated a fairly extensive questionnaire asking them to bring as much information as possible, preferably actual copies of whatever Christian literature they knew of in Japanese. The conference proved to be extremely helpful, although the picture of available literature was discouraging, but challenging. We had only been able to find about twenty-four titles of anything currently in print, ranging from simple tracts to the Scriptures. Even these were in pathetically short supply.

When leaving Japan, the leader of TEAM had kindly driven me to the airport. I can feel the strength of his handshake yet and see his penetrating appeal as he looked at me and pleaded, "Please be sure to return. Do not let us down."

The facts I had gleaned and the challenge they presented were shared quickly with our CLC fellowship in North America, Britain, Australia and elsewhere. We seized every opportunity to present this astounding challenge before as many of God's people as we could reach by spoken word and through the printed page.

The following year, 1950, things began to fall in place. Before the year ended, Ray Oram, from Bristol, England, responded to the call for personnel and headed to Japan as CLC's first representative. He went by way of the States, for this advance was to be the responsibility of CLC North America, and Ray's visit would give us opportunity to consult together. Once again, we were totally cast upon God to see us through. We needed His wisdom and His provision every step of the way. Just how did we expect to develop a literature work with hardly any literature in the language of the people?

We would major in English literature.

I had found during my visit that almost all Japanese pastors and Christian leaders read English. Scarcely any of the many helpful study books and commentaries had been put into Japanese, so all theological training had to be done using English books.

Then there was the Army of Occupation. We had a wonderful opportunity to get good Christian literature into the hands of American youth who were the mainstay of the occupation forces in Japan. Many young men found Christ as their personal Saviour during their time of service in Japan. Some, who were Christians, caught the vision of missionary service and, indeed, a number of missions actually were started during the fifties by many of these very men who had served their country overseas. The Far Eastern Gospel Crusade was one such group.

Things began to improve quickly as missions did their best to get something written or translated into Japanese, so within a couple of years we began to give serious thought to opening Christian bookstores. By the time Ray and his wife, Margaret, whom he married in Japan, were ready for furlough in 1955, three bookshops had been opened: in Kyoto, Sendai and Tokyo.

One veteran missionary in Japan was Miss Irene Webster-Smith, a remarkable Irish lady whom the Lord had used over her long years of service to bring the Christian gospel into many of the higher circles of Japan's elite, even to the Empress. Years earlier she had been able to obtain a house with a sizeable piece of land located in the university area of Tokyo. Her burden had always been to work among students, and because of the new freedoms in post-war Japan, she saw her opportunity to establish an active Christian student center right in the heart of this main university area. By 1955 her goal was reached, and a beautiful, modern three-story building facing the main street was completed. Along with an auditorium and other meeting rooms for the students, a bookstore had been planned. Miss Webster-Smith approached Ray Oram requesting that CLC be responsible for this bookcenter in the student building.

It was opened and dedicated just hours before the Orams sailed out of Yokohama for Britain and their first furlough.

Bob and Dorothy Gerry, who went to Japan as WEC missionaries, took over from the Orams and continued there until 1979. Under their wise leadership the work has grown by leaps and bounds. Bob still makes occasional visits to Japan in his capacity as CLC International Secretary and is always heartened as the ministry continues to move forward under the direction of Peter and Joy Horne and a capable national committee.

The bookshop is still in that same building, although the building itself has been enlarged and added to several times. An important change for CLC took place in 1973. At first we were disappointed when the governing board of the Student Center advised us that we would have to move from our location on the right side of the main entrance to the left side, but it proved to be God's opportunity.

The move enabled us to modernize our display and plan a better layout of the shop, making it more attractive. We were also given room above the shop where we were able to develop a much more extensive English literature center. Later we were a little chagrined when we learned the reason for this move.

The board had contracted with McDonald's, an American hamburger chain. Apparently it was much easier to enlarge the area we were occupying to accommodate this McDonald's Company. We moved only to find that on our other side another American food chain—Mister Donut—was to open! This made three companies in the food business side by side—Mister Donut and McDonald's looking after physical needs, and right in the middle The Bread of Life bookshop looking after spiritual needs!

The result for CLC? Unbelievable! Thousands of students pass our door every day, but when we were on our own only a trickle found their way into the Christian bookshop. The students were in too much of a hurry to stop. Now that there are two eating houses, they do stop. Then, after their repast and in a relaxed frame of mind, they take time to come and browse in the Christian bookstore.

The increased outflow of literature, including the Scriptures, has been phenomenal. Many days we have to restock the shelves with Bibles and Testaments two or three times. The Bible Society tells us that this store is the largest single distributor of the Scriptures in all of Japan! What thrills us is that possibly 80 per cent of those Scriptures, and a very high percentage of the other Christian literature, goes into the hands of non-Christians, many of them students.

CLC now has a second Japanese bookcenter in Tokyo, plus the English bookstore located in the Student Center, as well as a flourishing wholesale division serving more than seventy Christian bookstores and the CLC centers located in seven other cities—Hiroshima, Kanazawa, Kumamoto, Kyoto, Nagoya, Okayama, and Sapporo. A bookmobile operates in conjunction with each center, getting vital Christian literature into the country areas. The publishing program has grown steadily.

Thankfully others have carried the heavy end of publishing, notably TEAM's Word of Life Press. Whereas thirty years ago there were less than twenty books available, today there are something over 3,000 titles of good Christian literature ranging from the Scriptures, including newer translations, to evangelistic books, commentaries, study books, devotional titles and a good variety of reading material for youth and children.

Most of this is still translated material, although thankfully national authors are making a much bigger contribution.

Our team of workers has grown significantly from one worker—Ray Oram—in 1950 to over sixty workers in 1981, most being Japanese. God has brought to us choice and capable Japanese fellow workers, each dedicated and enthusiastic with an ever-growing vision of the literature ministry, not only for their homeland but in other parts of the world.

CLC Japan has made a vital contribution to the work in Brazil, where more than a million Japanese reside. To help get the multi-language phase of the Brazilian work started they sent sizeable supplies of Japanese literature as an outright gift. CLC Japan also fully supports Mrs. Saito and her son, Samuel. She served with CLC in the Sapporo center for about four years and is now capably handling the Japanese literature program from our Sao Paulo International Bookstore in Brazil. So CLC Japan now has its own missionary serving overseas and expects to be sending more trained workers to other parts of the world in the years ahead.

The Hawaiian Islands also challenged them. Here thousands of fellow countrymen live, as well as other Orientals.

Then came action.

Along with Bob Gerry two Japanese CLCers surveyed the situation and in 1978 Japan took the initiative by opening a book-center in Honolulu and supplying Japanese, Chinese and Korean literature. CLC U.S.A. added about $10,000 of English stock, and Japanese-born Miss Eiko Soronaka, now an American citizen, went to Japan for several months of training in the Tokyo store. She is now in charge of the Honolulu center, which opened its doors in May 1978.

Japan's world interest grows, and with it, prayer and practical help. In 1979 they sent a bookmobile to the young CLC work in Sri Lanka as a gift and a token of their interest in this land of new opportunity. During the decade of the eighties they expect to continue their involvement in the expanding CLC worldwide.

Our beginnings in Japan were feeble indeed. In the natural we would have preferred to have planned and provided substantially, but that wasn't God's way for us. Beginning simply has almost become standard procedure, so any glory in later success goes to Him. Certainly of the work in Japan we can say without hesitation, "He has done great things whereof we are glad—and the best is yet to be!"

Literature work in any part of the world is, in a sense, a hidden ministry. We sow; God gives the increase. Yes, it is a faith enterprise, to be sure. Not always do we see tangible results, although we are encouraged by the evidences of the "fruit of our labors" which do reach us along the way. People do find Christ as Saviour; they do grow in the faith; they do share their faith in personal witness; they do become involved as full-time literature missionaries or in some other phase of Christian ministry— all as a direct result of the printed word put into their hands somewhere along the way. Then sometimes the end results are seen in a bigger way.

This was so in the fall of 1980.

Billy Graham and his team again visited Japan. Over a two-week period campaigns were held in several cities, culminating in the 40,000 seat stadium in Tokyo. In each city the crowds overflowed the auditorium capacity. Thousands responded. Statistics show that the numerical results of these days in Japan outstripped any previous campaigns in any part of the world! Percentage wise, results elsewhere have ranged from a low of 3 per cent to a high of around 7 per cent. These days in Japan produced an amazing almost 13 per cent. Surely this was Japan's hour in God's planning, but it might never have been possible had there not been years of faithful, dogged sowing of the seed— the Word of God, spoken and printed. To God be the glory. GREAT THINGS He has done.

CLC Japan continues its forward move. In 1980 a planning committee was created and five-year goals set, which include consolidation of all existing functions, increase of personnel, both national and international, and at least two more bookcenters with mobile outreach. Although it cannot be planned by any committee, expectations are high that the decade of the eighties will see increased harvesting as more and more Japanese respond to the gospel and share their faith with others.

Celebrating thirty years of literature ministry in the country, a special meeting was arranged in December 1980. Eighty pastors and guests attended, joining their hearts together in recognizing the good hand of the Lord over the years now gone, expressing personal gratitude for what the ministry has meant to them, and indicating their determination to continue upholding the CLC ministry and its anticipated growth and expansion in this new decade.

11

ALL ARE EQUAL

There were more lessons to be learned as the work continued to expand. We were now clearly established on the principle of being an interdenominational work, serving the literature needs of all; of being an inter-mission service agency where we could help; and of being international in scope. Now, we saw that we would also become an interracial mission.

This is easier said than realized, not because citizens of other countries would be unwilling to cooperate with us, but because of our foundation principle of fellowship whereby we recognize the oneness of the Body of Christ. Were we really ready to accept people of other nationalities on a full fellowship basis totally free of prejudice? In theory, yes. In practice, that might turn out differently.

I remember well the occasion when the Lord shook me up about this issue. It happened this way. For a number of years there had been a remarkable ministry of revival going on continuously in Africa in the country which was then known as Ruanda. News of this continuing move of the Spirit was filtering through to many countries.

In the mid-forties I had the privilege of spending several days with one of the leaders of this work—William Nagenda. He came to London at the invitation of Norman Grubb, along with another African. William was very fluent in English and an able expositor of God's Word, particularly relating to this message of renewal.

I remember being very favorably impressed by these two brethren. They spoke with considerable authority, although I was disappointed that they did not tell us very much of the actual story of this Ruanda revival. Rather, they ministered to us in just the same way they did to their fellow Africans. The standard of their message was high. Inconsistencies in daily living could not be tolerated. The Holy Spirit would not countenance *hidden dishonesty.* They were convinced that the Holy Spirit demanded total honesty, not only in individual living but also in individual witness and personal ministry. If they felt any person was living below these standards they would boldly challenge that person. "My brother, I sense pride in your heart." "My sister, you appear very frustrated." "Young man, there is evidence of disobedience in your life." "Young woman, you are not allowing the Holy Spirit to control your emotions." They would urge immediate repentance which would bring immediate cleansing and immediate release from the problem. Then would flow again the abundant life of the indwelling Spirit of the living God.

Now that was all well and good in Africa, but when these two brethren began to apply these same methods to those of us in England, that was something quite different. They expressed great gratitude for the missionaries who had brought the gospel to their country. That pleased us. However, to them the gospel was not just a matter of sins forgiven and peace with God, but it was a matter of holy living and a true integration into the family of God as active members of the Body of Christ.

Agreed, this was good doctrine. We could accept it as such, but to apply this in such a practical way was something which we questioned. I did. Surely it was the work of the Holy Spirit alone to convict of any irregularity in Christian living. If the Holy Spirit through the Word revealed some area of weakness and sin, then we would certainly make adjustments, but we were unwilling to accept this *interference,* this kind of meddling in personal matters, coming from these African brothers. Did they not know their place? Did they not know there was a limit to how far they could go?

Then the Holy Spirit began His convicting ministry. I was able to see that it was not a case of African brethren going too far, but of me being unwilling to go far enough! After all, I did believe in the Body of Christ. I did believe that this body would be made up of people from every tribe and nation and tongue. That's why my heart and soul was in the missionary program. Still I was holding it as a belief, a doctrine—I was not accepting it as an actual, operating, day-by-day fact of the Christian life.

Thankfully through that experience a change in my heart on this attitude did take place. I must admit I never did follow through in repenting to the point of telling these two gracious brethren of my sin of pride, criticism and limited acceptance of them as members of the Body of Christ. William is now in heaven, so I will have to wait until I meet him there to remedy the matter, although perhaps penning it now in this book will be acceptable. Certainly that change in my heart has borne fruit in the growth of the CLC. One of the six Guiding Principles in our current International Constitution states it succinctly: "We are a fellowship of God's people drawn from various denominational and cultural backgrounds. We therefore allow no national or racial prejudices or exclusive denominational or doctrinal emphases in the life and ministry of the Crusade." Today we have nearly six hundred workers drawn from fifty-one nationalities in the service of CLC! And we love all of them.

Of these, perhaps five hundred have actually applied for membership in the Crusade, completing their application forms and spending a time of orientation and training in the literature ministry. Of course, the same principle of oneness in the Body of Christ applies to all who serve with us in the work.

Those who have become members of the organization are welcomed in any part of the world. They can share in staff meetings in any country. They can assume leadership or other positions of responsibility in their own country as the Holy Spirit witnesses this to the local staff. They are also free to serve cross-culturally in any other part of the world and are considered just as much missionaries as those of us from the West. Indeed, there is no position in the Crusade, including serving on our International Council, which is out of bounds for any member of our worldwide international fellowship. Our present Council is comprised of seven nationalities. Admittedly most are from the West. Brother V. M. Abraham from India is one of the exceptions. Actually the only thing which restricts some from being eligible for such service is their inability to speak English. Our hope is that this can be rectified during this decade.

On the surface, this appears to be an exciting accomplishment, but working out this principle of oneness in the Body of Christ is something that all of our fifty-one nationalities have to grapple with. In most countries there are distinct ethnic groups, and we have to learn how to work with each other, trust each other, and respect each other, recognizing that the Holy Spirit indwells all His temple. This is true even in smaller countries, such as in the West Indies. In Trinidad, for instance, there are five distinct ethnic groups—African, Indian, Chinese, Syrian and European. In larger countries, such as Indonesia, where the people are spread over several thousand islands, the whole setting and way of life in each is quite different. A number of our Indonesian workers have been sent from their home island to another and have found themselves in an almost totally different country.

We also have to guard against accepting a worker into a position of leadership because his ethnic background. Our qualifications can only be those of the Spirit. Does this worker evidence true maturity of the Spirit? Will he be unbiased in his leadership? Will he be ready to serve the needs of all the workers whom God has appointed him to lead? Can he live above any inferiority his background may have given him?

I personally can testify to this very point. As an Englishman I have served the greater part of my leadership with Americans and Canadians! I gladly testify that my fellow workers in North America have been very gracious to me personally. I can look back to more than thirty years of service in America with very happy memories. Not that everything at all times has been smooth sailing! No, we have had our battles, our disagreements, our sharp differences of opinion, and yet I have never sensed that my nationality was important as we grappled together with the problems until we could finally say "Thus saith the Lord" on the point we were discussing.

Over the years several books inspired by the work of the Spirit in Ruanda have been published by CLC. Two, specifically, are *The Calvary Road* by Roy Hession and *Continuous Revival* by Norman Grubb. Both of these authors took time to visit Ruanda and fellowshipped with the Christians there. Obviously, they learned some personal lessons and were anxious to share these and the wonderful reality of a workable, continuous revival with God's people around the world. Both these books are still in demand and enjoy wide circulation. *The Calvary Road* has been translated into more than thirty languages.

Their message continues to meet the needs of hungry hearts, but an interesting thing happened some years ago.

William Nagenda, Roy Hession and others visited the States and spent some time with us at our Fort Washington, Pennsylvania headquarters. They asked that the words JESUS ONLY be displayed prominently in the auditorium, for they had a growing concern that people were talking about "The Ruanda message," whereas to them there was no such message. It was just a case of making Christ totally central. They were concerned that many were putting *things,* even doctrines and Biblical interpretations, in place of Jesus only.

William felt that this was true of Roy Hession's book *The Calvary Road.* He was concerned when a lady wrote Roy indicating that she was being so blessed by the book that she actually put it under her pillow at night! To William this indicated that the book was becoming a fetish. Certainly it was not a case of JESUS ONLY but of *The Calvary Road* and JESUS. So he strongly urged me to take the book off the market and cease publishing further editions. We gave his request prayerful thought but were not able to agree. Just because one or two people were going too far did not, in our judgment, justify withholding the book, for it was bringing blessing and liberation to many.

Here was a case where dear Brother William had to submit to

the teaching he had expounded in England. Rightly, he shared his concern, but he also had to submit to the way of the Spirit as expressed through the fellowship—in this case the fellowship being just a few of us who were considering the matter together.

We see this same principle operating in country after country. We have to watch against letting the culture of our country stand in the way of our obedience to our one and only culture as members of His family—the way of the Spirit. This applies even in simple things, too.

One of our newer Japanese workers faced this problem during the 1980 Billy Graham campaign in Tokyo. CLC shared with others in having book tables. We also were given permission to go up and down the aisles prior to the start of the service with books and Bibles. But this young man was gripped by the we-don't-do-this-in-our-country syndrome, and on his first day sold hardly anything. Then the Holy Spirit spoke and this young CLCer recognized that his attitude was nothing more than personal pride. He just didn't like doing this. So the next day he went forth in the boldness of the Holy Spirit and from then on became our best aisle salesman!

Yes, I fear it is sometimes true that CLC is publishing books which are actually beyond our own daily experience. So pray for us. We sincerely want to be known, not only as publishers of "deeper life" books, but as people who through life, lip and literature are manifesting the manifold grace of God in all areas of our daily lives.

SECTION III

A TREE...BEARS FRUIT IN HIS SEASON
Psalm 1:3

*And he shall be like a tree planted by the rivers of
water, that bringeth forth its fruit in its season; its
leaf also shall not wither, and whatsoever he doeth
shall prosper.*

Psalms 1:3

12

THE ISLANDS BECKON

In the first eight years and two months since CLC officially started on November 1, 1941 we had seen the work established in eight countries—U.K., Canada, Australia, U.S.A., Dominica, Uruguay, Germany and Liberia—giving us a foothold on five continents. The decade of the fifties was to see further rapid advance. The work would be established in twenty-one more countries, and CLC North America would carry the major weight of the expanding overseas program during these next ten years.

During 1950 a second country in Europe was entered—Belgium. A store in the bilingual city of Antwerp was opened and a good ministry developed. Unfortunately, we have not always been able to hold the ground gained on every occasion. At the time of this writing fifty-four countries have been entered by CLC, the newest being Finland, where we took over an existing bookstore in the city of Helsinki on January 1, 1981, but over the years we have withdrawn from eight countries. We anticipate that some of these will be re-entered during the eighties, along with opening new countries where CLC is not currently operating. Belgium is one such country. We had to withdraw from the work because of lack of personnel.

As John and Ethel Davey completed their furlough and returned to Dominica our eyes were again focused on the West Indies. Two areas were before us—Trinidad and Jamaica—but we were uncertain which was to come first and just counted on our Captain to guide. Interestingly, things happened almost simultaneously. John's increasing burden was for Trinidad, and he had set Easter of 1951 as the goal for the Davey family and Lizzie Miller to transfer from Dominica to Trinidad. Because John had no experience in opening new CLC countries, he asked if I would meet him in Trinidad and help in this new undertaking. So in January 1951 I left Philadelphia and motored down to Miami. Funds in CLC for this trip were not available, so I agreed to accept the responsibility and would personally watch the Lord provide. I set out with $16 in my pocket! As I had expected, He did supply, mainly through a few church meetings on my way down to Miami.

In those days I was not very familiar with air travel schedules, and I rather naively assumed that all I had to do was to go to a travel agent and buy my ticket! This I did while in Miami. If I remember rightly it was a Thursday and I wished to reach Port-of-Spain, Trinidad, by the weekend. Imagine my frustration when I was told that there would be no flight until the following Tuesday, and even then it would mean an overnight stop in Kingston, Jamaica. This proved to be in God's ordering, for the stop in Kingston brought me in touch again with my earlier Sunday School teacher, Harold Wildish. Harold would be instrumental in bringing the CLC ministry to the island of Jamaica before the year was out. The work has been maintained under the leadership of George DaCosta for the past thirty years and is now continuing in the hands of a younger man, a fellow Jamaican, John Keane.

The next day I arrived in Trinidad. John Davey was at the airport to meet me and we immediately began our strategy discussions for our stay in Trinidad. I also shared with John the interesting developments of the last few hours while I was in Jamaica. Subsequently John played a significant part in the development of the literature ministry there for a number of years.

Our hosts in Trinidad, Hedley and Emma McLachlan, were keenly interested in seeing a literature ministry develop in their island and gave us every encouragement. Hedley was Assistant Postmaster General, so he knew the island and its people thoroughly. Each morning we would consult together and then compare notes at the end of the day. We were anticipating two things—a house for the workers and shop premises for the beginning of the ministry. Even though we were in touch with key people, particularly in Port-of-Spain, no answer came to either need.

While concentrating on the capital city, we also took time to visit most of the island, traveling many miles by buses. Whenever visiting distant post offices, Hedley took us along in his car. This enabled us to see much more firsthand.

Our time in Trinidad came to an end, still without much success, and we wondered just what the Lord had planned for CLC here. One thing had become increasingly clear. Our travels throughout the island convinced us that a mobile ministry would have to be part of the literature thrust. Because no store premises had yet become available we felt that perhaps the start should be made with a bookmobile. In leaving the island we had three faith targets before us. First, the provision of a bookmobile; second, a home for the Davey family of four and Lizzie Miller; and third, a good store location.

Knowing that God would lead step by step and that by Easter, just three months away, at least goal number two would become available, Hedley and other local businessmen continued the search. After a few days in Dominica, I returned to the States by way of an eight-day visit in Jamaica.

Naturally I reported on my trip at one of our regular joint prayer sessions at our Pennsylvania headquarters. All were enthused and agreed to stand in faith for the three goals. A day or two later a young lady, a candidate for service in India, came to talk with me. She had been praying regarding the need for a bookmobile and the Lord had challenged her to become personally involved.

This was her story.

As she prayed the Lord had checked her up regarding earlier promises made in connection with her giving during the time she was a student at the Prairie Bible Institute in Canada. Because of other financial needs, including saving money for her journey to India, she had not fulfilled her pledged commitments while at Bible School. Now with this urgent need for the vehicle in Trinidad she knew the Lord was asking her to fulfill her obligation and make the total sum available towards this need. I urged her to go cautiously, although I did encourage her to meet her previous promise to the Lord through the PBI missionary program. I also counseled her against any "on-the-spur-of-the-moment" emotional reaction, though I appreciated her concern. We agreed to leave the matter for a few days of further careful thought and prayer. She had not mentioned the amount.

When next we met, her conviction was even stronger. God had told her clearly that He wanted her promise to Him to be met and He wanted the funds to be applied to the Trinidad need. What more could I say? I asked what amount we were talking about and she said $750. I was dumfounded, having expected the answer to be $50 or so, because this amount was more than half the price of the brand new station wagon we had our eye on! I was both humbled and jubilant.

That dear lady is still in God's service and has spent many fruitful years in India, but her investment in Trinidad continues to produce dividends. She has laid up treasure in heaven.

Word went off immediately to John Davey and the vehicle was on the road with its life-giving literature in a matter of weeks. Our strategy proved to be correct, for the mobile outreach gave us a thorough knowledge of the island and the areas of greatest need.

Goal number two had been realized, too. The home of a Nazarene missionary family could be used for one year during their furlough. This made possible a bookroom until goal number three was achieved some months later, when 63 Abercrombie Street became available. Part of the premises was being used to make caskets for the dead—now they would also provide spiritual food for the living! We remained in these premises for some years, during which time a second center was opened in the southern town of San Fernando. It was quite small and in an arcade, but in the seventies rapid changes took place.

A piece of land on Abercrombie Street, nearer the center of the city, was purchased, and a lovely two-story building erected. With that move completed the work in Trinidad began to leap forward. The San Fernando center was moved to a much better location at the entrance to the same arcade, giving us frontage on the main street. A mobile ministry based on this center has operated for a number of years. A third center was opened in the town of Arima. Because it is right in the center of town it has developed into a vital ministry, especially among young people, even though it is located on the second floor.

Our goals for the eighties include seeing a mobile ministry develop from each center. Other methods of outreach are anticipated which may include a fourth bookcenter.

At one time we did have a center in the far south of the island. On one of my later visits I met a dear brother, now an outstanding evangelist, who remembers that shop in Point Fortin very personally. He was going through a spiritual valley experience when one day he happened to visit the bookstore and found two books which interested him. One was Oswald Smith's *Passion for Souls* and the other Oswald Chambers' *So Send I You*. He testified very emphatically that those two books revolutionized his spiritual life and became foundational to his present evangelistic ministry. Such incidents could be repeated over and over again from every center in every part of the world, for books continue to influence the lives of people in many and varied ways.

In the next seven years eleven more countries were entered and three of these were in the West Indies. A Scottish couple, John and Jessie Buchanan, lived in the South American country then known as British Guiana (Guyana since 1970). John headed up the hardware department of the Booker Company. As keen and active Christians they were particularly interested in working with young people. Consequently the need for Christian literature in the country became increasingly apparent to them, so John urged John Davey to come to British Guiana and investigate the possibility of opening a center in Georgetown.

This was accomplished in 1953 and it remained an active ministry for almost twenty years, but then the situation began to deteriorate. All books coming into the country were censored by the government and getting supplies became increasingly difficult, so in the early seventies CLC withdrew from Guyana and another mission took over the bookstore activities. Unfortunately this did not last, for when the missionary had to leave, the literature work came to a standstill. A trickle of Christian literature continues to get into Guyana because some local Christians are doing their best to keep a small supply in hand. CLC is keeping a watchful eye on the situation and will be ready to return to Guyana as soon as restrictions are lifted.

The same is true of the work in British Honduras, now known as Belize. That same year, 1953, a start was made in the capital city. Some years later we handed over this work to the Gospel Missionary Union. I believe that literature ministry continues to this day.

Four years later, in 1957, a call came from Barbados. I had been in the island the previous year, when I made a promotional trip throughout the Eastern Caribbean for the forthcoming *Caribbean Challenge* magazine which CLC Jamaica began publishing that same year and which continues in circulation to this day.

While in Barbados I was approached about the possibility of taking over a small literature work which a missionary of the Plymouth Brethren had been operating for some years. His health was not good and he planned to return to his homeland but wanted to see the literature work continued. When I returned to Jamaica at the end of my *Caribbean Challenge* promotional trip I shared this call with our team there, but what could we do? Where was the personnel for such an opportunity?

The John Daveys were due to leave shortly for their overdue furlough in Australia. It would seem that nothing could be done for at least another year, but it did not seem right to postpone action. The challenge became personal for John and Ethel Davey. CLC's foundational principle of sacrifice again came into play. The Daveys would postpone their furlough for another year! They would move over to Barbados and get the CLC program started, anticipating that by the time they did go on furlough other workers would be available to take over from them.

But the Captain had other plans.

During this year it became increasingly evident that Barbados could serve as the main base for any future developments in the Eastern Caribbean. So, after furlough, the Daveys returned to Barbados and made this their permanent base until the mid-1970's, when they transferred to Canada after thirty-three years of active ministry in the West Indies. The bookroom had been moved to a central location on Broad Street, although this was abruptly terminated when fire gutted the entire building. We moved to one temporary location and then to another, until the early seventies when we settled into a new, permanent complex on St. Michael's Row.

If Barbados was to become a center for the Eastern Caribbean, it seemed necessary to consider adequate housing, possibly building to our own specifications. The Daveys accepted this as a further personal opportunity. A piece of land became available and John put months of his own blood and sweat—and perhaps some tears—into building Faith House. The name was appropriate, for the Daveys had agreed to assume responsibility to pray in the funds for this undertaking. God honored that stand, and on dedication day in 1963 the house was opened to the glory of God with all bills paid!

It was expected that this building would become a center for training new workers, most of whom hopefully would come from the West Indies. It continues to serve this purpose, as well as providing housing for workers and visitors who come from the other islands and from other parts of the world for consultation, guidance and spiritual help. After the Daveys left for Canada, Phyllis Trim from New Zealand carried on this responsibility until 1980, when Bill and Marge Almack and their family transferred from Trinidad to assume the task of superintending the Eastern Caribbean work, which is now active in seven of the islands—Trinidad, Barbados, St. Vincent, St. Lucia, Dominica, Antigua, and French Martinique.

Just what the Lord has for the work in this decade is not clearly spelled out; one thing is certain: more workers will be needed—men and women truly called of God. As in the days of the Acts, they must be "men of faith and of the Holy Ghost." Because of the element of business built into the CLC ministry, it is more imperative that those who serve with us in any part of the world are truly called of God and, with singleness of purpose, are always ready to respond to the voice of the Captain. There is so much more needing to be done, and which will remain undone until people rise up and do God's will, fulfilling the "good work which God hath before ordained that we [they] should walk in."

There is, however, a growing problem in many parts of the world.

The age of affluence is upon us in many countries. With the higher standard of education, young people feel that they are entitled to a "good job," with its corresponding "good pay," and they will search and travel until they find it. Still the example set by our Captain and the standards for discipleship clearly given to us in the Scriptures remain unchanged. They apply to every generation. Those of the first generation who accepted the implication of the Great Commission have passed on to us, by the preached and printed word and by personal example, the unchanging foundational principles for the fulfillment of that Great Commission. No hand must be taken off the plow.

Today's generation could be the completing generation for, thankfully, the gospel is spreading rapidly to the farthest corners of the earth. The task of completion and consolidation belongs to the church worldwide. It is the unique privilege of those of every nation to turn their backs upon the tempting affluence of the age and to devote themselves to the task. True, we do not have to return again to the simpler days of forty years ago when our desks and tables had to be nailed to the wall to keep them upright! We can be thankful for the new tools and better equipment in this day and age. If used in the same spirit of sacrificial simplicity of our Captain and His first followers, the task can be completed before this century has run its course. This must be our goal.

As in CLC Japan, our colleagues in the Caribbean have been responding to the Great Commission overseas as well as in their homelands. The Hudson Changs of Jamaica served for a number of years with CLC in Guyana and Trinidad. Guyana in turn has sent its missionaries. Rose Burrowes now serves with CLC in Montreal, Claire Chichester in Panama, and for a number of years Janet Bacchus (now Mrs. Felix Durand) served in Antigua. She and her husband are now watching for the Lord's new assignment for them, possibly again with CLC. Then, Delores Wason from Trinidad (now Mrs. Darrel Primus) helped build the CLC work in St. Vincent in its beginning days. We look for others in this part of the world to go, not only to their nearby neighbors but to the very corners of the earth, ideally fully supported by prayer and finances from their home church and local friends. The 1981 goal of CLC international for new workers stands at 153. By the end of the decade we hope to be a thousand strong, with full-time literature workers busily getting the word around, plus an ever increasing number of volunteers who give hours or days as they are able. The work would not be where it is today without them.

13

SIMPLE BEGINNINGS

For the first five years of the 1950's we concentrated on developing the work in North America, rather than continuing our overseas expansion. There were no journeys other than the one to the West Indies described in the previous chapter. Of course, we maintained our interest in all the overseas work, particularly those countries in which North America had a major responsibility.

During this time Britain took the overseas initiative, planting the CLC banner in two more countries of Europe—France and Italy—and then in 1954 stretching halfway around the world to the great sub-continent of India.

In every case the beginnings were simple. Indeed they had to be because there never was an abundant supply of either personnel or finances. We were always on the stretch. Every once in a while we would stop to review the situation. Were we really right in moving ahead so quickly? Wouldn't it be better to concentrate on the work in hand, building, consolidating, and strengthening before moving to fresh territory? We surely had to depend on the "wisdom which is from above" every time. And we are still asking the same questions today, but we can now look back on twenty or thirty years of experience to see what these simple, struggling beginnings have developed into.

Take France as a case in point.

It's beginnings could hardly have been more primitive. Writing an article for *Floodtide* in 1957 Jean Treboux put it this way: "We were led to establish a very insignificant bridgehead in an old and humble house in the small town of Marguerittes, surrounded by its vineyards and olive trees. It lies in the south, only five miles from the ancient city of Nimes, made famous by her huge, skillfully-built Roman arena, into which bullfights are still attracting thousands of people."

The start was painfully slow. Although the work officially started in 1952 it was not until 1957 that the first bookshop was opened—in the city of Rennes. It is still there, a vital testimony reaching out into the whole area of Brittany, northwest France. Next year it will celebrate its twenty-fifth anniversary! Since this opening day on March 15, 1957 seven other centers have been added—St. Peray, Toulouse, Strasbourg, Grenoble, Montpellier, Anduze, and the main headquarters in La Begude de Mazenc. A very sizeable publishing program in French has developed and a vast mail-order department reaches, not only across France, but into every French-speaking area of the world.

Yes, the beginnings were simple enough. The thrust of CLC France in its first five years was tract distribution, door-to-door colportage, bookstalls at market places, and even displaying colorful text posters on street walls where such things are officially permitted. Their little Citroen van also carried these gospel posters on it, silently proclaiming their living message.

One day a young engineer doing atomic research read the posters when the van was parked in Nimes. He was still there when Jean Treboux returned and he shared that he needed comfort because his child was dying. After a talk and prayer the young man went on his way, the glad possessor of a copy of God's Word. Three weeks later the Trebouxs learned that the child, who had been given up by the doctors, had been restored to the family in full health. He and his wife were grateful and invited Jean into their home. Both had many questions but they continued searching diligently as they read the Bible together night after night. Of course, their search was rewarded.

The work in France began with a small supply of literature valued at about £80 ($400), but today the ministry ranks number four in the total literature output of our forty-six countries, exceeding one million dollars in 1980. Yes, we are glad we didn't wait until there were adequate funds to do the job. In God's strategy, the mobile outreach with the market work, the door-to-door visitation, the poster ministry and the publishing program were all necessary. Maybe that young engineer and his wife would not have been reached except for the poster on the Citroen van. So we take courage and are glad for the simple beginnings. This has so often proved to be the strategy of the Spirit—the way of the Captain for each occasion, giving ample scope and needed training for our expectant faith.

These pioneers of nearly thirty years have now handed over the responsibility to younger people. Idris and Andree Davis took over the leadership of the work in France in September, 1980 and are continuing, under God, in the same spirit as Jean and Marcelle Treboux to press the battle to the gate, advancing into new towns and cities of need. Three are on their immediate agenda—Lille, Paris, and Marseille. Indeed the long-range vision of CLC France has been to establish bookstores in fifty of the major towns and cities of the country. May the Lord reward the team with many additional workers to fulfill their immediate and their long-range goals.

And what of the Trebouxs? Now nearing seventy, they must relax and take things easy! Not so. They plan an extended visit to French-speaking West Africa. Their first survey journey is likely to take them to Senegal, Gabon, Togo, Benin, and Congo Brazzaville, with a return visit to Cameroon. As an autonomous field within our CLC fellowship, France is responsible for the oversight of the work in Cameroon and the Ivory Coast in Africa, as well as the small work in French Guiana, South America. It will assume oversight of the expected new developments in Africa. Little has truly proven to be much, for God has most surely been in this ministry of CLC France from its inception right to this very moment.

The same is true in the work in Italy. This began under Don Teal's leadership. However, when he accepted another assignment, the Lord used a gentle lady from Scotland, trained in Rees Howell's Bible College of Wales, as His instrument to develop the work. Jean Henderson went to Italy in 1954 and two years later the first bookshop was opened in the city of Florence. It was small but strategically located—almost opposite the Galleria Academia, which houses some of Michelangelo's famous sculptures. In recent years an addition has made the center even more influential.

Jean is not with us now. She had seen five of our six centers opened and a mobile ministry and publishing program come into the visible. And then she was called to higher service. She had served Him joyously and faithfully right to the end. On Thursday she was still busy in the literature ministry. On Friday she was in the hospital on the operating table. On Monday she was in heaven! What a soldier she was, always on the firing line. I remember traveling with her by train from Milan to Florence. Soon she was in conversation with fellow travelers, sharing the joys of the Christian life. Tracts were passed to one and another. Never a moment was lost witnessing and working for her Master, and her works follow her.

The team of some twenty dedicated workers now under the leadership of Ernesto and Ruth Schmitt carry on the program. They are an international group—Italian, Swiss, Dutch, British, and American, with the expected addition of a couple from Sweden.

This work must grow substantially in this decade, for among Italy's almost 58 million people only about 350,000 are considered Protestant Christians. Of course there are true believers in Catholic circles, but, even so, probably less than one percent of the total populace could be considered truly born-again, functioning believers. Thankfully the door is wide open for new missionaries. In CLC we must see our ranks doubled during this decade so that we can continue to expand this vital literature ministry in Italy.

The present work must be strengthened through our six centers—in Milan, Naples, Florence, and Perugia on the mainland and in Messina and Palermo on Sicily as well. The mobile ministry must be strengthened and expanded to reach all the national

Trade Fairs and other key market places; the publishing program must be increased, for today there are still less than 1,000 titles in Italian; the mail-order ministry across the country must be extended; and new centers must be opened. Italy's fourth largest city, Turin—with a population close to one and one-quarter million—is an immediate goal as soon as workers are available. Our eyes are also on establishing a permanent base in the capital city of Cagliari on the island of Sardinia. CLC's yearly visits to this area indicate that the need for a permanent literature ministry is imperative.

This rather bleak picture of Italy's spiritual condition is indicative of most of Europe. It has been stated categorically that Europe is the most neglected continent. There are more evangelical Christians in Zaire (previously known as Belgian Congo) than in Belgium; more in Madagascar than in France; more in Brazil than in Portugal. Indeed, it is estimated that there are probably a quarter of a million towns and cities in Europe without any evangelical church.

But I have digressed, though the need of this neglected continent must not be passed over glibly. God give us ears to hear, eyes to perceive, hearts to respond, and wills to become involved.

14

GOD KNEW WHAT HE WAS DOING

Faith is not a guarantee against trouble, it is a guarantee against defeat. Faith is never more tested than when adversity overtakes us. This is particularly true when our immediate family is involved.

Donald David was born in Madras, India, into a Christian family. At the age of twelve he gave his heart to the Lord after hearing a missionary speak on John 14:6. Two years later he met with an accident which, within a month, brought him to the brink, when he was given only twenty-four hours to live. As with Job, it would seem that God's will did not include death for Donald, but neither did it include immediate healing. For many months Donald was totally bedridden, and this gave him plenty of time to search out God's purpose in saving him. Up to this point he had his own ideas of what he was going to do with his life.

But now the Captain was speaking.

Donald was doing a lot of reading. One book was particularly challenging. It told how D.L. Moody started the Moody Colportage Association to provide good, inexpensive books. Donald was fascinated and began to believe that in some way he, too, would be involved in a Christian literature ministry. So in 1946, after several years of being an invalid, he started a small bookroom in Madras, under the name of Evangelical Literature Service. It was far from encouraging. Some days not a soul would cross the threshold. After several years of slow progress, he felt the need for training in literature work and was greatly encouraged when he received a letter from CLC Britain, suggesting he spend several months in London to gain more general knowledge and experience.

During his time with CLC in Britain, Donald heard young people testify to God's call to serve Him in one country or another. This interested him, though it did not seem to have any personal significance.

Next, he visited America for several months and met with Christian publishers on this side of the Atlantic. While in America God spoke again, this time through the story of the lad who gave his lunch to Jesus and, as a result, a multitude was fed. Donald sensed that God was saying to Him, "If you also give what you have to Me and step out in faith, I will use it to bless multitudes in India."

Donald's answer? "Yes, Lord, I will give everything to You and trust You completely."

The first test of faith was immediate. He must have money for his return to India. He would tell no one of his need but trust God alone to supply.

He did, and Donald returned to India via England. There he shared with the CLC fellowship in London how God had led, and that he was now ready to join CLC and return to India as a member of the Crusade, if they were agreeable. They were, for this was surely a confirmation to CLC Britain of the present involvement they had in that land.

As usual in these early days of growth, the wisdom of CLC's action was questioned. Was it really right to try and start a literature work in the vast land of India through a single young woman? For in 1951, Ida Howlett had been sent, first to North India for language study, and then to Calcutta to get on-the-spot training and experience through an existing Christian bookshop in that city.

On his return to India, Donald wrote to Ida suggesting she visit Madras and see his little book ministry, which now had become the first CLC bookcenter in the country. It had been operating for its eight years under its own name. All agreed that the name should be retained, so in 1954 CLC India was registered under the title Evangelical Literature Service, as an Indian missionary society under the Society's Act.

Now things became complicated. CLC Britain had received a very special request from the young work in India. Donald David, the Indian, was asking permission to marry Ida Howlett, the young lady from Britain. Could CLC carry its interracial policy a step further?

Most missions looked with strong disfavor upon inter-marriage. Should CLC conform? We went to the Word and could find no restricting guidance, but we did write suggesting caution, sharing openly some of our concerns (prejudices?). We went even further and requested some procedures which we felt would allow time for things to find their own level. After all, the heart does act strangely sometimes! They submitted to our suggestions willingly, which only strengthened our conviction that these two fine young people were sincere in their dedication to the Lord and in their uncompromising allegiance to the call of God upon them for the Christian literature ministry in India. There was a ring of reality and wisdom in what they were now proposing.

After approximately six months of "testing," God's will for this couple was strengthened and confirmed. In the light of their testimony the British staff gladly gave their permission for this union. When Phil Booth, the new British leader, was visiting India in 1954, he shared in the happy occasion. As Donald put it, "Oneness of vision and burden for the work to which God had called Ida and me finally culminated in the happy bonds of marriage." They and we have never regretted this decision. Indeed the exciting growth of the work during the next twenty years would be a direct result of this union of East and West in both spirit and purpose.

But, in 1978 they were separated.

Earlier, in 1973, Donald, Ida and their three growing children were transferred to New Zealand where Donald assumed the leadership of CLC. The next five years saw the literature work in that country greatly expanded. Donald had never been robust in health since his accident as a lad of fourteen, but never once did he let his physical limitations hinder his wholehearted and untiring involvement in the plan of God for his life through the literature ministry. He soldiered on bravely and uncomplainingly until in December, 1978 a heart attack laid him low and a few days later took him directly into the presence of his Lord and Master, whom he had served so faithfully. What a welcome he must have received.

And what a living memorial he has left behind. To that first struggling little bookroom in 1946, eleven more have been added. All but one remain to this day, though three have been passed on to others. India was the first country to have two CLC bookshops in the same city—Madras.

Now they have achieved another first.

When in 1979 the brand new headquarters building in Madras was completed, the plan was to transfer everything from the old building. Because of the nearness of the Christmas season and because most customers would be much more familiar with the old location, they felt it wise to keep both the shops operating, even though they are only about one-half mile apart. All were surprised that sales in the old location actually surpassed any previous year, and sales at the new location were surprisingly encouraging. Consequently, both centers continued to operate, and after testing things for a full year, the 1981 Annual Conference agreed to maintain all three centers indefinitely!

Along with the bookshops other literature programs have developed. CLC India is now the largest supplier of Christian books in English, both imported and printed in the country—and at least one hundred million Indians speak and read English. They also publish books for the thirty million Tamil-speaking people of South India and carry stock in several other languages, including Hindi, the national language. Other things have resulted from this. An extensive mail-order program reaches all across the country with an annually updated catalog. They also wholesale books to the other bookstores and literature outlets. For a number of years a bookmobile was attached to the Madras center and served the over three million people of metropolitan Madras, as well as penetrating into the Tamil-speaking area to the south. A busy print shop is maintained in Bangalore, and in 1980 this was greatly strengthened by increased equipment sent as a gift by CLC U.S.A.

After the Davids left India the leadership was entrusted to Nobel and Coral Massey, the very first Indian couple to join the ranks soon after the official CLC/ELS work started. The big development under Nobel Massey's administration was the construction of a three-story building in Bangalore which brought together the bookshop and the print shop. This change of location and better working facilities caused both aspects of the ministry in Bangalore to grow in a big way.

Early in 1975 the mantle of leadership fell on V.M. and Lelah Abraham, who were at that time heading up the work in Bangalore. Indeed it was V.M. Abraham who gave oversight to the construction of the new building there. During their first term of service two significant developments took place. In August, 1977 a branch shop was opened in the city of Trivandrum, the capital of Kerala State, which incidently boasts of having received Christianity in the first century.

And then in 1978 the biggest faith project of all was launched—the headquarters building in Madras. The following year it was completed and on November 14, 1979 was dedicated to the glory of God and to the memory of Donald J. David.

But this building in itself is also a living testimony to faith, a faith which was untiring in its expectations and never wavering when the pressures mounted. It could be called "Miracle Building," for right from the start the stand of faith was tried and tested. Field Leader V.M. Abraham reported on the day of dedication:

> Shortly after we began negotiating for the 14,000 square feet piece of land on Vepery High Road, the government clamped on the Urban Land Ceiling Act which prevented any sale or purchase of surplus land.

The new ceiling act stood like a wall of Jericho before us. We continued in faith and received assurance from several portions of the Word. But we had to believe and wait patiently.

Then, miracles began taking place.

A new government came into power and among other things amended the Land Ceiling Act. This immediately made the transaction possible for us. During the waiting period a Christian architect prepared a beautiful plan with all the necessary drawings to the satisfaction of the municipal authorities. Finally, in about nine months we received the building permit. Our hearts rejoiced and our faith was greatly strengthened.

On August 4, 1978 nearly eighty people gathered at the site to witness the turning of the first sod, which marked the beginning of construction. A Christian builder undertook this project for us. The first thing we did was to dig a good well and the Lord gave us plenty of sweet water.

Then, we encountered the "giants in the land." The work on the foundation was hardly started when there was an acute shortage of cement. Our request to the government authorities was submitted and we were overjoyed to receive the permit in just three weeks. Truly God was working on our behalf. And He continued to do so just as we expected. The rainy season had set in and water began to rise in the deep foundation-column pits. The monsoon was advancing. The situation looked hopeless and we helpless, so we prayed again and asked the Lord to give us sunny weather for two weeks so that we could complete the concreting of the foundations. The Lord graciously withheld the rain until the work was completed! Then, the windows of heaven opened and the heavy rains helped in curing the concrete!

When we began the project the available finance was very meager compared to what the total need would be.

However, looking to the Lord and counting on His faithfulness, we had launched out. Many people appreciated our action and gave us their support spiritually and financially. And, while all this was going on the Lord continued to bless our day-by-day literature ministry to such an extent that a substantial part of the finances could be drawn from our own resources. And our own workers, too, gave sacrificially to see the project come alive.

During 1979 prices of building materials continued rising. Scarcity of cement and steel increased. It looked as though as each day came, a new giant raised his head in our path. But the Captain of our salvation was always ahead of us. As construction progressed the Lord kept supplying the necessary materials and funds. Right in the beginning the Lord had given us His promise, "My God shall supply all your need according to His riches in glory by Christ Jesus." As a fellowship we claimed this promise and continued trusting God to meet every need for the completion of this project. There were occasions when our faith was shaky and doubts crept in. But our God remained faithful and saw to the completion of the project which He had begun.

Now we have one of the best and most attractive Christian bookshops in India, attractively furnished and ideally situated. Our warehouse has plenty of light and air. The squirrels, rats, cockroaches, silverfish, etc., may find life rather uncomfortable in our new warehouse!

V.M. Abraham concluded: "It is a joy to be in this wonderful new building and to serve its Giver more earnestly and effectively than ever before. Truly our God has 'done great things for us and it is marvelous in our eyes.' He is indeed the God of the impossible. To Him be glory and honor!"

On that bright November day the three hundred or so people who had gathered to share in the dedication were surely standing on holy ground. Because of rising prices the final cost of this building exceeded $100,000 but that day no bills which had been submitted were unpaid. It was not only a dedication day but a day of glad thanksgiving to our miracle-working God.

Yes, God did know what He was doing when He dealt what, except to the eye of faith, appeared to be a harsh blow to young Donald David. Now on this dedication day there was concrete evidence. This building represents the largest and most widespread literature ministry in the whole of India, and its new facilities are making possible fresh advances across the land. As more young people from within its boundaries respond to the call of God and share the literature vision, we will see more bookcenters established in city after city, more good books published, and more people reading, responding and learning as they find Jesus Christ as their personal Saviour and grow stronger in the faith and bolder in their witness.

Not only does this fine headquarters building in Madras stand to the glory of God, it is also a lasting testimony to the living, vibrating work of the Spirit through consecrated Indian flesh and blood, for CLC India is a totally indigenous operation.

15

RESEARCH IS PRIMARY

While these specific developments were taking place, requests for help continued to come from many other parts of the world. Many were from South America, which indicated to us that the time had come for another overseas research journey. So, in early March, 1955, I was on my way south for a six-week trip which would take me to more than a dozen countries.

Up to this time CLC was established in only one Spanish South American country—Uruguay—although news of our activity there was already spreading to the Argentine, Chile and Brazil. Everywhere on this journey, the concern and question was the same from missionaries and nationals alike. How can we improve the literature ministry? In what way could CLC offer help?

By the time I returned to Fort Washington, my notebook was full and my heart aflame. One thing seemed abundantly clear—CLC must prepare for a sizeable involvement in both Spanish and Portuguese South America.

Of course, literature work was already being done in all the countries I visited, but without exception, the feeling of those engaged in it was that the surface was hardly being scratched and that more help was urgently needed.

Take Brazil, as an example.

My contact was David Glass, whom I had known about in a general way because his parents had been missionaries in Brazil. His father had carried on an extensive colportage work, spreading the Scriptures far and wide throughout the country. He recorded the story in his book *The Bible for Brazil*. I had read the book and now was privileged to meet his son, David, in San Jose, Costa Rica, at the beginning of my journey. About fifty missionary representatives and one or two Latin Americans met together in the Latin America Mission Bible School to discuss the need of setting up a literature fellowship to help resolve some of the overlapping problems and improve the literature ministry throughout Latin America.

I met David again in Rio de Janeiro about a month later. He was still concerned about the inadequate supply of vital books in Portuguese and the poor distribution throughout Brazil. We sat for hours in his office and in his home across the bay, discussing Brazil's new day of spiritual growth which accentuated the need for a much more vigorous Christian literature program. He, personally, was making every effort to do more and was in the process of opening a second bookshop, this time in the city of Belo Horizonte.

The thing which surprised me was his insistence that CLC should come to Brazil. No, he did not see this as overlapping or competitive. That would only be so, in his judgment, if we would open a CLC bookshop in a city where another one was already established. There were so many cities and large towns, David insisted, with no evangelical literature witness.

Before I left the country I heard the same story again, when I spent twenty-four hours at the Unevangelized Fields Mission headquarters in Belem in north Brazil. Charles Sarginson urged that CLC come quickly and establish a bookcenter in that rapidly expanding part of the country. The only promise I made in response to these many urgent calls from country after country was that I would share what I had learned with our CLC fellowship worldwide but particularly in North America and Britain. As the Lord gave direction and personnel became available, we would take appropriate action. However, in my heart I knew our Captain had a plan for CLC in South America.

The opportunity to share the South American situation with our colleagues in Britain came within weeks of my return to Fort Washington. It was almost seven years since we had left England,

and with things developing so fast on both sides of the Atlantic, we felt it wise to plan a return visit for consultation and for deputation.

So the Adams family sailed from New York for England on the *Queen Mary* at the end of April, 1955, arriving in time to share in the British CLC Annual Conference. These annual conferences bring together almost the total fellowship from all the branch centers, as well as the main base in London. This was, therefore, a unique time to share what God had been doing during the past seven years in North America, including, of course, the recent visit to South America.

While I was busy with Crusade affairs and the deputation, Bessie and the two girls were able to spend time with relations. This was good, for it has since proved to be the only time that the four of us would be together in the "old country." Our younger daughter, Janet, has been back several times but our older daughter, Margaret, has never returned to England since that visit. When finally she does make it, it will be in company with five others—husband Bill and the four children, David, Jimmie, Kimberly Bess and Heidi Joy Janet, too, looks for the day when she can again return, for English blood runs thick in her veins! She also will have company—husband Tom, and the two children, Jeffrey and Jennifer.

16

THE FAMILY AND CHRISTIAN SERVICE

This matter of families and Christian service is something that has to be grappled with. Our Lord made it very clear in such passages as Luke 14:25-35 that He demanded total commitment even when he spoke to the masses, not just to the inner circle of disciples. But total allegiance does not annul the responsibilities with which He entrusts us in the course of a lifetime. If children are God's gift to us, then we are duty-bound to fulfill our responsibility meticulously. We are instructed to train our children in *the fear, nurture, and admonition of the Lord.*

Total allegiance to Jesus as our Lord, Master and Captain includes discharging our responsibilities well, whether it be raising children or working in an office or factory. *Do all things to the glory of God* is an all-embracing directive of the Scripture.

Yet, could it be that sometimes we fail to fully communicate, especially at the family level?

Bessie and I believe we can.

In our Christian world today we are so caught up dotting eschatological "I's" and crossing theological "T's" that we have lost the wonder and reality of "Christ in you" being our glorious hope. It is the daily life we live which really communicates much more powerfully than mere words. Frankly, I do not remember much about our family devotional times in my growing-up years. I am sure we had them, but any fruit from them was minimal. What did make maximum impact on my three sisters and myself was the life of Jesus which touched our lives every day through the person we proudly called "Mother." Actually she was quiet and rather reserved, but she lived her life with joy and with enthusiasm, and the four of us were unconsciously caught up in the excitement.

Let me share with you some of the last words she penned, dated March 27, 1950: "My darling girlies and Sonny, it is a joy to get your loving letters, and I know how grateful you all are to me as I tried by God's help to be a loving father and mother to you all. My prayers were always, first for your spiritual life, second, your health, and then to try to give you a better standing in this life than I had. I do praise God that I have been spared to see this....Now my dear ones, the doctors (three of them) have just been and they gave my tummy another try, and one would gather that there will be an operation. So, dears, I want you to know if this is to be His will, then I just rest in His loving arms. We all know His ways are best, and I am sure He will undertake for me and should He see fit to spare me a few more years to be a praying partner in His great harvest field, that will be all to His glory. But it is a grand comfort to be ready to go, and as you say, Doris, any sacrifice we have made for Him is but a drop in the ocean compared to what He has done for us. I am so glad that I never tried to hinder any of you children's call to His service. Go on, dear ones, give all for Jesus—'All my days and all my hours,' etc. It is only the fully yielded lives that the Lord can use. It is the life that counts, and may Christians so live as we remember each day a Book of Remembrance is being kept to our account—that keeps us near to His wounded side. I can truly testify He has been more dear to me than any earthly tie—the One who has only known all my desires and all my sorrows and all my joys through these many many years.

"Now I am feeling tired of writing, so...."

And my dear sister, Doris, who sent me a copy of this and two other letters Mother had written during her stay in the hospital, added, "These were the last words penned by our precious mother—we laid the poor tired body to rest on May 3 after a triumphant entrance into the presence of the Lord she loved so dearly and served so faithfully."

See what I mean?

Much the same could have been written about Edward Miners.

So both of us had almost unconsciously received training in how to raise our children. Our lives, because of constant separation (on one occasion almost six months), were turning out quite a bit differently, but the principle of living Jesus enthusiastically before our children was the same.

Of course we read our Bibles together, usually after the evening meal so that it could be without rush. As we read we kept our eye open for our *WT* and then we each shared our findings together. *WT?—Wonderful Thought!* Something which had meaning and which we could lay hold of personally. It was great fun.

Then we prayed together. During the mealtime we had shared the day's events—what had transpired at school; what had transpired in the office or over the telephone; the good things God was doing personally and in the CLC; if I was soon to be off again, where I was going, who I would be seeing, what I was trusting the Lord to do, and so on. These were the sort of things we prayed about. Did one of the girls need something—a new dress or winter overcoat? Let's tell our heavenly Father about it. Let's remind Him of His promise: "Seek ye first the kingdom of God"—I know what you need—"and all these things will be added unto you." On the strength of this we prayed expectantly, and what fun we had together when the answers came!

What was the result of this on-the-spot training?

Both girls voluntarily elected to go to Columbia Bible College in South Carolina. Before doing so they had a year or two of working, just to put into practice some of the things they had learned at school and to learn about the "world out there," for they lived rather sheltered lives at home and with all the other families at the CLC Fort Washington compound. In her teens, Margaret wanted to start a Bible Club at school but could not obtain permission. So "Mum, Dad, could I have it here at home?" she asked—expectantly!

"Sure thing, great idea," was our spontaneous reply.

A bit inconvenient? Yes, when once each week (and some-times more often) the living room (and it seemed the whole house!) was taken over by anything up to thirty young people. There were plenty of ways around that "problem," and our hearts bubbled over when we saw all that was happening, especially when some of these young people accepted Jesus personally. This went on for eight years or so, for when Margaret left for Bible College, Janet took up the task of keeping this house Bible Club going while she, too, did a spell on the outside—at one time keeping two jobs going. This continued for another six years during her service with the Bible Club Movement, following graduation from Columbia Bible College. She also initiated the Bible Club ministry in several local high schools and again saw a number of these young people converted, some going to Bible colleges.

And today?

Both are in full-time Christian service. Margaret and Bill (whom she found at CBC—or was it the other way around!?) have been serving with CLC for the past twelve years in Jamaica and Trinidad. They are now in Barbados overseeing the CLC work in the seven islands of the eastern Caribbean. Janet now serves with Tom, a graduate of Westminster Theological Semi-nary, with Mission to the World in southern Mexico.

The secret, we believe, is that we see life as a whole, not separated into spiritual and secular, Christian service or a busi-ness career. Then, everything will balance out. It will dovetail perfectly and flow in one continuous stream of life with Jesus at the center. Bessie and I can testify that no part of our CLC ministry suffered because of family responsibilities. We have a strong feeling that our two lovely girls and their wonderful fami-lies feel the same, agreeing that they lost nothing during their years of upbringing because they, not of their own choice, had to be part of an active missionary society which kept their parents fully involved and often meant days, weeks, or months of separa-tion. We base this assumption on the kind of letters we get from them and the birthday and anniversary cards which come year after year, always with added personal words of appreciation. Certainly we miss each other and have not had the joy of being around to see all the grandchildren growing and maturing, as I suppose is the ambition of all grandparents! However, we do count it all joy to be in the service of the King together.

17

PERSISTENCE PRODUCES

During our time in England I had the privilege of meeting Timothy Ree, a fine Korean Christian who was continuing his education at Edinburgh University. He spoke English fluently and we learned later that he was quite a key figure in Korean evangelical circles. Tim had taken time to come to London to share his burden for Christian literature in his country.

Our discussions and subsequent correspondence culminated when Tim Ree returned to Korea in 1956 ready to begin the CLC ministry there. The going was not easy, although a bookstore was started and a publishing program begun. Roy Hession's *The Calvary Road* was one of the first books to be translated and published, and there were others including some written by Tim Ree and other Koreans. An attempt was also made to produce a nationwide interdenominational monthly magazine. But no aspect of the work really blossomed: perhaps because Tim Ree was so busy with other Christian responsibilities, or perhaps there were basic misunderstandings between us. Correspondence can be misunderstood so easily, even among our own people, but it is much more problematic when corresponding with those of another culture, where thought patterns are quite different and the same English words can convey two different meanings.

Ultimately, it was clear that an on-the-spot visit was needed.

One other significant thing had come out of our time in Britain. In discussing our rapid growth, it was becoming apparent that sooner or later we would need better coordination. Perhaps an International Office would be useful, or, at least, an international figurehead who could help handle the various calls for assistance. In a rather loose way we agreed on two international policies. First, that CLC Britain would continue to be responsible for developments in Europe and in India, and CLC North America would assume responsibility for developments in South America and the Orient. Any further expansion in Africa and elsewhere would be considered on a country-by-country basis. The second agreement was that I should attempt a sort of coordinating ministry along with my other responsibilities. Hopefully, as a result of this, we would get clearer light about the need for an international guiding body later on.

Because of these decisions, the developments in Korea became a responsibility of North America and, therefore, a visit to Korea was planned for 1959. Regretfully, following that visit, I had to recommend to the North American staff that CLC terminate its operation in Korea. That was a hard and disappointing decision to make, for my visit had convinced me that the need for a strong literature program in the country was clearly evident.

We kept Korea on our prayer list and watched for the day when we could return. This came several years later when Harry and Ingabrit Weimar applied to CLC for service in Korea. Harry had been in the country during his time in the navy and the burden to return and help in its evangelization never left him.

After language study a second start was made, this time in the city of Taegu. The Weimars worked hard and their grasp of the language improved considerably. Harry had many opportunities in local churches and they both gave their best to the literature ministry with the city bookstore, some further publishing, and a mobile ministry to the rural areas.

But once more, after several years of struggle, we had to face the probability of withdrawing from the country. This was confirmed when, during their furlough, Harry indicated that in returning to Korea he would go as a "regular" missionary to work with various groups and perhaps to do some further church planting. For some unexplained reason it seemed that getting a literature program really rolling in Korea was easier said than done. Other groups were also having difficulties, and so CLC was not alone, but this was cold comfort and in no way justified our leaving the country to let it work things out on its own. The need for Christian literature was as urgent as ever.

It was almost ten years later that the situation was brought to our attention for the third time; and once again, it was through a Korean brother. While Young Kwang Park was in America continuing his theological education, a copy of our *Floodtide* magazine came into his hands. He had never heard of CLC before, but seeing this magazine was devoted almost exclusively to the world-wide literature ministry, he was immediately alert. On the inside back cover there is always a list of countries where CLC is operating. Rev. Park scanned this list but was disappointed to find that his country was not included, so he wrote to us asking why.

We replied, giving him a brief history of our two attempts and assuring him of our continued prayerful interest in the literature needs of Korea. We invited him to come and visit us at Fort Washington, and this he responded to without delay. In forceful terms he insisted that a group such as CLC was urgently needed in his country. He told us that he was ready to become involved on his return to Korea later that year. He knew of other Koreans who would also want to help and he was sure that money within the country would be available. He was adamant, convinced that a Christian literature program could develop quickly. It would include writings by himself and other Koreans and the publishing of these manuscripts. The one urgent need was an adequate supply of English books, and for this he appealed to CLC for help. We wished him Godspeed and sent him on his way with a donation of $5,000 worth of English books. He had happily selected the titles from several American catalogs, including our own.

This dear brother lost no time implementing his ideas. The first letter we received from him after his return to Korea was on printed letterhead boldly displaying Christian Literature Crusade! A bookstore was started in a busy section of Seoul, and a publishing program was immediately set in motion. All of this was made possible by the funds he had been able to obtain from other like-minded Korean Christians.

CLC was now in Korea for the third time.

Once again we had started without the foreign missionary, and I must admit we watched the developments with a cautious eye. Thankfully, there was growing evidence that this dear brother and the team of workers he gathered around him really meant business. One sold his home and put all the money into the work. Others made similar gestures and all worked long hours sacrifically, taking only a minimal allowance in return. They knew that the Lord's work needed haste, sacrifice and faith. They lived and labored expecting results. Still, they did not want to go it alone, and urged us to send a missionary couple to help them, especially on the English side of things.

By this time Young Kwang Park had put his brother, Young Ho Park, in charge of the bookstore. He spoke some English and understood more through his reading. Young Ho indicated a readiness to obtain training and experience with CLC in America but was unable to obtain a visa, so we arranged for him to take his training in London, which proved to be beneficial in more ways than one! There was a Korean young lady, Kie Soon, also in Britain. She had spent several years in Germany as a nurse, and during her stay in that country had found Jesus Christ as her Saviour. She felt a strong urge to return to Korea to help in this new literature ministry developing in her country. Now with Bible School in Scotland completed, she was a CLC candidate in training for her future literature ministry.

Young Ho was able to obtain a visa to England and the *few months* visit actually lasted almost *eighteen months*. It included a short term at the Glasgow Bible College and culminated on a happy day in June, 1976, when Young Ho and Kie Soon were united in marriage at a Baptist Church in south London close to the CLC headquarters in Upper Norwood.

With their return to Korea the work has gone forward from strength to strength. I had the privilege of seeing it firsthand at the end of 1976 and was very impressed, although all agreed that a missionary couple was still needed. Unfortunately, we have not yet been able to respond to this request. We decided in 1978 to link the work with CLC Japan, giving them the oversight of CLC Korea. Several visits have been made to Korea and Young Ho has also made one visit to CLC in Tokyo. On Peter Horne's last two visits he became increasingly enthusiastic about what he had seen and heard, because the literature potential in this country is tremendous.

The work has grown rapidly. There is the main bookstore in Seoul and four bookcenters elsewhere. The publishing program continues to leap ahead with about eighty titles now in print. Because of this rapid growth, the need for a main base became an urgent necessity. In 1980 the workers set a faith target to see a piece of land purchased that year for the anticipated headquarters building. Everyone realized that this would be a costly undertaking, for land is very expensive in Seoul.

God honored their faith. By early December a piece of land with a two-story house came to their attention. It looked hopeful until a technical snag developed. Then in January an even better property was found, only two years old and with more floor area. With settlement completed, dedication at the end of February 1981 drew an overflow crowd of interested friends. On the ground level, two offices, a bookstore, and the warehouse now operate. Upstairs, a three-bedroom apartment is occupied by the Young Ho Park family. There is also a large room suitable for meetings.

The total project cost under $100,000—much less than the staff had expected. Within two months this amount was in hand—approximately one-third of it from Korea and the rest coming from several CLC countries. Of course, owning the building immediately released them from the previous high rents of the other locations.

So, with ever increasing confidence we can say that CLC Korea is there to stay this time!

18

TO AN ISLAND NATION

One more significant development in Crusade growth during 1955 must be mentioned. Just ten years earlier, on August 17, 1945, Indonesia declared its independence from Holland, although it was not until December 27, 1949 that The Netherlands formally recognized this. Thirteen years later the western part of the island of New Guinea became Irian Jaya, completing the picture. It is a sprawling country of 13,276 islands lying between the mainland of southeast Asia and Australia, stretching 3,300 miles from west to east. Not all the islands are peopled, although Indonesia is the world's fifth largest nation with a 1980 population of 155 million.

When independence was declared less than 7 per cent of the people could read, but the new government quickly grappled with this handicap. An extensive educational program was launched. Schools were built and immediately filled to capacity with eager young learners.

This was the situation CLC's first two workers found when they arrived in October, 1954. Willard Stone, in his mid-thirties, was new to this part of the world, but Grace Chang, in her mid-fifties, was in her element. Both had to learn the language, but Grace had a head start for she had begun her missionary career when she was only nineteen years of age, arriving in China in 1920. Spending at least eighteen of her years in Chinese villages gave her a good grasp of the language and a real affinity with the Chinese people, so she gravitated immediately to the Chinese segment of Indonesia's population. Of course, she did have to learn the national language.

You may ask: Why start a Christian literature work in a country with such extensive illiteracy?

We had responded to the urgent call of a Swiss missionary, Heini German-Edey, who along with his many responsibilities, which included starting a Bible School, was importing literature into the country, mainly in English. There was a fair supply of Dutch literature, but a pressing need for Chinese, Javanese, and other vernaculars. However, the number one priority was to produce easy-to-read books in the new Indonesian language which the government was determined to make the national tongue.

Taking over of the stock which Heini German-Edey had in hand, the Christian Literature Crusade officially began in Indonesia on January 1, 1955. While Willard Stone concentrated on his language study, Grace Chang was able to give much of her time to the needs of the Chinese. News quickly spread that CLC was planning to provide literature for all the people, but it was the children and young people who were uppermost in their minds at the beginning, for we would have to start almost from the ground up since very little was available in Indonesian.

This meant a change in our normal priorities. CLC's number one task right from its inception had been distribution, for this was the congestion-point everywhere. Even in Britain this was true. The head of one Christian publishing company in England emphasized this to Norman Grubb years ago when he said, "Distribution is the bottleneck. We are held up with what we publish because we cannot be sure of the books getting to the people.... If this new literature work [CLC] is concentrating on distribution, you are hitting the nail on the head." But you cannot distribute books which are not yet in print.

Quickly CLC settled down to this new challenge. Competent translators were put to work and a Chinese printer—a keen Christian—set aside some of his regular work to undertake our printing needs. This was the Lord's provision, for at the time, print shops could take on extra business only six months of the year. The other six months were taken up with government printing, especially educational books for the schools.

One serious handicap most printers were experiencing was inadequate typesetting facilities, so our printer suggested that if CLC could import a typesetting machine that would help to solve the problem. At that time a religious group had more chance getting such equipment into the country than a business, because it could be paid for with hard currency. He agreed that it could be installed in his print shop and that it would only be used for his own needs when CLC work was not in hand. Mr. Tanutama really caught the literature vision as he saw the amount of work we were able to channel his way. At one time almost 80 per cent of his work load was Christian books, Sunday School supplies, tracts, etc., ordered by CLC.

When, some years later, CLC registered with the government as an Indonesian missionary society, Mr. Tanutama was appointed Chairman of our Board, and he continues to serve in that capacity to this day.

Our preoccupation with publishing did not hinder distribution, although we had only the one bookcenter in the city of Surabaya, which is the largest port on Java, Indonesia's most populated island.

This was significant because boats from many of the other islands, large and small, were constantly coming and going. Keen Christians from these islands came to the bookstore. How glad they were to find the books. How sorry they were that there was no such Christian literature center on their island. How excited they were when we suggested that they become book agents. We would start them with an initial supply of stock, which they would replenish on their next visit to Surabaya. The idea caught on quickly and soon several hundred agents were the backbone of the distribution program, most of them servicing other islands.

This released Willard to concentrate on publishing as well as giving general oversight to all other aspects of this young and rapidly growing ministry. Things greatly improved for him personally, and for the work, when Dorothy joined Willard in 1959. They had met during his training days with CLC in Fort Washington. She bravely traveled on her own to Singapore where they were married. When they returned to Indonesia, Dorothy quickly settled into language study, homemaking and sharing the growing load with Willard, particularly giving secretarial help with English correspondence.

Grace was also busy on several fronts and always bubbling over with excitement. She lived her life expectantly. Indeed she often referred to herself as "Day-by-day Grace"! Never a dull moment with her! One of her first letters early in 1955 was so typical:

> My heart is full of praise and thanksgiving today and I want to start by telling you about direct answers to prayer.
>
> Yesterday we packed our first order of books to be taken by a Christian worker—new Christian—for sale at the market....Another wonderful answer to prayer has been the sale of a great number of Bibles and books in Indonesian and Javanese—about sixty Javanese Bibles, seventy Indonesian, forty English, seventy-eight Chinese, making a total for one month of over two hundred and forty Bibles and New Testaments.
>
> In the past months four pastors in different cities have set up book tables in their churches. They have all sent-for their second consignment and three others have taken their first consignment. The work and benefits are spreading out to distant cities.
>
> This past month we have had at least six different pastors who have made a special two and a half hours' bus trip just to come here and get books. A few days ago two came all the way from Jakarta at the other end of the island. 'We have no such place in Jakarta,' they said. It is no wonder that they appreciate the books—they have longed and hoped for them so long. To them it is worth a long trip by bus just to get Christian books.
>
> Again this month literature has gone into three seminaries and also into two large schools on another island.

An order came last week from a Javanese church for sixteen thousand evangelical picture tracts for children— just off the press in Indonesian! Another pastor sent two orders for books.

We received our first batch of Sunday School pictures from the U.S.A. to be pasted in albums....The demand was so great...many requests had to be turned down. We could have used two or three times as many.

So the letters would come with their exciting news and never-ending challenge—more, more, more must be done. Remember, too, that what the above letter records was all being done in the first eight months of CLC's entry into the country. No wonder Grace and Willard were excited and full of praise.

This was the pattern for the next fifteen years, but early in the seventies a change in strategy developed. By now more groups were publishing, so more books were available. The CLC team felt the time had come for a return to our normal distribution pattern. Publishing would not be dropped, but more time and money would be channeled into the bookstore ministry.

Thankfully, the number of national workers was increasing and they shared the vision of reaching out to the other islands. By 1981 thirty-two Indonesians were in the CLC ranks, and more were applying. This steady increase of workers made possible the opening of new bookcenters. One of these was in Jayapura on the island of Irian Jaya, over 2,000 miles from our main base in Surabaya.

Grace Chang, though now in her seventies, pioneered this advance, assisted by a fine Indonesian couple. She was fascinated by the crowds and the constant activity in the market place, so she made this her first objective. A suitable location was found and the CLC stall brought living literature to the people of the market place. What a busy place this proved to be right from opening day. Later a good store became available in the general shopping area and this, too, has been successful, but not at the expense of the market stall which is particularly busy in the evenings. The market stall is essentially for the people of the town, while the bookstore, also serving local people, caters to the whole region. Missionaries from the hinterland get their supplies from the bookstore, much of it being sent in by the Missionary Aviation Fellowship planes. This, too, gladdened Grace's heart, for she lived to see the printed word going out far and wide.

Just what her plans were for April 12, 1980 I do not know—more of the same, I am sure. But the Captain knew.

This was to be Glorification Day. Grace was busy in the shop that morning, but suddenly she was gone—directly into the presence of the One she had loved and served so vigorously for sixty years. She was seventy-nine, in her work clothes, and with her "boots" on when the call came. What a welcome she must have received!

Since her home-going the work continues to expand. By the end of the year, another market stand was operating in Abepura, about fifteen miles inland. She must have trained her Indonesian workers well, and now her mantle rests on them. They have taken up the torch she passed to them.

Another interesting development of the work in Indonesia has been bookboats. We were challenged by this need after the first visit of Operation Mobilization's ship *Logos*. It was unable to dock in Jakarta and had to remain out in the harbor. There were also government restrictions which limited the various functions of the ship's ministry considerably, but one thing became clear—even without government restrictions there were few ports in Indonesia which could handle large ships. Another thing was clear—so many of the smaller islands were almost totally neglected. Many had only a very limited gospel witness; some none at all. The solution was obvious: a fleet of boats, rather than large ships, operating under Indonesian registration and manned by Indonesian crews.

It took a number of years to bring this vision into the visible. It began to crystalize when we learned of an experimental boat built in Papua New Guinea of cement reinforced with wire mesh and steel rods. This type of ferro-cement boat could be built very inexpensively and with local talent. Better yet, God was preparing some young Indonesians to assume responsibility for this boat ministry. They built the boat in Surabaya as a faith project and were encouraged by seeing the Lord provide as each need arose. They took navigational training and finally the day came when all was ready. Nearby islands were visited first. The boat operated well, but the response from the people was the most encouraging, as they listened to the message preached and as they happily obtained reading material for their spiritual needs—many of them for the very first time. Then the crew took the long two thousand mile journey to Jayapura, making this their base from which to visit many of the islands in the east. Unfortunately the boat was lost in 1980, when the motor failed in a severe storm as it approached the small island of Pulau Liki, about 250 miles from Jayapura. Thankfully there was no loss of life. Some of the cargo was saved, but not the Bibles or books. Another boat—indeed several—should be in constant service as inter-island gospel bookboats manned by teams of God-called Indonesians. Hopefully this can be accomplished during the eighties.

Meanwhile, this boat ministry is operating on the rivers of some of the larger islands in another way. CLC Indonesia cooperates with three boats plying the rivers of the large island of Kalimantan (Borneo). The *Ebenezer,* the *Tobiasi,* and the *Bunga Holfer* concentrate on a medical-evangelistic ministry, and they also carry a good stock of literature supplied by CLC. Because they are often tied up for long periods while medical needs are met, CLC has now (1981) purchased a smaller boat so that Mansur Poniman can visit places not served by these boats. While he is away his wife, Mamiek, looks after the shop in Palangka Raya, as well as keeping her eye on their little daughter, Grace.

All this is so exciting and the results tremendously rewarding. Indonesia has the largest Muslim population of any nation, but the Christian church here is still considered one of the fastest growing in Southeast Asia. By far the greater proportion of the existing work and expansion is in the hands of God-fearing Indonesian leadership.

Visas for the international missionary are not easy to obtain (though not impossible), but more personnel from overseas are needed. Working side by side with the maturing nationals they together can keep the ministry pressing forward. Even as I write, thought is being given to opening their tenth bookcenter, this time in Pematang Siantar on the island of Sumatra.

This city is about a three-hour drive south of Medan where the CLC shop opened in 1978. In less than two years this operation became self-supporting and continued its amazing growth all through 1980, which will enable it to assume some of the financial responsibility for the proposed new center in Pematang Siantar when the Captain's time comes. It was in this general area known as Toba Batak that some early Christian missionaries were martyred years ago. What a privilege CLC will have to establish a vital Christian literature center here. What a joy to be a service agency to the growing Christian church in this area. Truly the blood of the martyrs has proven again to be the seed of the church. God's ways are past finding out, but exciting to be involved in!

How thankful we are for the mature Indonesian workers the Lord is bringing around us, who not only adequately handle one bookcenter but reach out to other needy areas, as we see in Jayapura, Palangka Raya and Medan. I am sure that something similar is happening in all of our centers. The Willard Stones took a one-year furlough in 1979/80, and the rather natural question persisted—how will things go during their absence? The 1980 Annual Report from Willard answers that question. The personnel increased, the publishing program progressed, and distribution increased 33 per cent—all under the careful leadership of Frans Kairupan.

The future looks very promising, for there is still more ahead as the CLC team in Indonesia looks forward to opening a center in the Ambon area of the Molucca Islands. They live expectantly out there, too!

19

OVERSEAS GROWTH UNLIMITED

The final four years of the fifties saw nine more countries entered, three in South America, three in the Far East, and one each in Europe, Australasia, and the West Indies. The developments in two of these countries, Korea (1956) and Barbados (1957), have been told in previous chapters. In three of these years I spent time overseas helping in the continuing growth of the work.

The first journey in 1956 took me to the West Indies for three months. This was to help plan and promote the monthly *Caribbean Challenge* magazine, preparing for the first issue which appeared in January, 1957. The full story of this faith venture has been recorded in Norman Grubb's story of CLC's first twenty-one years entitled *Leap of Faith,* which is still in print. The need for this magazine had been sparked by the then very popular *African Challenge.* CLC was circulating about 10,000 copies each month of this gospel paper throughout the English-reading areas of the West Indies and Central America. Because of the multi-ethnic structure of the people of the Caribbean, the need for a specialized publication became growingly evident—so we acted.

After an encouraging start with the first two issues, circulation continues to be around 30,000 copies each month. This in itself is another of God's miracles, for in spite of hurdles, roadblocks and limited personnel, it is still in circulation, having entered its twenty-fifth year of continuous production with the January 1981 issue and outliving many similar efforts such as the French *Envol* and the Spanish *Vida.* There is a great potential for the *Caribbean Challenge,* and more workers both for the editorial staff and islands-wide distribution can make the difference. In February of 1981 Nancy Boerman from the States joined the editorial staff. That is good. As this decade unfolds maybe we shall see a progressive climb in circulation. Then many more people across the area will be blessed by the monthly message of this magazine.

The following year I was back in the Caribbean and in Central America, but this year also saw the work begun in Austria by two dedicated sisters, Elizabeth and Helga. They caught the literature vision when two members of the British CLC were visiting the country some years earlier. Subsequently they went to a Bible School in Germany and then to London for training and to improve their English. On their return a bookshop was opened in Graz, after a battle with the authorities to obtain various permits.

Elizabeth and Helga von Ferenchich will soon have completed twenty-five years of faithful service, which has included getting literature, by the mail and by other means, into Russia and some of the other European satellite countries. A growing mail-order program and mobile outreach is enabling the ministry of that one store to reach far and wide. The Krauter family from Germany, who joined the work in 1979, is part of the reason for this increase, but more workers are needed. Then consideration could be given to opening bookshops in other cities and expanding the mobile outreach.

Books continue to play a vital part in Austria as some find salvation and then use literature as a tool for witnessing. Two years ago two families in one village were converted and immediately began to share their joy. One year they purchased three hundred carefully chosen books to give away as Christmas presents to friends and neighbors. Another year they ordered about seven hundred Scripture calendars, mainly for their business customers. There is a fine group of Christians in this village today. Encouraging fruit indeed.

This same year, 1957, also saw us back in the Orient. As we have mentioned earlier, calls were coming constantly from many parts of the world, for the fact of CLC's existence and what God was doing through this young organization was spreading rapidly. I fear that some expected CLC would be the immediate answer to the literature needs in their country, but it is not that easy, especially when many languages are used and literacy is low. I am sure some have been disappointed because CLC did not produce as they had hoped. Maybe they had been given to understand that we had ready-made answers, only to find that we had no magic wand! We, too, have been disappointed that some countries have not gone ahead as well as others. Notwithstanding, we have persisted and have seen some remarkable "resurrections," for ministries as well as people must often pass through a "death" before the glory of resurrection life is experienced.

A number of young missions in the Philippines had urged CLC to come and develop a nationwide literature ministry. Ray and Margaret Oram responded to this invitation. Their experience in Japan would help them, though the situation was very different in the Philippines. While we were still waiting for the Lord's leading to establish a bookstore in Manila, we were able to get one started in Cebu City in time for Christmas, 1959.

But then something new developed.

The Far Eastern Gospel Crusade was one of the missions which urged CLC to come to the Philippines. They were already involved in literature work and had started a small print shop. When their printer returned to the States for medical attention, the mission asked Ray if he would supervise their printing program. Later they asked him to take it over completely and passed all the equipment to CLC. This became a full-time responsibility and slowed down our normal distribution ministry. As production in two or three of the main languages grew, it became increasingly clear that we faced a major decision. Either we should pull back on printing and return to distribution, or set distribution aside for the present and major on production.

Two events gave us the guidance we needed. After a two-year absence Dick LeBar was ready to return to the Philippines with his family and to the printing ministry. They would transfer to CLC if this was agreeable with the two missions. It was, and so they came. Soon after their return an $8,000 gift was received in Fort Washington earmarked for a new print-shop building in the Philippines. Our course was set. We would give our best efforts to the printing and publishing program even though this was a departure from our norm, and at the same time we would keep the distribution need on our hearts and watch for the day when this, also, could move forward.

With this settled, suitable land for the proposed new print shop, which would include two apartments for the staff above it, had to be found.

In 1959 I was in the Philippines to help guide the work through these transitions, but as yet no land had been found. The Orams, the LeBars and Eric Parsons were living in separate houses, two of which were owned by the same landlord, but the print shop was still at the FEGC compound. Much of my time was spent looking for land but nothing materialized. It seemed that I would have to leave the country without having reached this objective, for I was to visit Japan and Korea before heading back to the States.

Then it happened. I was being interviewed at the Far East Broadcasting Company studio, sharing some of the impressions I had gleaned during my visit. I was asked about CLC's immediate objectives, and I mentioned our need to find some land for our print shop and the building program. As soon as I was back in the Oram's home, the landlord of the other two houses came over to see us. He had been listening to the FEBC broadcast. "Why not buy my piece of land?" he asked. Well, we didn't know he was thinking of selling, and I must admit the idea had never crossed our minds. Though it was not on a main highway (which had been our hope), it was very close to the main road to the north and within walking distance of both the FEGC and the FEBC operations, which we felt would be a distinct advantage. Now within a day or two of my departure, I knew where CLC would be based in the Philippines.

We are still there today, though because the FEBC later developed a much bigger print shop, we recently sold our equipment to them and phased out the printing side of our work. These had been good years and much vital literature in several languages had been produced. We had been able to assist many missions and churches with their printing needs, but it seemed clear that it was now God's time for us to return to distribution.

We now have a nice bookstore on the property and have developed a mobile ministry. Though Tagalog, now known as Filipino, is the official language, English is still widely used, and there is a greater desire on the part of the young people to use it today than ever before. Spanish is also used quite widely. Because most of our personnel were serving in the print shop, they were not suitable for this distribution program, so we are beginning again, building another team of Filipinos who share this vision and have responded to the call of the Lord to become involved. This is the task which Neil and Jean MacKinnon from Scotland are grappling with. Along with building the new Filipino team, they will welcome other international personnel. God will do it. Resurrection day is at hand!

Indeed it is!

Since this chapter was written (February, 1981), a fine couple, Paul and Josmena Mortiz, and their five teen-age children joined the MacKinnons in April, 1981. Paul has been in an evangelistic ministry and is currently the Sunday pastor on FEBC radio. At the same time a young lady who just graduated from the university as a librarian applied to CLC. Her name is Josie Colangoy and she is now getting on-the-spot experience in the CLC Manila bookcenter.

Yes, indeed, there are some exciting things ahead for the literature ministry in the Philippines.

All four countries opened in 1958 were the responsibility of CLC North America, so we kept busy laying the initial plans through correspondence. Only cursory information had come our way about Thailand, though it did indicate that a definite literature need existed. Then a letter from Bob Sjoblom, a Christian and Missionary Alliance missionary in Bangkok, brought things into sharper focus. A copy of the *Floodtide* magazine had come into his hands and he wanted to know what plan CLC had for that country.

The outcome of continued correspondence, and then face-to-face discussions when Bob and Muriel were on furlough, led to their amicable transfer to CLC.

The start was, as usual, simple, but ultimate goals were always kept in mind and prayed over. From the beginning, literature in three languages was stocked—Thai, Chinese and English, but because the range of Thai literature was inadequate, we soon became involved in a publishing program in this language.

20

A MINISTRY IN THAILAND

The total CLC program in Thailand, at this time, was centered in Bangkok. But with the coming of another couple from Australia, Bill and Kath Devine, two new developments took place. A second bookcenter was opened in the up-country crossroads city of Chiengmai and a mobile ministry based on that center reached out to some remote villages. Because of the very poor roads getting to these places, a four-wheel-drive Land Rover was later used for this more rugged mobile program. Literature was in steady demand and evangelistic and Bible teaching opportunities abounded.

Unfortunately, the Devines were not able to return after furlough, and in 1980 Kath was called to higher service where another "Well done" awaited her. So far no replacements have been found to take up the task which this couple carried on so faithfully. It is just another of the many unfulfilled opportunities awaiting God-called volunteers in Thailand as well as in almost every country of the world.

With the coming of the cassette age, the possibilities for hinterland ministry in Thailand have greatly increased. CLC Bangkok began to make available inexpensive playback machines (recording facilities were not needed), and cassettes were prepared by various mission groups. Thousands of tapes are in constant use today, and undoubtedly this method of mass communication will continue to make a significant impact for many years.

In 1979 another big development took place. Our present field leader in Thailand is Kjell Bonerfalt from Sweden. He and his family are supported by the Orebro Mission, which whole-heartedly backed their involvement with the CLC ministry. Indeed, a very happy agreement has been worked out between the two missions, which may lead to further cooperation of a similar nature in other parts of the world.

Nothing was being done in south Thailand, so Kjell Bonerfalt made a survey trip, and he became convinced that something should be done. And done it was. With the financial help of the Orebro Mission, a branch store in Hadd Yai was opened in April, 1979. At year's end Kjell reported that, because of its good location, the bookstore had attracted many non-Christian customers. Even visitors from Malaysia and Singapore find their way to it, and many good contacts have been made. This has continued throughout 1980, and a new goal is before them—a bookmobile. The workers are convinced that with a good vehicle on the roads a greater impact can be made in the whole of south Thailand, and even into north Malaysia, since there is a constant movement of people across the borders.

A long-standing goal of the Thailand team has been to have a more permanent location for the bookstore in Bangkok. Indeed, this highlights a problem we face in most countries. With land and property values rising constantly, landlords often raise rents, only grant short-term contracts, or have other reasons why they do not wish to renew leases. This is always disappointing, especially if years have been spent building contacts and establishing a solid ministry. There have been occasions when we have been unable to find suitable alternate premises. The only satisfactory answer is to own property whenever possible, so that we cannot be moved at the whim of landlords or changing circumstances. When this has been possible, it has been done on a carefully calculated basis, with a goal of completing the transaction within seven to ten years. I will return to this matter in a later chapter.

So it was in Bangkok. After several moves, each time improving our location and general appearance, we were able to rent a three-story building ideally located on one of Bangkok's main streets. We were granted a ten-year lease, with the bulk of the money having to be paid in advance (something over $20,000) and then just a nominal monthly rent.

However, a combination of circumstances indicated yet another move. In 1976 the owner of the building offered a substantial rebate on our original investment if we would surrender our lease—we had about three years to go. With the fall of Viet Nam, and the possibility that Thailand could be next, it seemed wise to accept this offer and use the funds, at least for the immediate future, in the newly developing work in Hong Kong.

The ministry in Bangkok would continue, but we would now concentrate on distribution of Thai literature while still stocking books in Chinese and English. However, we had to be content with an upstairs showroom in the same general area. We missed our good storefront and window display but persisted in faith that one day we would again be at street level, for it is from the foot traffic that most of the non-Christians "stray" into the literature center.

Thankfully the general situation in the country did not get worse. Indeed, things stabilized and this encouraged us to keep faith high regarding a better location—hopefully this time in our own building! So we added "work" to our faith and kept searching.

Finally we were able to work out a proposition with the Christian builder of a new three-story building. Again with the financial help of the Orebro Mission, we transacted the purchase of this building. Things ran a little behind schedule, but in October, 1980 we took possession of "our" lovely new building. Immediately there was a marked improvement as more people began finding us and obtaining some of the living literature that we have to offer. Now there will be no escalating rents or compulsory moves. We can settle down to increasing fruitfulness among the more than 4 million people of Bangkok, and through improved outreach, to the nearly 50 million citizens of Thailand.

A trickle of literature from our Bangkok center reaches even further afield to the neighboring country on the west—Burma. Perhaps one day we will be able to do more when government restrictions on the importing of Christian books are eased. Certainly the need is there, and the growing church should have better access to Christian literature, especially because English is widely used.

However, within the last few years we have been able to make an indirect contribution to the Lisu people of north Burma. Orville and Hazel Carlson had ministered to the Lisu people during their years with the Overseas Missionary Fellowship and were keenly aware that the Lisu Bible needed revision. They were back in the States facing retirement when, instead, the Lord gave them redirection!

Hearing that CLC had an urgent need for help to allow the Bob Sjobloms to transfer to the Philippines, they offered their services and returned to Thailand to take over the management of the CLC bookstore in Bangkok. They threw themselves wholeheartedly into this new assignment, and at the same time kept in close touch with their friends in Lisu-land, paying them an occasional visit.

As a result, the burden for Bible revision was quickened. The Carlsons made contact with other missionaries who had worked with the Lisu people and also with some key Lisu Christians, following which the tedious, time-consuming task of revision began in 1976. As the work progressed it became necessary for all concerned to be together in north Thailand close to the Burma border. Slowly all sixty-six books of the Bible were completed. This first draft needed further revision, followed by the task of typesetting, which fell to Hazel Carlson, who spent long hours each day before the specially prepared IBM typesetter. Next came proof-reading, with some slight revisions, and back to the IBM. Then art proofs for actual printing were prepared. By mid-April, 1980, Orville Carlson completed proofing these and all was ready for printing.

The British Trinitarian Bible Society had agreed to print the Bibles, so on April 26 the Carlsons flew to Britain to carry the precious cargo and discuss the final details with the Secretary of the TBS.

One final problem remained. How to get the 10,000 finished Bibles to their faraway destination. God had the answer, we were certain. Ideally the Carlsons should take them to Burma and organize the distribution, but only seven-day visas were being granted to visitors. More time would be essential, the Carlson's reasoned, for things move slowly in Burma. So, faith claimed extended visas from the God who had brought them thus far along this road of revision.

Their faith was rewarded when, by February, 1981, two visas had been granted, the Bibles were en route by ship, and plans for the actual distribution were being worked out. The following month the Carlsons were in Rangoon to clear the shipment through customs and get the Bibles upcountry. In early April they sent this cable: *Mission Accomplished.*

The timing was perfect, for a situation had developed which was undreamed of when the revision program was launched four years before.

The new religious freedom allowed by the Chinese authorities in 1979 was bringing new hope and release to the Lisu people of China. Letters from the Burma Lisus reported that Lisus from China were coming to Burma hoping to get Bibles. The China Lisus say that they now have peaceful living conditions. For thirty years they had been silent, but in 1979 they were allowed to celebrate Christmas. They are now allowed to have Sunday services again, and they can even sing the songs of Zion while they work in their fields!

In J.O. Fraser's wonderful book *Behind the Ranges,* he tells that the first penetration of the gospel to these Lisu people "behind the ranges" was because a young lad obtained a copy of one of the Gospels when he came over the mountains to trade. On his return the book was read by and to the people. They believed what they read and acted upon its instructions, and when the Frasers arrived in Lisu-land years later, they found a church already established! How they must be rejoicing in heaven today as they see the Lisu people still hungry for the living Word, and as they have witnessed the remarkable provision which has now been made through the untiring efforts of the Carlsons and others. It is indeed the Lord's doing and marvelous in our eyes.

21

ENLARGEMENT IN SOUTH AMERICA

The continent of South America continued to be on our hearts as a Crusade since my extended journey in the spring of 1955, and our concentrated concern and prayer brought rather rapid developments in the year we are now reviewing—1958.

The small team of CLCers in Uruguay had been strengthened by the coming of Jack and Rachel Roeda. Just before graduating from Columbia Bible College they had contacted CLC, sharing their interest in the literature ministry in South America. After a few months of orientation and preparation at our Fort Washington base, they headed to Uruguay for language study and on-the-spot experience in the Montevideo bookstore. Actually the Argentine had been our original target when the Crusade first began in South America, so in due course Jack made occasional visits to Buenos Aires. Through these visits the way opened for the Roeda family to move across the River Platt and take up residence in Buenos Aires which, at that time, was the largest city in the southern hemisphere.

There were already a number of Christian bookshops in the city, but each seemed to be linked with a denomination. There was room, we felt, for an interdenominational bookcenter. We obtained a very central location in a downtown arcade and are still there today, although the work has never blossomed into what we had hoped. One thing we have learned from this experience is that a dead-end arcade with no throughway is not conducive to attracting the pedestrian traffic. It does not give adequate exposure to the shopping public.

Our present workers, Raul and Rosa Roldan, have soldiered

on bravely, waiting patiently for the tide to turn. In 1981 a bookmobile made possible a wider ministry to other parts of greater Buenos Aires and beyond, especially servicing book tables at special events, churches and conventions. Their older son, Jorge, is assisting in this mobile outreach. It is still an uphill climb, even though the unbelievably high inflation dropped in 1980 to 213 per cent from the previous year's 230 per cent. That is right, two hundred thirty per cent inflation! (It was 350 per cent in 1976!)

This same year the call came from Chile. The work began with a colportage ministry. Later a Chilean pastor asked CLC to take over the little bookcenter which he was operating. The Roedas moved to Chile after furlough, mainly because Rachel was having severe problems with asthma, which was probably aggravated by the pollution of Buenos Aires. Two new centers were opened during the sixties, both in arcades, one in Santiago, the capital, and the other in Concepcion, about three hundred miles to the south. Some years later we had the opportunity to purchase the Concepcion center, which had proved very success-ful right from the beginning because it had a constant flow-through of people.

However, in Santiago we ran into the problem of having to move. At that time the Bible Society's premises became available for purchase. We were interested, but not overly happy about the location which was quite a distance from the main shopping area. So we continued to search the city's shopping streets, but without success. It seemed that the Bible Society premises were the only answer, yet there was no settled peace in the hearts of our workers, and time was running out. Our final decision had to be given to the Bible Society the next day, March 23. Then, during a final prayer time together (of course there had been many along the way), the urge came to search once more.

It was the Captain's voice.

Sure enough an excellent corner store had just been put on the market. Indeed, the owner, who lived in the Argentine, had come over that very day in the hope of getting a quick sale, as he needed money urgently.

His story was fascinating—and confirming. He, too, had a very strong urge to travel to Santiago on the 23rd. Normally he would fly, but he could not get a flight. For some unknown reason the bus company put on an extra bus—an express direct to Santiago which would arrive at midday instead of the usual time of midnight. Between the departure time of this special bus and the regularly scheduled one, some political problems arose and the Argentine government put a temporary ban on international travel, so he might not have been in Santiago for several days. As it was, the unscheduled special bus arriving at midday gave time for the owner to meet us, whereas coming on the regular bus, even if it had not been banned, would have meant a delay until the next day, March 24—and we would have settled with the Bible Society! Who put that urge in his mind? When this man heard our side of the story he, too, was asking the same question. Our testimony made a real impression. He returned to the Argentine with a book we had given him and with a question calling for an answer.

Our folks had looked the place over and the witness was immediate and unanimous. This is it. It had lovely display windows on both streets, a full basement, and other attractive features. It was located within two blocks of the post office communication tower, which was known by everybody and considered the exact center of the city. Beyond these premises were a number of government office buildings, such as the Employment Bureau, Pension Office, and Main Post Office, places well known and to which a constant flow of people gravitated. It was ideal in every way. And the price? Just two thousand dollars more than the Bible Society building! Yet a greatly superior location with about one-third more space, so we were ready to talk business with the owner when he arrived later that afternoon.

We have been there since 1977. The large basement allowed us room to greatly increase stock and begin a wholesale service to the other bookstores throughout the country. Our two bookmobiles draw their stock from this center and there is ample office space, not only to handle the book operation, but to organize the itineraries of the two vehicles. Unfortunately, owing to rising costs of maintenance and gasoline, the longer trips have been cut back considerably in recent months. However, some of this outreach is continuing, using local buses. Along with book tables in churches, an extensive gospel film ministry has been developed. For many years three radio programs each week have been handled through the CLC office, with all follow-up correspondence cleared through the CLC mail address. Never a dull moment in CLC Santiago, to be sure!

The Temuco store was opened in 1978. It is just one more story of the perfect timing and detailed leading of the Captain.

For eighteen months or more, requests had reached the Santiago office for CLC to open a store in Temuco, a city with an unusually high proportion of evangelicals. It has several Bible Institutes, and headquarters for a number of national churches and missions are located there. Its people keenly missed the previous bookcenter, which had closed leaving a real gap. At the workers' Annual Conference the previous November, the staff had agreed to respond to this persistent call. Eduardo Moreno was sent to do the initial investigation. Empty premises were available, but the key money and rents asked were beyond what CLC could do. Alan Harris joined Eduardo and they continued searching. Nothing witnessed.

Then they came upon an empty shop on one of Temuco's busiest streets, though there was no indication that these premises were for rent. No doubt the terms would be out of this world, they thought, but you never know until you try. So they traced down the owner, whose son was soon to open a business there. Indeed, it was the son they finally met and he confirmed what had been told them. The store was not available.

After a few minutes of further conversation, the young man said to Alan Harris, "You are from La Crusada, aren't you?" The previous year he and his fiancee had been in the Santiago store — and Alan had served them! The owner of this store and his family were keen Christians. When they knew why the store in

Temuco was needed, they were delighted and agreed to pray that CLC would find something suitable.

Pray they did, discovering through the inner urge of the Spirit that they would have to be part of the answer! Gone must be their own ambitions. God wanted their shop for His business! That same day they reached Eduardo and Alan by telephone, and met them again an hour or so later.

God likes prompt obedience!

The terms they offered were most generous. Key money was less than half of what could have been asked, and the monthly rental was considerably less than that being obtained for other commercial property in this prime part of the city. Isn't God good? Or should we put it another way? Isn't God glad when He finds members of His body operating their lives on the principles of the kingdom, which enables Him to bring into the visible His "good and acceptable and perfect will"? In this case, His will was an adequate building in which He could carry on His literature business! Yes, He always needs bodies—redeemed and sanctified—through which to continue His program of reconciliation, generation after generation.

This dear Chilean family had given God their best, for when Eduardo and Alan looked over the shop they found it was ideal. It included two large display windows, adequate floor space and a mezzanine floor with room for offices, another area suitable for a lending library or a counseling room, and a place for fellowship in a relaxed atmosphere, perhaps over a cup of coffee. They couldn't have designed it better themselves!

What this present decade holds for CLC in Chile, I do not know. We must keep moving forward, but more personnel, both Chilean and international, are needed. The church grows unbelievably. A recent survey concluded there are at least 250 evangelical churches in the greater Santiago area, and so it is all across the country. Approximately 20 per cent of Chile's nearly twelve million people are now evangelical Christians. Not all are truly born again, perhaps. Not all are totally committed disciples, maybe, although there is much bold witnessing and energetic proclamation of the good news. For this very reason the distribution of Christian literature is of paramount importance today. These zealous young people need to "grow in grace and in the knowledge of the Lord." To grow, they need food, and vital Christian books are the heaven-sent manna to maintain and mature the Christian life. They are essential tools for personal witnessing, too.

The third South American country where CLC's ministry began in 1958 was Brazil. Tom and Lily McClelland, WEC missionaries in Uruguay, responded to the Captain's directive and transferred to CLC to undertake the formidable task of establishing the literature ministry in Brazil.

Again it was an unpretentious beginning—a bookroom on the fifth floor of a downtown skyscraper in Porto Alegre. Though not exactly what we would have chosen, it did produce some lasting fruit. One customer, Claudio Ely Espindola, purchased a Bible, found the Lord, and matured in faith through good books and fellowship with Tom and Lily. Not surprisingly, Claudio and his wife, Carmen, learned about CLC and of the McClellands' hopes for the literature ministry in Brazil. Their interest grew and Claudio began to offer advice and help in practical ways. Some years later they recognized the Captain's voice directing them to join CLC. Today they are pillars in the expanding ministry, and at the beginning of 1981 they moved north to Sao Jose dos Campos to help establish CLC's new Administration and Training Center.

The following year a mobile ministry took books to the people of the interior, thus extending the influence of the bookroom in the city. The welcome received, the appreciation expressed, the eager purchases made, and the constant testimony of blessing and help were ample reward for the expenditure of time and energy which had been put into these trips, often traveling long hours on gravel and mud-packed roads.

Three years later, we moved to a good, ground floor shop right in the heart of the city. We are still there today and a much greater flow of literature continues to reach a wide area.

This was the limit of our ministry until 1965 when, strangely, we went to the far northeast and opened our second center in Recife, 2,500 miles from Porto Alegre. It was the beginning of steady advance, although it was not until the seventies that things really began to move. Six new centers were opened during the decade: first, further north to the smaller towns of Joao Pessoa and Natal, and then south to the major cities of Salvador, Sao Paulo, Rio de Janeiro and Sao Jose dos Campos.

Our goal for the immediate future is to establish a main base for centralization and overall administration. It will include a training center for new workers, not only from Brazil, but also from Chile, Argentina, Uruguay and other countries. This is likely to be located somewhere near our Sao Jose dos Campos bookstore, which is situated between Sao Paulo and Rio de Janeiro, right in the heart of industrial Brazil. Undoubtedly this decade will also see more bookcenters opened, increased publishing in Portuguese, and further mobile outreach.

Each of the stores has its own unique image and ministry, along with the main task of getting books out. Often there are specific reasons for this.

Two things, in particular, drew us to Sao Paulo. First, this city is the hub of the publishing industry in Brazil. Then the mix of nationalities and languages in Brazil's fastest growing city (approximately ninety languages are spoken) presented a challenge—and an opportunity.

One of the larger language groups is the Japanese with over a million strong. In a way, we had a built-in answer to this situation—first, because of our ready access to Japanese Christian literature which could be supplied through CLC Tokyo, and then because Mrs. Chieko Saito had served with CLC in the Sapporo center for about four years prior to her marriage. She and her husband had taken up residence in Brazil, but after his death, Mrs. Saito suggested to CLC that she (and her son, Samuel) would be willing to stay in Brazil and help distribute Japanese literature to her countrymen. This witnessed to the CLC staffs in both Brazil and Japan, and so the stage was set for the beginnings of a multi-language ministry. Japan generously sent the first consignment of books (about $10,000 worth) as an outright contribution and took on Mrs. Saito as "their" missionary, agreeing to trust the Lord for her support each month.

Today Sao Paulo stocks Scriptures and Christian books in about sixteen languages and is always willing to try to supply other language needs. In a recent letter Victor Cardoo mentioned that, in a matter of days, twenty-one nationalities visited the International Christian Book Center, which is our name in the city. It was quite a list—Japanese, Arabs, Germans, Italians, Chinese, Egyptians, Canadians, Koreans, Russians, Dutch, Americans, Argentinians, Mozambiques, Paraguayans, Mexicans, British, Bolivians, Lebanese, Chileans, Peruvians, and Swedes. Of course, plenty of Brazilians are always in and out. What a mission field in one comparatively small location. What a ministry to "hidden people," all in less than one week. Come they do, week after week, the whole year through.

No wonder our team there is thrilled with what they are privileged to do. As Victor further commented in his letter: "To know that we can bring books from across the world and place them in the hands of these people is a blessed experience. We have always been concerned with providing good Christian books for the people in their mother tongue. One of these recent customers said to me, 'This book store is a real blessing. I just love coming here!' "

It is a different kind of service in Rio de Janeiro. Along with the retail bookstore, we operate an extensive wholesale department, sending the merchandise to almost every Christian literature outlet in the country. A larger percentage of books have to be imported from Portugal, the U.S.A., and elsewhere—and importing can often be very frustrating! Being able to obtain books from one source within the country is greatly appreciated by the bookstores, by the churches, by the missionaries and by people in the rural and remote parts of the country who can order by mail, using our increasingly comprehensive catalog.

Then, there is Recife. Different again.

A local pastor has a daily radio broadcast and is seen on television each weekend. He felt the need to contact some of his hearers face-to-face. But how? Where? Could CLC offer any suggestions? We could and we would. A small air-conditioned room with an attractive waiting area toward the back of the shop was made available to him without charge.

And there was more.

Four mornings a week, at seven o'clock, he used the shop as an auditorium. To make this possible all display furnishings were fitted with castors. At the end of each day these were pushed to one side, and more than one hundred chairs were set in place. Then each morning, with standing room only, right out to the doorway, the place was filled with about one hundred fifty people. Many had heard of the counseling room and the morning Bible studies in the CLC premises over the airwaves.

The idea caught on.

Why, asked a missionary from Scotland, go to all that trouble for just one service in the morning (remember, he was from Scotland!)? Could not the facilities be used for Bible studies in the evenings also? Brilliant thinking! And so it was arranged. Of course, a sort of fringe benefit for CLC is that all these people are constantly in touch with a supply source of good Christian literature. CLC is indeed a service ministry in more ways than one. Who said literature work was dull and unexciting? Away with the idea! We get out of everything we do in life and in our Christian service what we put into it. When the "we" is the combination of the Holy Spirit operating through the willing, human channel, there is no telling what can happen—even in a downtown bookstore!

The Porto Alegre premises are used in a similar way. There it is the custom for stores to close for two hours during the midday. One time when I was in the city, local pastors were meeting at the store during the midday break for fellowship, and to pray for each other's ministries, for revival, and a new visitation from the Lord.

In Joao Pessoa there is an active ministry among university

students. In Salvador a dozen or more telephone callers each day ask for guidance about specific problems, and prayer is offered. The center in Sao Jose dos Campos has a public prayer room in which nine people found Christ as Saviour in its first year of operation.

Thrilling! Each center is different, and yet their combined effort is seeing lives touched all across the country. In a very special way, the centers are rallying points, uniting God's people in living fellowship, using the ever-influential printed word.

Then, there is cooperation when special events are organized. Undoubtedly the Generation '79 Congress for Youth has been the most far-reaching to date. Over five thousand young people and about five hundred pastors converged on the Anhembi Exposition Pavilion in Sao Paulo for this seven day convention, the largest youth congress ever to be held in Latin America. They came from all twenty-two states of Brazil and from Argentina, Bolivia, Peru and Uruguay.

The organizers of this Congress knew that literature would be essential, and they graciously gave the task of providing it to CLC. In the allotted space of one thousand square meters we set up a comprehensive multi-display in Portuguese, Spanish, English, German, Japanese and Korean. Unfortunately, they misjudged the demand in some of these languages. Korean books had been air freighted from CLC Seoul. By the second day of the Congress they were gone! During the seven days more than $45,000 worth of living literature had changed hands. High on the list was a commentary on Colossians, followed closely by Bible dictionaries, other commentaries, concordances and so on. It had kept the team of nine CLCers from four centers, and some fifteen volunteers, busy fourteen hours each day, but they were rewarded by the constant, warm appreciation of the young people. For many, this was the first time they could select their books from so many different publishers in one location! Local people suggested that this proved the need for an "evangelical supermarket" in Sao Paulo! Maybe that should be another goal for CLC Brazil!

This type of cooperation by CLC has been extended also to the Operation Mobilization ship *Doulos* on its two visits to Brazil. Extraordinary things are constantly happening, all testifying to the mounting interest in spiritual things by the people of Brazil—80 million of them under twenty-five years of age. Multiplied thousands are being won for the Lord week after week.

But Brazil's ministry reaches even further afield.

One of the policies of the Crusade is that each country or cluster of countries, such as the islands of the West Indies, work toward administrative autonomy. A number of requirements must be met to bring this about. Among them is financial stability, so that the local work is maintained from within the country and does not require outside subsidy. Brazil meets this requirement, not only through the flow of money generated by the distribution program, but because the churches and individual Christians are beginning to rise to the responsibility of financially supporting Brazilian personnel called into full-time Christian service within the country. Now, they are beginning to recognize CLC's ministry as a home mission needing their prayerful backing and financial support, even though the work began through the efforts of the foreign missionary. They see the Scriptural principle of financial involvement in all phases of the Christian ministry within their country.

Individuals, too, are embracing this principle. One successful Brazilian businessman saw the need of renovation in CLC's Recife store and paid the complete cost of having it done. Later, when advance into Sao Jose dos Campos was being considered, he gave a substantial gift toward this need. These are all significant signs that the growth of the church in South America is not just numerical. One recent estimate places it at 11 per cent, nearly four times faster than the growth of population. It is also growth in accepting and applying the principles of the kingdom on a corporate church level and as individual members of the Body of Christ.

There is another encouraging sign—a willingness to accept responsibility beyond their own borders. The Great Commission is the responsibility of the whole church. Brazil is now seeing this and is beginning to encourage her young people to respond and to become involved as Ambassadors for Christ in any part of the world, as well as standing behind them with prayer and finances when they do go.

CLC Brazil, as an autonomous country within our international fellowship, is active in this adventure of sharing. They have recently assumed oversight of the work in Uruguay, Argentina, and Chile, thus relieving CLC U.S.A. of this responsibility. This is proving to be much more acceptable. The workers in these three countries find they have more in common with their fellow Latins. Even the Portuguese and Spanish languages are more or less interchangeable. And, of course, this leaves CLC U.S.A. free to concentrate on the calls for help coming from other countries.

Brazil has also become a sending country. One young lady, Enedy Da Silva, has served one term with CLC in Mozambique, East Africa. She is now considering a further overseas assignment with CLC in Guinea Bissau, West Africa. Both of these countries are Portuguese speaking. Indeed more than one worker is needed, for CLC Brazil has now accepted the 1980 request of the International Council to assume responsibility for the literature ministry in Guinea Bissau. When the door opens again in Mozambique, no doubt this will become Brazil's opportunity, too.

Of course, this does not rule out the possibility of people from other lands serving in these two African countries. Nor does CLC Brazil's autonomy mean that workers from other countries are not needed in Brazil. Remember, we are international and interracial. All we ask is that God's call has a clear witness, to the individual and to the fellowship.

Let me make one point clear. The Crusade does not believe that the missionary must work himself out of a job. Yes, he must learn the art of delegating and training fellow workers in the country where he serves so that they can take on more responsibility—and finally take on his task. Then what? Can he return to his home country, smugly declaring MISSION

ACCOMPLISHED? Indeed not. As each task is handed over to others, the missionary is released to develop another phase of the work, and then another and yet another. There is not one of our forty-six countries where we have reached saturation point. There is always more which *can* be done and which *must* be done.

The clarion call is clear to all, to national and international personnel alike—"Come over and help us."

SECTION IV

A FRUITFUL BOUGH...WHOSE BRANCHES

RUN OVER THE WALL
Genesis 49:22

Joseph is a fruitful bough, even a fruitful bough by a well, whose branches run over the wall.
Genesis 49:22

22

AUSTRALASIAN EXPANSION

We move on to the decade of the sixties when the pace of international expansion slowed from the hectic growth of the previous ten years.

You will have noticed in our story thus far that after the initial beginnings it took a few years for the work to take root in most countries; but with stability assured, advance, especially in the larger countries, was the order of the day. This is where our overall growth has been most evident during the past twenty years.

We will now trace our way through the sixties, visit the twelve new countries which were added to CLC's international expansion, and record how the Lord led us to consolidate the worldwide program through the formation of the International Council.

First we must step back for a moment to the last six weeks of 1959.

For a number of years missions in the Papua Territory on New Guinea had been requesting CLC to "come over and help us," but it was not until November 16, 1959 that we were able to respond. On that day New Zealanders Maurice and June Thomas arrived in Port Moresby. They had served a short term with CLC in the Philippines but had to take an early furlough because of injuries Maurice had sustained in a car accident while on a book trip.

In their homeland, they learned of the call for help from Papua and volunteered to begin the literature ministry in that territory. Again the timing was right. The government of Australia had accepted responsibility to groom the people of Papua for independence, which came in 1975. Here was a new nation— Papua New Guinea—in the making; literacy was on the increase; books were the order of the day. Once again it seemed that CLC had "come...for such a time as this."

It was clear that Port Moresby would be the logical place to establish the main base for this new literature thrust, and a start was made through the kind help of the Salvation Army. They were operating a small bookroom but gladly handed this over to CLC. This became June Thomas's responsibility while Maurice was kept busy with outreach. The Australia-based Campaigners for Christ also allowed CLC to use their building on Koki Beach for a bookroom. This is the main market center for Port Moresby, where thousands of people from many tribes come from miles around in their boats and canoes to do their marketing. Manning this bookstall kept Maurice busy.

Still calls came from further afield, so Maurice took time to visit many of the missions, setting up book agencies operated mainly by keen Christians from Australia who lived in the territory.

Then further yet. In response to other requests for help, Maurice Thomas made a survey trip to the Solomon Islands and then to other islands to the north as far as Fiji. He always carried what he considered to be ample supplies of literature, but on several occasions he was very disappointed. What he considered "enough" was quickly taken, sometimes by just one contact, so that he had no supplies for all the other people he would meet before returning to Port Moresby. Everybody was so overjoyed at the prospect of having the source of their literature needs so readily at hand.

All this indicated that a good building in Port Moresby was essential and that became the Thomases' next goal. A piece of land in Boroko, a suburb of Port Moresby, was purchased, and a fine two-story building erected. The work continues to this day, based on the shop there which is now under the leadership of Harold and Priscilla Hinton. Literacy is still on the low side, about 35 per cent, but the younger generation is rapidly improving the educational standard. Apart from the more remote tribal areas, the country is considered "Christian." Much remains to be done to help the people mature in the faith, and Christian literature has a significant part to play in this.

There were other New Zealanders joining the CLC ranks at this time, which indicated the need for the Crusade to have a recruiting and sending base in that country. In 1960 this goal was realized when Alec Thorne took up the challenge. He had known pioneer missionary work in West Africa and had seen, firsthand, the need and fruitfulness of the printed page.

This was the first time that CLC work began without literature! New Zealand was well provided with good Christian bookshops. Its people are great readers. Indeed, they led the world at that time, for more books per capita were purchased by New Zealanders than by the people of any other country. Then Alex saw a way to begin a service ministry with literature. A good number of Christian bookstores were buying CLC publications direct from Britain and the States, so why not make this easier for them, he reasoned. Why not import the books in quantity and wholesale to the bookshops?

This he did along with his other duties as Home Base Secretary, receiving and remitting funds, sharing the CLC vision in the churches and Bible schools, and seeing new recruits join the ranks. One of these had a vision for a mobile ministry in the South Island, although this never materialized. Neither did any CLC bookshop come into being until the 1970's.

By this time Donald and Ida David had taken up the leadership. With their long years in India, the literature vision was ever with them. The wholesale department had been maintained over the years and had grown steadily. That was good, but where was the direct-to-the-public ministry through the bookshop, they mused. That was their hope. It turned to substance in the mid-seventies, when the owner of a small bookshop in Auckland asked CLC if they would be interested in taking it over.

This was God's answer to the Davids' prayers, but because

there was another larger bookshop in the same street, they decided to move to Henderson where there was no bookcenter.

A year later a similar opportunity came their way in the town of Palmerston North. Both centers have seen steady growth in the outflow of Christian literature and, as is true in all our centers, there is a constant ministry to needy hearts.

Under Donald the deputation ministry was increased and bore fruit. Some young people caught the literature vision and applied. Indeed, over the years CLC New Zealand has made a proportionately sizeable contribution in personnel to our overseas ministry in the countries of the West Indies, Venezuela, Brazil, Chile, the States, and elsewhere.

With Donald David's passing in 1977 his wife, Ida, has bravely held the work together through correspondence and general office routine, although most of the public deputation ministry, for which Donald was so capably equipped, came to an end. Ida has done what she could, especially ministering to women's groups. At this writing Alan Harris, on furlough from Chile, has been helping, and Bill Ching is serving as interim leader until the solution for ongoing leadership is found. God will do it. He has His man for the task, and the Christians of New Zealand will continue to respond, adding their vital contribution to the completion of the Great Commission.

A new phase of my own overseas travel began at this time.

Our two daughters, now in their teens, were maturing to the point that Bessie could accompany me. Not only was this a great personal delight but it widened her ministry and influence. She was able to get alongside the lady workers, sharing their lives and offering counsel and encouragement from the Word and from her own experiences. Her positive attitude, her gentle but firm advice, seasoned with an abundant outflow of genuine love and affection, has ministered life again and again. She is a much loved and respected member of our worldwide fellowship. Even when communication has been difficult because of the language barrier, Bessie has found the secret of "speaking" from the heart to the heart, a great gift indeed; one that has been a tremendous strength to me in my own personal battles over these forty-three years we have been in harness together.

Our united travel began with a visit to Jamaica in 1960 to share in their Annual Conference. It was a blessed time as we renewed fellowship, reviewed the ministry over the past nine years, and projected into the future. Jamaica was already reaching out "overseas" to the Cayman Islands, to British Honduras (now Belize), and to the island of St. Kitts, where Jamaican-born Sylvia Wallace organized the take-over of a small bookshop in the capital, Basseterre. (This ministry is now back again in local hands.) They even considered establishing the CLC ministry in Nassau in the Bahamas, although this never materialized because of lack of personnel.

Things were also continuing to develop with the CLC team in the Eastern Caribbean. Under John Davey's leadership a bookshop was opened in Castries, St. Lucia, this same year and in St. Johns, Antigua, the following year. Both of these are still active today, though not in the same premises. As we have noted before, our beginnings in the early days were usually simple and unpretentious. Then, as the work took root, we have been able to improve both location and premises. We are certainly happy with our present-day bookshops in these two islands. The flow of life and literature from them is making a visible impact on the Christian witness throughout the islands.

Indeed, we are touching an even wider circle, particularly in the tourist meccas of the world, as many of these lovely islands of the West Indies are. Most of the tourists would be considered prosperous. They enjoy a good share of this world's comforts. They have money so they can buy the souvenirs, trinkets and expensive merchandise offered in abundance. Still, many have not found the satisfying secret they are unconsciously searching for and which money cannot buy. Often in our Christian bookstores they "get on the scent," as it were. Some, thank God, have made the great discovery right there in the bookcenter or in the quietness of their hotel room while reading the books they purchased—and have returned to tell the story of their joyful discovery. News like that brightens the day for the CLC worker, I can assure you.

23

A MAJOR OVERSEAS DEVELOPMENT

Five exciting things, in particular, happened in 1961. We have already mentioned one—opening the bookshop in Antigua, the ninth Caribbean territory to be entered. It even made front page news in the local paper! Indirectly a number of these advances, including this one into Antigua, have been a direct result of the *Caribbean Challenge* distribution ministry.

The second adventure was the erection of our administration-warehouse-print shop building in Fort Washington, but it was another battle of faith. We knew we were on target in considering this project. There had been too many clear evidences as we prayed, planned, and saw earmarked funds coming in. Construction began in September, 1960—and then was stopped because the building permit was refused due to the reluctance of the Zoning Board. After several months of negotiations, the permit was granted, and once again we watched construction begin— this time for real! Dedication Day was on September 23, 1961. Dr. Clyde Taylor of the Evangelical Foreign Missions Association, of which CLC is a member, gave a stirring address.

Not everything was completed by that day. The electricians and others still had work to do, but we were humbled to be able to announce to the Lord's glory that all bills which had been submitted had been paid. It was a proud moment for all of us.

The next happening was more personal. It marked another milestone for us as a family—we received our U.S. citizenship! It had come about because our daughter, Margaret, had lost two job opportunities because she was not a citizen. It seemed fairly clear to us that both our daughters would make the U.S.

their home, and we wanted to do everything to help them. Now that they have found themselves American husbands, this little detail has worked out well for them!

The fourth development was undoubtedly the most significant, for it resulted in consolidating and strengthening our international outreach.

For some months I had been corresponding with some of our overseas leadership about the possibility of an informal get-together. It seemed that this could be tied in with travel plans which were already anticipated. Some would be taking furlough. Others wished to visit other countries in the interest of their own program. One such was Jack Roeda who was planning a visit to Spain to discuss with Christian publishers the wider use of their literature in South America, for by this time Jack was heading up the CLC program in Uruguay, Argentina, and Chile.

So Jack and I headed for Europe with the first stop in Spain. This was a return visit for me since, you may remember, this is the country where, in one way, the whole overseas CLC venture was started, when I visited there as a teenager more than twenty-five years earlier. On this present visit I was going with eyes and ears full of faith and expectation. Surely the Captain would let us know if CLC was to have a share in helping to meet the literature needs of this country.

Our contact upon arrival in Madrid was George Verwer and his young Operation Mobilization. What a blessing both Jack and I received as we fellowshipped with this keen firebrand for God and his lively team, who were sold out to God and firmly dedicated to the ministry of Christian literature. I am tempted to digress, for his is yet one more record of twentieth-century, God-inspired adventurism which is having an impact around the world. It is an amazing story.

We traveled on through several European countries including France, Belgium, and Holland. All this was good preparation for what awaited us in London.

About twenty-four of us, including Bessie who had flown direct to London, met at the Crusade headquarters in Upper

Norwood. We were a representative group covering several areas of operation—the Far East, South America, the West Indies, Europe, and our three home bases, Australia, North America, and Britain. Indeed, Africa was the only area not directly represented.

For three days we considered many aspects of the work, concentrating particularly on those of mutual interest and concern. God gave real light. We had held our first conference focused solely on international affairs.

The following week our findings were shared with the British Annual Conference. All agreed that God had given much new light during these two conferences, but now the recommendations would have to be considered by each of our fields at their annual conferences. Their findings were to be forwarded to me, as I was still acting as International Secretary since the experimental appointment in 1955. With this information in hand we would then be in a position to analyze all the recommendations, formulating any new policies upon which the whole Crusade could continue to move forward with renewed purpose. However, this would take much longer than anticipated.

The one concrete outcome of all these deliberations in London was that an International Secretary should be appointed and that I should continue in that capacity for the present. However, an even stronger conviction which surfaced was that the International Secretary should be freed from all other duties. What the growing Crusade needed was not just a man at a desk trying to coordinate world affairs through correspondence, but one who would be free to visit the countries, sitting down in an unhurried atmosphere with the leader and his workers to discuss the problems, needs and opportunities facing each area.

It took many months for all the answers and recommendations to come. There seemed to be general agreement by our worldwide fellowship, but it was clear that more discussion would be necessary. There was, therefore, less than three years to plan and prepare for this transition which, it was hoped, could become effective by the North American Annual Conference in April, 1965.

The final specific development in 1961 was the opening of the CLC ministry in Pakistan. Miles and Beryl Sim were WEC missionaries in Pakistan and during their first term of service they were quick to see the pressing need for Christian literature. There were several things that indicated that the time was ripe for a literature ministry. Among them—the government had recently extended its educational program throughout the country and as a result, many more people were learning to read.

The Sims began to seek the Lord about any part He would have them play in making living literature available. During their furlough in North America (they are Canadians) they learned more about CLC and were interested to find that the Crusade was praying about the possibility of beginning a literature work in Karachi. To them it was now abundantly clear that they should transfer to CLC and help meet the literature needs of that country. As a final seal to this, a letter came from a group of missions in Pakistan inviting the Crusade to open up work in that country and, specifically, to establish a bookshop in Karachi.

On their return the Sims were able to rent a store in a suburban area of the city, but their ultimate goal was to find a center-city location. By the time I arrived in the country in 1965, Miles had contacted the Bishop of the Anglican Cathedral in Karachi. A small building on their property facing one of the main streets was being used by the Bible Society, but they were in the process of transferring their operation to the northern city of Rawalpindi. Bishop Chandu Ray was most gracious when Miles and I visited him, and the outcome was an agreement by the church authorities to allow CLC to use the premises. The Bible Society would continue to keep some of their stock in the same building.

This proved to be an ideal arrangement, and the work quickly began to take on a new dimension. It was particularly successful in the evenings when the crowds were in a much more relaxed mood—an excellent location, perfectly suited to our ministry.

Some years later, and after Bishop Ray had transferred to Singapore, we had to leave these strategic premises and return to the suburbs. We are still in this more restricted bookroom, and in the last year or so have made an all-out effort to find a more central location. Faith is not daunted, and we will persist in our search until suitable premises have been found.

There are indications that the Lord's time for a more concerted effort in the literature ministry is soon to take place. In 1980 Michael and Jane Shaw from Britain joined the team in Pakistan, and then early in 1981 Margaret Low from Singapore, who had received training with CLC in Hong Kong, also joined the workers in Karachi. As soon as the Shaws and Margaret are reasonably competent with the Urdu language, we will be able to greatly increase our outreach among Karachi's four million people. Indeed, we have already made a start by developing a more active mobile outreach to market places and other gathering points throughout the city. Our Pakistani co-worker, Emmanuel Chandi, who has served so faithfully and fruitfully with us for many years, is a great asset in this mobile ministry. This will also be a good experience for Michael, giving him greater opportunity to use his Urdu.

While the progress in the literature work in Pakistan has been much slower than in other countries, the combined ministry of house meetings, Bible clubs, one-to-one witnessing in the book-center, and the mobile outreach has been consistently rewarding and fruitful. Quite an accomplishment in a country where 97 per cent of her people's religious affiliation is Islam!

As an example, there was Edward. He was leaving for Saudi Arabia where he had obtained work. He had known about the Christian message for some time, without knowing the Author. Miles spent time with him, carefully explaining what it means to be born again. Edward prayed and received. He corresponds regularly with the Sims and is faithfully studying a Bible correspondence course which they send him.

A Catholic mother brought along her twelve-year-old son on one occasion. Beryl led him to the Lord. The mother was so thrilled. Now her two children attend the Bible club each week, and she regularly attends the evening prayer and Bible study.

A Parsee lady found the Lord. The following week she began witnessing in her office. She now makes good use of the lending library at CLC. Recently she gave a week of her vacation to help in the Daily Vacation Bible School.

Then there was the lady from Greece who had been witnessed to. She had had a dream which troubled her. She came again for help, read the booklet "Journey into Life," and as a result asked the Lord to come into her life.

These are just a sampling of recent contacts. All of them are encouraging evidence of the Holy Spirit's working in hearts and lives. In the most recent letter received more incidents were reported—some finding, others still searching. Yes, indeed, God is at work by His Spirit in Pakistan, and all across the world. On both sides of the "curtains" of man's making, the penetrating Holy Spirit is doing His reconciling work. Cell by cell the Body of Christ is being completed—from every nationality and tongue.

24

PREPARING FOR TRANSITION

Now that it had been agreed I should continue serving our worldwide fellowship as their International Secretary, two things seemed clear: except for any emergency I should postpone further overseas travel until I took up my new full-time duties three and one-half years hence; I should give as much time as possible to strengthening the programs in the States and Canada.

With our new Administration Building completed, time had to be given to consolidation in Fort Washington. We developed an attractive retail bookroom and strengthened our print shop and warehouse/shipping room with better equipment, for the demands on this continent for the type of literature we were publishing and handling was steadily increasing.

Considerable time was given to deputation, visiting churches and Bible Schools, to put the challenge and opportunity of the Christian literature program, in this increasingly literate world, before God's people. There were some real encouragements. Churches caught the vision, adding CLC to their missionary budgets, and young people sent for application papers.

By 1964 two further things became clear. Thankfully the number of people joining our ranks was increasing. Some were for the home ministries; others were candidates for the overseas programs. However, our housing facilities soon became inadequate and something just had to be done. We did have room on the land we owned so it was a matter of planning and building again. We knew that we must project our thinking—and our faith—into the future and finally decided on three buildings together. One would have eight efficiency rooms, mainly for the

single ladies, and two one-bedroom apartments—one to be used
for visitors or for our overseas personnel when passing through.
A number of distinguished friends have stayed in that "prophet's
chamber." Corrie ten Boom made it her "headquarters" whenever
she was in this part of the country. After all, CLC was her
original publisher, producing the first seven books she wrote.

Another building was to be for families and would contain
nine apartments. Between these two housing units would be the
community building with kitchen, dining room, lounge and auditorium on one floor, and a full basement for storage, laundry,
garage, workshop and boiler room, etc. The lounge would be for
our daily prayer sessions and the auditorium for a variety of
things, including our Annual Conferences and occasional public
meetings. This sizeable building program proved to be the largest
and most costly we had yet undertaken. It was begun early in
1965 and completed in late summer. That is sixteen years ago and
it is good we planned ahead. At the time it looked like an enor-
mous undertaking and perhaps a bit extravagant, but today we
are beginning to ask why we didn't plan and project further!
There are times when our total of thirty apartments are all in use.

In Canada, too, things began to happen. It had, you may
remember, actually been our second advance: Britain in 1941 and
then Canada in 1944, both in operation before the war had come
to an end. The start was a small bookstore in a suburb of
Toronto, but four years later we moved into the center of the city,
remaining there for five years. Then in 1953 the Lord directed us
to Montreal in the Province of Quebec, which seemed to be more
of a "mission field" than Toronto with its dozen Christian bookstores. Montreal, the Dominion's largest city, had no evangelical
bookstore. From a simple beginning in a semi-basement, the
ministry increased steadily, but in 1964 we were informed that
the building we were then occupying was to be demolished to
make way for a new road. Finding property in a good location
and at a reasonable rent was no easy task.

Then we discovered 1440 rue Mackay. A new nineteen-floor
apartment building with two shops at ground level had just been

completed and we were able to arrange a ten-year lease for one of the shops. On April 10, 1965 we moved into this new location. It was a veritable step of faith: a much higher rent, a store four times larger which would mean much more stock to fill it (another financial outlay), and an untried location with no other shops in that street a dozen or so blocks west of city center. There were some compensations. It was within walking distance of the main shopping street and of one of Montreal's universities. We knew our Captain had led. His hand of blessing would be on this new center—and so it has proved beyond our highest hopes.

In preparation for my release two other things happened. At the Easter Annual Conference in 1964 John Gross was appointed Assistant Director to work alongside me. The decision on his part had not been easy, for John and his wife Mary Anne were in charge of the Montreal store and they were loath to leave. Their hearts were in the work, and God's blessing was on their personal witness and their ministry in the city, but they submitted to the will of the Lord as expressed through the staff fellowship. In the following year John took over fully from me and became the new Director for North America.

Because of John's help as my assistant, I was freer to begin correspondence with the fields which were to be included in my first extended journey. When things finally shaped up, I found it would last more than ten months and take me to nearly thirty countries.

During these years Britain was busy advancing into four more countries: The Netherlands and the Ivory Coast in 1962; Egypt and Cyprus in 1964. These countries would be among the first I would visit on my forthcoming journey so we will return to them later.

The one country opened by North America during these same years was Portuguese Guinea in West Africa in 1963 (now known as Guinea Bissau). Perhaps the word "opened" isn't quite correct. Four years earlier the Worldwide Evangelization Crusade, the only faith mission allowed to operate in the country even to this day, had opened a small bookshop in the capital city, Bissau. The young, growing church was greatly helped by the good books which were now available in their country. During the day a flow of people came into the shop to buy the books and Bibles. Some sought spiritual counsel; many asked for tracts which they could use in their own witnessing.

With this bookstore as their base, many colportage trips were made into the villages, and the missionaries were much encouraged by the results. At that time Portuguese soldiers were helping to keep order and quell guerilla uprisings. These men were among the best customers. On one occasion a visit was made to an army camp. The soldiers literally stormed the bookstall, buying the Bibles and books, and soon everything was gone.

All this was tremendously exciting and it convinced the small team of missionaries that they should ask CLC to send workers, taking this responsibility off their shoulders, so that they could give time to church development.

Happily we were able to respond and, after language study in Portugal, Ron Evans reached Portuguese Guinea in 1963 with a view to gradually taking over the literature ministry in Bissau and throughout the country. He was later joined by Betty Broderick, his fiancee, following her language study in Portugal, and they were married in Bissau. Things went well under the Evanses' leadership. They had good rapport with the young people, and God's blessing continued to rest on the literature ministry. However, opportunities to get out into the countryside became less and less because of the worsening war situation, and when the call came three years later from Sierra Leone, the Evanses were moved to Freetown and began the CLC ministry in that country.

The WEC missionaries accepted this decision, though they were genuinely sorry to see the Evanses go—and indeed to see the CLC go, for we did not have any replacements. In spite of the limited opportunities for literature work in Portuguese Guinea, the WEC Field Committee agreed that the shop should not be closed; they would find ways and means to keep it going. CLC agreed to retain a link by sending a small monthly gift of $100 to help cover expenses.

Unrest in the country persisted for fifteen years, but in September 1974 Portugal recognized Portuguese Guinea's independence after ruling over the area for five hundred years. The name was immediately changed to Guinea Bissau and things gradually settled down. Since then there has been marked progress in the country's development.

Once again opportunities for gospel witness and Christian literature are plentiful and WEC is urging CLC to return. CLC Brazil has accepted this invitation, although as yet they have not been able to send workers. Of course, they need not come from Brazil. Under the aegis of WEC, international workers can obtain visas. The door to the whole country is virtually wide open.

The present WEC missionary, Kathleen Smith, and a capable national young man are doing a great job. The bookshop ministry is becoming truly international, as sailors of different countries visit it during their time in port, and others have taken up residence in the country.

Consider this which came in yesterday's mail as I was writing this chapter. It is part of a letter from Kathleen Smith, who was in the bookshop full time while Albino was on his vacation. "I have sold at least one Bible every day. Several Russians came in and bought Bibles in their language. They were thrilled, and one came back and asked if we had a book which spoke about the future....Scripture pens from CLC Brazil are very popular, as there are no pens on sale anywhere in Bissau. It is thrilling to go into the post office or bank and see them in use! When parcels arrive, people follow us from the post office and stand in the shop as we unpack. There is such a shortage of things here that whatever we put on the shelves is bought up quickly."

These are opportunities which must not be lost in our united effort to get the good news to the people of this small African nation, 66 per cent of whom are animists and 30 per cent followers of Islam.

25

AN INTENSIVE ITINERARY

Laying down leadership in North America after seventeen years was not as traumatic as it might appear. For one thing I was doing it in direct obedience to the clear instruction of our Captain. As you have noticed, during those years of leadership I had been very much involved with the expansion of the work worldwide. I had been overseas almost a dozen times, visiting some twenty-seven countries and revisiting Britain three times.

Now, as I left Philadelphia on May 28, 1965, I returned to Britain for the fourth time. This gave opportunity for discussion with the leadership there, particularly regarding some of the details of my new assignment, especially as it related to the proposed second gathering of some of our key leadership planned to be held in Bangkok in mid-September. The first had been held in London in 1961.

A three-day conference, prior to the regular British Annual Conference, had been arranged so that I could meet with several workers from our European countries. This was most helpful, because I had not been closely involved in these developments and was now able to catch up on happenings in this part of the world. It also prepared me for the next phase of my journey—to Europe.

After these two helpful weeks in Britain, I left London for The Netherlands on June 14. The CLC work in this country was still experiencing growing pains, having started in 1963 under the direction of two Hollanders, Ineka Stuiver and Nollie Durivou. The store in Amsterdam was very attractive, and the ministry there had grown quite rapidly, so it would not be long before more room would be needed. I was thrilled to hear the testimonies of local Christians of just what this new literature ministry in the city meant to them and to meet some who had received specific help through the books and the personal ministry of the two CLC ladies.

I moved on to Germany, France and Italy, but had to miss Austria, as it had not been possible to obtain flights in the time schedule allowed. But I promised Elizabeth and Helga that visiting Graz would be a priority next time. I was encouraged by what I saw of the progress being made in these three countries and was delighted to learn of the goals each team was reaching for during the next few years.

The next stop was special, and one I had looked forward to for many years. Algeria was where my sister Gladys and her husband, Eric, had served; first with the North Africa Mission and then as missionaries with the Plymouth Brethren. They were now living in Algiers, and I had four delightful days with them. During my visit I was able to learn about the literature situation and to fellowship with the workers of a small Christian bookshop in the city, run by the North Africa Mission. It was tough going and the shop has since closed. The situation all across North Africa continues to be discouraging, as modern day Ishmael still mocks Isaac and rejects the Christ which he foretold. I did meet one or two Algerians who knew Jesus in a personal and saving way. Handfuls of Christians are scattered in all the countries of North Africa, and many of the younger generation are searching for truth. They study the Bible and complete correspondence courses supplied to them through the mail. This seed is bearing fruit.

My next stop was Egypt. Here I was joined by Bob Hiley from London, for things were beginning to take shape for setting up a CLC ministry in this country. Since this advance was the responsibility of the British base, it seemed good for this on-the-spot review of the situation. A fine German couple, Gerd and Erica Leuchtman, were soon to head up this work. They were living in Cairo and were busy with the language, but they were now to the point where plans for the future must be laid. We had received helpful advice from the Anglican Canon currently serving in Alexandria, and in his judgment, he felt that CLC would do well to start there rather than in Cairo, where some literature ministries were already functioning. The three of us, Bob, Gerd and myself, paid a visit to Canon Douglas Butcher for face-to-face consultation, and then we looked at possible shops in the town.

Some months later CLC opened a small shop in Alexandria, and a fine Egyptian Christian, who had served with the Bible Society for a number of years, became manager. Unfortunately the Leuchtmans had to leave the country. They had failed to obtain their permanent residence visas, probably because the Bonn government had recently recognized Israel and tension between the two countries was quite high. However, I had been impressed with the strength and virility of some Christian groups in the country, particularly in the capital.

On July 3 Bob and I flew on to Cyprus. Just the year before CLC Britain had agreed to sponsor a literature work under the management of Levon Yergatian, an active Armenian Christian and a citizen of Cyprus. By the time we arrived Levon had a bookshop operating on one of the main shopping streets of Limassol, carrying supplies in English, Greek, Turkish and Arabic. This work continues to this day, though it is now linked with an indigenous ministry which has branched out in several directions, including operating a Christian school, all under Levon's enthusiastic leadership.

In 1980 CLC returned to Cyprus in a rather indirect and unconventional way, which may yet prove to be quite significant. A literature work originally based in Lebanon has moved its operation to Cyprus, where there is greater freedom to distribute Arabic Christian literature to all of the Arabic-reading world. They were hard pressed for competent Arabic-speaking personnel and invited CLC to help.

No personnel were on the immediate horizon, but in sharing this need with the WEC we learned of Aleta Matthews, one of their missionaries with thirty years experience in the Arab world! When the Cyprus situation was explained to her she responded affirmatively. CLC U.S.A. sponsored Aleta and she is in Cyprus, helping this Arabic literature program. Perhaps this is just the beginning of greater involvement in the future.

From Cyprus it was on to Lebanon for both of us. Because of our growing burden for the Arab world and our direct involvement in Egypt, we were keen to get a clearer picture of the publishing program in Arabic. At that time our main link was with the Arabic Literature Mission based in Beirut. Later we had a closer link when the Leuchtman family took up residence in Lebanon, and Gerd worked with the ALM for some years. It was an extremely useful visit.

The next eight days were full of meaning, for we were right in Bible lands. When in Cyprus Bob and I had visited an ampitheatre near Salamis. Our imagination took us back to New Testament times. We could "see" Paul with Barnabas and John Mark, preaching his heart out to packed audiences, not only there but all across the island to Paphos. We were surely on holy ground.

And so we were as we left Beirut by taxi headed for Damascus. Yes, we walked down the street called Straight—and straight it is, too! We met an American from Texas coming in the opposite direction. He, too, had been looking for the house of Judas where it all started. It was all so real. We were literally "being followers," as we walked the same cobblestones as did Saul of Tarsus in those memorable days of long ago. The hymn we sing so often in our fellowship sessions came alive with new meaning: "How wonderful it is to walk with God along the path that holy men have trod."

Then, we took another taxi across the desert. The Dead Sea was on our left as we began to climb up to the City of Jerusalem. What thoughts flooded our minds and hearts! How alive the Bible became during those next few days as we walked the streets, climbed the Mount of Olives, and looked toward the same city which He had addressed nearly two thousand years before our visit, "How often would I...but ye would not." We were humbled as we "sat where He sat" and determined never to waver but, with our Master's flint-like steadfastness, continue to play our part in fulfilling His Great Commission.

The objective of our visit was Haifa on the Mediterranean. A young American Israeli had visited CLC in London, indicating his readiness to operate a bookshop for CLC in Israel, possibly in Haifa. It would be a multi-language ministry, because the Jews flooding into Israel were from many countries and could not speak the official Hebrew language. The need for such a literature center was confirmed as we talked with others, and by what we saw as we walked the city streets. Unfortunately this never developed, though that young man still lives in Israel and continues to be active in Christian ministry.

Since then another very effective literature work, with a concentration on publishing in Hebrew, has developed under the able leadership of Victor Smadja, and CLC has contributed to this work from time to time. In his last letter reporting on the activities of 1980, he reminded his readers that "literature...is almost the only way of evangelizing in Israel." During the year there has been an increase in the mail-order service, with about 1,000 books ordered, mainly by adults. In door-to-door distribution the picture was encouraging: 6,200 books and 160,000 tracts in Hebrew; 4,000 books and 10,000 tracts in Arabic; and 2,600 books in English and other languages. (The word "books" includes the Scriptures.)

Victor's further comments, coming from one who lives and operates as a citizen within the country, are truly meaningful: "As nations are being polarized for or against Israel, we are made increasingly aware that the end of the age is near, and that the day of opportunity is swiftly passing. How shall we excuse ourselves if through our slackness or preoccupation with other things we fail to reach our contemporaries with the good news of salvation?" How, indeed? And not only in Israel but all across our world.

We parted company now, Bob returning to London and I heading for Pakistan. Our days together had been mutually helpful. We had seen situations calling for concentrated prayer, faith, and untiring determination to help bring the message of hope found only in the One who, in this very country we were now leaving, had made it all possible by His own unswerving obedience to His Father's will. We remembered He had also *left us an example that we should follow in His steps.*

Because of canceled flights I had a three-day unscheduled stop in Iran, so I took the opportunity to get some rest, knowing my program ahead would be very full. As I walked the streets of Teheran my burden increased, and I recalled again the imperative of the Master—the MUST of getting the gospel *to every nation.*

This delay in Teheran confused things for the Sims in Karachi. They had been to the airport to meet me, only to find that the flight had been canceled, and they were unable to get a satisfactory word from the airline about the next flight. When they finally did get word there was a three-hour difference between information and fact!

I arrived early Saturday afternoon—and waited and waited and waited. There was no phone at the bookstore, so I could not make contact with Miles. After an hour or so a taxi driver, sensing my predicament, I believe, approached me. He spoke good English. That was a relief! We arrived at the bookstore only to find it closed as were the other shops. Then I discovered my mistake. I had failed to bring the home address of the Sims, never thinking I would not be met at the airport or would not find them at the bookshop. Nobody in the area knew the address of "the man from America." One person thought it was in a certain area a mile or so away, so off we went searching but without success.

I suggested to the taxi driver that anytime we saw anybody who looked American, we should stop and ask. And, of course, I was expecting the Lord to direct our steps, and He did. Some six hours after I had arrived at the airport we found the house. Beryl was there looking bewildered. Miles was not. He was somewhere in town searching at hotels for Ken Adams!

The next day there was another test. I had been booked to

speak at the morning service of the big Scots' Church in Karachi, and in readiness for the service I needed something out of my small zipper briefcase. But where was it? Slowly the truth dawned—on a small shelf under the dashboard in the taxi!! Passport, ongoing tickets, etc., were all there in the taxi!

We prayed and decided to put first things first. I was on the King's business and had a job to do. No good getting "all het up." Faith knew He would have a solution, and He did. I was standing at the church door after the service greeting the people when I saw Beryl Sim running to the church, beaming and almost shouting the good news, "The taxi driver is here and he has your briefcase." Thank you, Master!

The incident left me with a determination that one of the jobs of the new International Office would be to prepare an international address and information book! This we now do and it is updated every year.

I spent two weeks in Pakistan. How good it was to fellowship with Miles and Beryl, and with Clara Bort, a graduate of Philadelphia College of Bible. She was still busy with her Urdu studies, but she was already having some good contacts with some of the Pakistani women along with assisting in the bookshop.

It was during this visit that I met Bishop Chandu Ray, which finally resulted in our renting the small building which the Bible Society had been using.

I had deliberately arranged to stay a minimum of two weeks in most of the CLC countries I was visiting. I wanted to see things, not just talk. I wanted to get the feel of each country: to learn what was being done; how the gospel was getting to the people; what part Christian literature was playing in this; what needed to be done to make it more readily available; and what were the problems to reaching these goals? Well, we haven't found all the solutions in this country of strong Muslim affiliations, but as I have already reported, things are looking brighter, and we will keep pressing forward.

The next segment of my journey was twenty-seven days in India.

26

INDIA—A FASCINATING COUNTRY

India is a fascinating country. I was first introduced to it when I arrived in Bombay, the country's largest city (its 1981 population exceeds six million), and began to feel the press of people. It is, I believe, the most thickly populated major country in the world, with one-third the area of China, into which are crowded over 672 million people in comparison with China's 1,039 million. Putting it another way, India has less than one-third the area of the United States, with three times as many people.

Still God's Word and work go forward. The ministry of the Gospel Literature Service in Bombay is encouraging evidence of this. Concentrating on publishing, their presses were busy producing literature in several languages, and they continue to do so today. It is a vital, well-ordered operation.

After a forty-eight hour train journey to New Delhi, I had to wait several hours for my train to Dehra Dun. It was late afternoon, the time when a number of trains converge on this important railway junction, and I watched as vendors prepared for an evening of business. Soon my eye caught the books. Several large tables were being filled with them, and when the task was nearly completed I went over to browse, for the greater proportion were in English. I was shocked at what was being offered. I was embarrassed and angry. The filth of the English publishing world was there, and a large portion of it came from the United States of America. What right had this Christian country to export filth and pollute the mind and soul of India's readers? And of the world—for no doubt they were also flooding every available market. Unfortunately things have worsened in the English publishing countries, too. The purveyors of pornography have succeeded in flooding the home markets with their degrading merchandise. The magazine racks and bookshelves of drugstores and general bookstores in the States and England—particularly at airports, railroad stations and long-distance bus terminals—overflow with it.

Where were the uplifting books which would bring the claims of Christ and His wonderful message of hope to India's readers? Not there on that railway bookstall. I pondered the matter for the next several hours as I continued my journey toward the small bookshop in Mussoorie, nestled in the foothills of the great Himalaya Mountains which peak at Mt. Everest. CLC had taken this over some years earlier from the Mussoorie Book Society. The main service of this bookshop was to the missionaries. Many of them spent their vacation there, away from the heat of the plains. The shop is still there, although its clientele has changed because there are so few foreign missionaries in the country. A growing number of tourists now visit the area for the same reason, and their literature needs are met through the efforts of Living Bibles International, which has made this the center for their translation work.

In Calcutta I visited the Christian bookshop where our own Ida Howlett (who later became Mrs. Donald David) had served during her early days in India. It is a living testimony in another of India's needy cities. It was in Calcutta that I also understood the full meaning of the hymn I had sung so often in my Sunday School days, "The heathen in their blindness bow down to wood and stone." We arrived just after the actual sacrifice of an animal had been completed. Blood was everywhere and so were bits of its fur and flesh. People "in their blindness" had purchased a piece of the animal and taken it into the nearby temple to offer it to their god, in hope of some absolution for their sins. I presume they were also using the services of the priest in this ritual. The place was very dimly lit and we were not allowed to get too near, but we could see the forms of people bowing low before their idol-god. Actually you didn't want to stay too long, the smell, the flies, the filth, the very atmosphere, all were so repugnant. We left with sorrowing hearts, the imperative of the Master again ringing in our ears and hearts—"Other sheep I have, them also I *must* bring."

Here in India I saw another demonstration of the darkness, this time at the end of life's journey. It was late in the afternoon and the day's work was nearly done. Some of the fires were still smoldering. Another was soon to be ignited as the family and relatives, dressed in their finery, sat around waiting. Maybe they were praying. I don't know. We didn't stay to see it actually happen. We did see the funeral pyre in place with the feet of the departed loved one protruding. Soon it would be ablaze. The family would watch and wait until finally there was nothing but ashes. Then would come the great moment when those ashes would be committed to the sacredness of the mighty Ganges. Yes, India desperately needs the message of hope for her people in life and in death.

Thank God, there is a brighter side. While in Madras, India's fourth largest city and the home of CLC's nationwide literature ministry, I spoke at the large Methodist church where Dr. Sam Kamaleson ministered so powerfully for a number of years. He was away the Sunday evening I was there. The place was packed to overflowing, and people crowded around the doors and windows—a total of seven or eight hundred. I was told that people respond openly to the message almost every Sunday— they did that Sunday, too. It seemed like the early days when people were "being added daily."

The same was true at Bakh Singh's church in Madras. I had already ministered at another church in the city and then was whisked off by Donald David to the Bakh Singh assembly. When we arrived just before eleven o'clock the place was packed, indeed overflowing, and I could hear the voice of a preacher resounding out into the church compound. Donald saw the question in my eyes and assured me that all was well. There were usually at least three preachers each Sunday. After all, the service had started at nine o'clock and would not finish until sometime around one o'clock!

There must have been more than a thousand people there, alert and intent, taking in the message. Then came communion. What a precious time! How real His lovely presence! What a joy to be sharing with my brothers and sisters of India, all of us members of the same Body, one in Christ Jesus our Living Head!

Then came my turn to speak. It was a new experience for me. I have spoken through interpreters many times, but this was different. There were two interpreters. My English was first put into Tamil by one brother and then another repeated the same thought in Hindi (I think it was). That had happened, of course, with the previous speakers. Every Sunday the messages are heard in at least two languages. This Sunday three languages were in use. No wonder the service took four hours!

Similar services in different parts of India were being held simultaneously, as part of the far-reaching ministry of these Bakh Singh Assemblies, all of them the result of vigorous evangelistic efforts by a team of gifted preachers. My soul was rejoicing.

I experienced similar evidences of God at work as I traveled to other cities. There was our bookcenter in Vellore, right in the main entrance of the great Christian Hospital and Medical College. People from all over India come to that hospital along with some of their relatives, so we carry literature in several of India's fourteen main languages. There is also the book trolley which is taken from ward to ward. What a ministry these books are having to those who are "imprisoned" within the walls of this wonderful Christian institution.

While in Bangalore I fellowshipped with my colleagues in the small bookcenter there, and saw the mobile unit in operation— this time a two-wheeled motor bike with book boxes firmly secured at the back! It was amazing how much could be carried. I also saw another phase of mass communication in operation. Gordon and Millie Bell, with whom I stayed, were heading up the studio of the Far East Broadcasting Corporation where tapes were prepared in a number of languages and then sent to the main transmitting center (at that time) in the Philippines. How good to know that the airwaves were carrying the good news, penetrating into some of the remote areas of the world. Remote they may be, but the transistor radio has found its way there! Yes, even poor people have ways and means of buying what they really want, including the radio and the books!

The Gordon Bells kindly drove me high into the Nilgiri Hills or Blue Mountains, so that I could visit our small bookcenter in Ootacamund. On this journey I had a firsthand view of life in the jungle. There were no lions or tigers, but elephants roamed in stately procession, taking their daily dip in the nearby river where we had stopped to have our lunch. There were also monkeys and their kin aplenty, full of chatter. Higher up the Hills were the orderly tea plantations. They fascinated me too.

On my way back to Madras I visited several Bible Schools. Theodore Williams was Principal of one of them. How good to see these fine young people being carefully trained and prepared for Christian service in their home country. They listened well as I shared the need and opportunity of literature with them. Some are in our ranks today.

So my four weeks in India ended. I was rejoicing in what I had seen and learned of the accomplishments of the gospel; I was stirred in spirit as I saw the scope of what yet remained to be done; and I was profoundly grateful for the contribution we were privileged to make in getting the message in print to India's readers. We were following in the steps of one of India's early pioneers who had spent so much of his time in literature work translating the Scriptures—William Carey.

27

THE STRATEGIC MOMENT ARRIVES

Perhaps the most important and far-reaching event in my itinerary took place at a holiday camp about one hundred miles from Bangkok, Thailand. The proposed conference had been planned for months. Now, in September 1965, it became a reality as eighteen delegates from eight nations, representing ten CLC countries, gathered at this retreat for two weeks of concentrated examination of many phases of Crusade activities. However, it was not an official international gathering. Most of the suggestions made at this exploratory get-together would have to be shared with all our fields. We did not know it at that time, but it would take almost five years before general agreement would be reached!

But a good start was made.

A first draft of the Constitution which we hoped could be acceptable to CLC worldwide was finalized. It brought together all important policy positions—the foundational one being: "The Lord is our God forever and ever. He will be our Guide, Helper, Deliverer and Provider even unto death." The Crusade, it was asserted, would press forward as an international and interdenominational missionary society for the spread of Christian literature, in which men and women, called of God from every nation, would march shoulder to shoulder. It re-emphasized that personnel from the West were still needed. This was to combat a growing feeling, in some circles, that because national churches in many countries were taking over full responsibility, missionaries would not now be needed. To us this was clearly erroneous thinking. Let me quote the statement on this point which the

Thailand Conference issued: "Missionaries from the West are still urgently needed, not to 'work ourselves out of a job,' in an unbalanced and unrealistic emphasis on indigenous policy, but to work loyally together in fulfilling the Great Commission." That was sixteen years ago. It is still our position in 1981. It will be our position always, for it is the Biblical position: All one in Christ; therefore, all "workers together with God" to complete the Great Commission.

I will not weary you with every specific detail. In general the Crusade, worldwide, continues to operate on the principles and policies which were hammered out at that conference. Minor adjustments have been needed from time to time, but the foundations remain intact to this day. For that we are profoundly grateful.

After the conference we all returned to Bangkok for two or three days before scattering. This gave us an opportunity to see the CLC bookstore and the other literature activities which, at that time, were operating under the guidance of Bob and Muriel Sjoblom. Even though CLC had been in the country only seven years, it was a very encouraging picture.

My next country was Indonesia. Willard Stone had been at the conference representing this country, so we traveled on together and spent a few days in Jakarta, the capital, seeing the literature work in that city. Willard had motored up from Surabaya in the bookmobile, so we drove back to Surabaya together, taking time to visit other literature ministries along the way, checking their stocks and picking up orders, for CLC was the largest publisher of evangelical books in Indonesia. It took us three days to cover the six hundred miles, but I did appreciate getting to see things firsthand. I was also impressed by the efforts being made by the government to encourage education. Schools were being built; potential teachers were being trained; literacy was steadily increasing.

In Surabaya I had an opportunity to see the progress in church growth and activity. I spent one Sunday morning, for instance, driving from church to church to see, with my own eyes, services in actual operation. I was fascinated. Every church was full or overflowing. I saw Sunday School classes being conducted on the sidewalk—there was just no room for them anywhere in the church building.

Another day I was shown how ingeniously one church was tackling needed expansion. So that there would not be any interruption in regular services, the existing church building remained intact, but on the extreme sides of the property new walls were going up. When the roof was finally in place, everything was set for the transition. The church had been in full use until late Sunday evening, even though it was now literally "inside" the new building! Early Monday morning, demolition started. When the congregation arrived the following Sunday their church building was at least 50 per cent larger than the previous Sunday! Of course, there was plenty of work yet to be done, but the services never stopped while everything was being completed.

Some churches were holding two and three services every Sunday morning and then again in the evening, with smaller groups meeting at different times during the week.

The predominant religion in Indonesia is Islam, although only 45 per cent are practicing Muslims. Hindus, Buddhists, and Christians have freedom to worship. During the years 1963-66, partly because of growing political unrest, the Christian church increased by 40 per cent. Today there are approximately fifteen million believers. Possibly the church in Indonesia is growing faster than in any other country of East and Southeast Asia.

We visited the Batu Bible Institute. I was delighted to see the young people being trained for the Lord's service. Some of them are the strong evangelical voices being heard across the country these days. Many of them serve in the smaller islands. Some are missionaries in other countries, for here again the Indonesian church is helping to fulfill the Great Commission...from their Jerusalem to *the uttermost parts.*

I left Indonesia on the afternoon of September 30, having spent a delightful day at the Overseas Missionary Fellowship base in Jakarta. Things seemed normal at the airport as I boarded my plane for Singapore. Imagine my surprise when I awoke the next morning to learn of the attempted Communist coup in Indonesia which had started in the early hours of October 1. This was resisted and crushed by the army under General Suharto, who emerged as the strong man of a new regime. The Sukarno government had been strongly pro-Communist, so General Suharto ordered the army to eliminate all traces of the Communist party. In 1968 Suharto was elected to a five-year term as President. He is currently serving his third five-year term.

Religious freedom has been maintained. This has enabled our own ministry to expand with our growing team of Indonesians. There has, however, been considerable restriction of missionary personnel. Few new visas have been granted in recent years and renewing visas has not been easy. Both Willard Stone and Grace Chang had been able to obtain permanent resident visas before 1965. This was before Willard was married. His wife, Dorothy, finally received her permanent resident visa in 1980!

Singapore's status had changed while I was in India. For almost one hundred years it had been part of the British Empire but became a self-governing state in 1959. Four years later it joined the Federation of Malaysia, but on August 9, 1965 it withdrew and has since been known as the Republic of Singapore.

So far on my journey I had traveled without my wife. Bessie had stayed in the States to be with our daughters during the summer, but after they returned to Columbia Bible College in early September she headed for Singpore, stopping off for brief visits with CLC in London and Bangkok.

While Bessie was undertaking that long journey on her own, I took off from Singapore for North Borneo, which had also become part of the Federation of Malaysia. The Borneo Evangelical Mission, based in Australia, had been corresponding with us about their literature needs, and this proved to be a good opportunity to talk with them. English was in steady demand in the large coastal towns, but the BEM were working in the hinterland and needed literature in Malaysian and in some vernaculars. We have since been able to help with supplies of Indonesian literature, as the Malaysian and Indonesian languages are very closely aligned. I am not just sure how helpful we have been with their vernacular needs.

Once again I was privileged to see the church in action; not only at the coast, where some of the congregation arrived in their boats for the Sunday services (no parking lot needed there!) but also deep in the jungle. The mission owned their own plane, so one day the missionary's wife and I climbed aboard the small, four-seat Piper and flew about a hundred miles into the jungle—the real jungle this time! The reason for the flight? A two-week convention for Bible study and leadership training had been planned, and the missionary was going ahead to help prepare the logistics for the three hundred people who were expected. The following week her husband and other missionaries would fly in.

How I wish I could have stayed! A few of the tribespeople were there already. How well I remember the hearty handshake of one brother and his enthusiastic verbal welcome. He was the real thing all right, with a well-tattooed face and body, long earlobes and weighty earrings, all having significant tribal meaning. Yes, he was the real thing, a radiant Christian and a gifted leader. He was my brother in Christ, who along with others of his family and tribe had walked the jungle trails for days, even weeks, so that they could study the Book and be better equipped to "teach others also." Many others were still on their way.

It was on the same trip I again saw the transistor radio in use, capable of bringing in helpful messages and good news from the Book of books. How I thanked God for those faraway Christian radio stations which were helping to make all this possible.

The pilot and I arrived back some six hours later, and as he climbed out of the Piper he said, "You know, Brother Ken, in the early days that round trip we have just completed would have taken all of three weeks!" Most of what I had seen was indeed the fruit of the walking pioneers, not the flying Pipers. It was the fruit of their "blood, sweat, and tears," mingled with their tenacious, faithful sowing, "declaring the whole counsel of God."

I flew on to Jesselton and Sandakan to fellowship with literature workers, meeting Mr. Willis who had been in literature work in Hong Kong and other places for many years. He must have been in his late seventies or early eighties, but was still actively engaged in both distribution and production.

From Sandakan I flew directly back to Singapore. My plane was on time and about three-quarters of an hour later Bessie's plane arrived, also on time. Quite an achievement—for her plane, although now coming from Bangkok, had originated in Rome. Well done, Air Alitalia. That was a happy reunion for both of us.

We stayed in Singapore over the weekend and again had opportunity to fellowship with some of the people in literature work. My impression was that the country was well catered to, and it was unlikely that CLC would be needed here, but I was wrong. In the 1970's Bob Sjoblom paid occasional visits to Singapore to find a market for books which CLC published in the Philippines and Hong Kong, and he discovered a serious gap. There are four main languages used in Singapore—Malay, Chinese, English and Tamil. In discussing the general situation with those in literature work, the one concern was the lack of a reliable wholesale base from which local needs could be supplied. All were experiencing irritating delays in obtaining their books, especially from England and America.

That is the gap CLC has been attempting to fill since 1976. There is still room for improvement, but appreciation has been expressed for what has been done thus far. Book agents in both Singapore and Malaysia are now able to obtain at least some of their stock from the CLC warehouse, and there are signs that this has helped to improve overall distribution in both countries.

I had hoped to make one more contact. A cousin of mine, Sidney Adams, was in north Malaysia, but it was not possible, in the time available, to get there and back, even by air. Sidney must have spent more than fifty years as a missionary in Malaysia. He is still there today at eighty-seven years of age. His dear wife, Ida, passed on some years ago, but they have done a great work for the Lord, and it would have been so nice to have had even a few hours together with this man of faith and vision.

28

THE FRUITFUL SECOND HALF

For the next two months there was a change of pace. From on-the-spot visiting of the mission field we would now be back on "home territory" so to speak. In these next two countries plans had been made for fairly extensive deputation.

From Singapore we went first to New Zealand. It was a joy to fellowship with Alec Thorne again. He had arranged a good number of meetings in the two principal islands. We enjoyed the warm reception given to us everywhere. New Zealand Christians surely have a heart for missions and are perhaps among the world's most generous in giving to the missionary cause.

However, there was one incident we could have done without.

As we were being driven through the town of New Plymouth to the airport, we were involved in an accident. The car was a total loss, but mercifully we were not seriously injured. Bessie spent a night in the hospital, having sustained a fractured rib, but the next day she was well enough to be driven back to Auckland, where she was given royal attention by Ivor and Rose Davies at the WEC headquarters in the city.

I flew to Wellington and continued on alone for the ten days of meetings which had been arranged in the South Island. Back in Auckland for final meetings, we were able to renew contact with Jack and Margaret Hume from England. We had worked together in my teen years in street meetings in Southend-on-Sea. These little touches with the past have always been enjoyed.

We had not visited the CLC centers, because apart from the small wholesale program Alec Thorne was doing and a colportage-book-party type of program carried on by Davida McKenzie, there were no CLC bookshops at that time. Nonetheless, we had been encouraged by the obviously growing interest in the Crusade's ministry, and we felt sure that someday CLC New Zealand would be more involved in the actual literature work. Ten years later that expectation materialized.

Next, we were off to Australia.

This time it was a combination of deputation and visiting the CLC ministry. The main operation was centered in Eastwood, a suburb of Sydney. Through a generous gift the Crusade had been able to purchase a few acres of land for a very modest price. It included one or two buildings which were put to immediate use, and a building program was started. Even before this could be developed, they had to move. The government needed most of the land for a new highway. At first this was disappointing, but soon the Lord's purpose became evident, for the money received from this transaction made possible the purchase of another piece of land, and the completion of an excellent all-purpose building containing offices, bookstore, warehouse, shipping room and a small auditorium, plus three staff houses and another building with room for candidates and visitors. This was certainly the Lord's way of providing CLC Australia with its national headquarters debt free.

At the time we were there Australia had three other bookshops: one in Parramatta, another suburb of Sydney, and two in Queensland, in the towns of Townsville and Cairns. We visited these centers during our deputation, and also traveled south to Canberra, Melbourne, Adelaide and some small towns. Then we flew to Tasmania to fellowship with the staff of the WEC Bible College and to speak to the students. I had also been privileged to speak at the annual public gathering of the Sydney Bible College.

Australia was making a significant contribution to the overseas program. They were responsible for the young work in Papua New Guinea and had a specific interest in Japan. Three couples were serving with CLC there, and John Davey was Australia's representative in the Caribbean.

file i-3

The work grew steadily during the rest of the sixties, but then the national program began to leap forward so that now, in 1981, they have fourteen literature centers. Twelve of these are in the eastern states of New South Wales and Queensland. In 1980 two other states were entered: Victoria, when CLC took over a book-center in the town of Geelong, and in Western Australia a book-mobile ministry started based in the city of Perth.

Another interesting development operating from the head-quarters in Pennant Hills, Sydney, is the School Library Out-reach. A mobile unit is used to take books to the schools, mainly in greater Sydney, to be placed in the libraries. The books are selected by the librarians and purchased by each school. This is an exciting ministry and hopefully will move on to other cities. How good to know that the school children have good Christian books available to them.

A new similar outreach is developing—the Hospital Library Outreach. This is made possible through donations sent in specif-ically for this purpose. A special list of suitable titles is available for hospital chaplains to choose from, and many are availing themselves of this opportunity.

The overall picture of CLC in Australia is very encouraging, and Brian and Una Gesling are to be congratulated for a task being well performed, as they give general leadership to this expanding ministry.

There is one area which needs improving. Currently they still have only three couples serving overseas: Ken and Joy Watson in Venezuela, the John Daveys now in Canada after thirty-three years in the West Indies, and Hal and Priscilla Hinton in Papua New Guinea. This is a concern of the Australian staff, and they are praying and believing that this will change dramatically dur-ing the next few years. They do share the responsibility of the work in Sri Lanka by channeling some support to national workers, Hugh and Christine Canagasabey, but where are the Australian young people who ought to be out on the firing lines, in some of the other forty-two CLC countries where more workers are urgently needed? *Rise up, O Australian men of faith!*

By mid-January, 1966, we moved on to New Guinea and rejoiced with Maurice and June Thomas in the exciting things which were happening there. Our two weeks were filled with opportunities for ministry, and Maurice and I made a tour of many of the towns where book agents were getting out the Word in print. Things are much the same today, with our one bookshop in Boroko continuing to reach out through the mail to these other centers, under the leadership of Harold and Priscilla Hinton.

Next to the Philippines, where Milan and Virginia Steffel were in charge of the printing program. Some distribution was being carried on through book tables but at that time the main emphasis was on production. Some were our own publications but a lot of printing was being done for other groups. All the Back to the Bible correspondence courses and others prepared by the Brethren were printed by CLC. Later on all the printing needs of the Asssociation of Baptists for World Evangelism were handled by CLC, and some of the printing needs of other missions, church groups, Philippine home missions and Bible schools were brought to the CLC print shop.

We greatly enjoyed our time of fellowship with the Steffels and the team of national workers, and we were blessed by what we saw God doing in the greater Manila area. On one occasion we went to speak at Faith Academy, the school for children of missionaries. We missed our way, so arrived late for the regular chapel hour. But that didn't matter. Just what set it going, I am not sure—I think a time of testimony had been called for—but one and another began sharing what God was doing in their lives. Sin was confessed, and students were testifying to the cleansing and renewing work of the Holy Spirit. This honesty brought other students to their knees. Not only did I not speak that morning but the day's schedule was canceled, and that thirty-minute chapel service went on for hours! Later some of the fruit of that day was seen when many of these young people went down to central Manila to hold street meetings and open-air youth gatherings—and many Filipino young people found Christ through those MK efforts.

Then it was on to Hong Kong, where the David Adeneys kindly took us under their wing. They had served for many years in China with the CIM/Overseas Missionary Fellowship and were now in an Asia-wide student ministry. For a number of years David had been urging CLC to come to Hong Kong, so this gave us an opportunity to look things over.

We could see big opportunities, especially as hundreds of people from mainland China continued to pour into this British Crown Colony every week. We also found a number of active literature ministries, so we were not convinced that CLC was needed. However we did assure the Adeneys we would keep an open mind and watch for some evidence that God did have a place for the Crusade in this strategic city, just ninety-one miles southeast of Canton. It is very much an international crossroads. That evidence came in 1976.

In Taiwan we stayed at the guest house of the Christian and Missionary Alliance, which was being managed by one of the new missionaries who traveled on the ship when I crossed the Pacific in 1949. How good to see him again and to fellowship with his wife and family.

Some good contacts were made with literature programs in Taipei and we were fascinated to see how busy the commercial presses were, pouring out all kinds of literature. Some of the books, I fear, were pirated editions, done without respect for international copyright laws. Taiwan had not, to this point, been one of CLC's objectives, but since our visit we have kept an open mind and eye on the situation. Indeed, at one time we did get some printing done there, and even had our name registered with the government! Perhaps that will be useful again in the days to come. At the present time some CLC books in both English and Chinese are distributed in the country.

Now we had reached our final month on this extended journey. The last two countries—Korea and Japan—would keep us busy for all of March 1966.

We have already outlined in previous chapters the progress which has been made in these two countries, so I will not go into detail again. The visits to Hong Kong, Taiwan, and now Japan and Korea were particularly meaningful to Bessie, because this is where her interest had been in her youth. It was sharpened considerably now that she was seeing things in person.

We spent the first ten days in Japan visiting the CLC cities to the south. They were not all CLC cities at that time. Take Nagoya as an example. A missionary from Sweden had been urging Bob Gerry to bring CLC to that city, but with our hands full elsewhere nothing had yet been done. Bob felt it might be good for us to meet this brother. At least it would give us an opportunity to see and hear what the situation was, and we could then add this city to our prayer list.

Instead, we did more than that. We actually looked at two or three possible locations, gathered facts and figures about rents and other costs, and came away convinced that God did want CLC in Japan's fourth largest city with a population of two million. Bessie carried this on her heart and shared her burden whenever possible until the goal was reached. We would have to see personnel and funds made available, for Japan was already on the stretch on both counts.

Whenever the opportunity arose, the burden of Nagoya was shared. During a missionary conference in an Atlanta, Georgia church, Bessie was asked to share some of the experiences of our recent travels. Nagoya was uppermost in her report, and it came across with such heart-stirring concern that the church put Nagoya on their missionary budget, and for years $50 per month designated for "the bookstore in Nagoya" was sent to our Fort Washington office. The store is there today, and the literature radiating light and life still flows, producing results. What a good investment that church made!

I think of one young lady who came into another southern Japan store during that trip. She had been searching. She had talked with a pastor of a nearby evangelical church, but still she could not fine "something" to which she could commit herself. Then she passed the bookstore one day, and there in the window was the Japanese translation of Paul Rees's book *Christian,*

Commit Yourself. She stopped in her tracks. "Commit yourself." That was just what she wanted to do, so she stepped inside and purchased the book.

Light began to shine as she read. She returned to the pastor. Now two books were examined—the Bible and *Christian, Commit Yourself.* There was more light, and finally it produced radiance as she committed herself to the Christ of both books. Now as a Christian, Bob Gerry told us, she had become one of our best customers, buying more books to help her grow—and books and tracts which she could put into the mail and send to her relatives. Books are bringing life and light and then are being used as tools for witness, so that they continue to bring light and life to others. Powerful is this printed page!

So it was in store after store; we saw evidence of the effectiveness of the ministry of the printed word.

Before visiting the stores to the north of Tokyo we spent ten days in Korea. The Harry Weimars were there, developing the CLC bookstore and publishing ministries in the city of Taegu. Again, it was the same story. We could only stand aside to "see the great sight" of God at work in towns and cities wherever we went. I had the joy of ministering in several churches and the response was gratifying. In one large church in Seoul, Bessie sang, "There were ninety and nine that safely lay...but one was out on the hills away...." Even though it was sung in English, the joy of the Lord shone through. There was a rapport in the Spirit. Joyful faces were everywhere, and when it was over there was a murmur of amens and hallelujahs. The Holy Spirit, through Bessie, had communicated. You could tell by the radiant faces and the warm expressions of appreciation after the service was over.

The Christian church everywhere can learn much from God's people in Korea. It is not the perfect church, but there are a lot of perfectly good things they can teach us. Unfortunately, there are the counterfeit Moonies and others who preach a "gospel which is not a gospel." But that is to be expected. The devil will see to that.

Well, we were home at last—on April 1, of all days! I think we really had two of them! It was a very quick flight. We left Tokyo at six o'clock the evening of April 1, and arrived in Philadelphia two hours later at eight o'clock on April 1! Apparently it was the International Dateline that had us all confused! Actually it had taken us some seventeen hours of non-stop traveling—the jets were due to start operating later that year.

We were tired and we were happy: happy for all that we had witnessed of God at work in His world and happy to see our two lovely daughters again. They were home from Bible College for the spring vacation and were at the airport to meet us. Then, when we arrived home, we thought we had entered the wrong house! The place had been redecorated—new carpets were on the floor, new furniture was everywhere. What expressions of love from our CLC family, our own family and our church family, for this transformation had been a combined effort. The love of Jesus shone through everywhere. It lives in our memory and in our hearts still.

29

A BURDEN SHARED

Within months of our return from overseas we began an extensive deputation ministry. One journey took us as far as Washington on the West Coast and to many of the northern states. Another trip took us to the South—Florida, Georgia and several other eastern states. Then the last trip was made to New England and other points to the north, including Canada. These were busy days. In increasing measure, the vision of the literature ministry across the world was being caught by churches and individuals.

This called for some kind of regular communication, providing fuel for intelligent prayer. The result was our monthly *International Viewpoint* which first appeared in May, 1967. It was nothing pretentious, just a single sheet giving a dozen or so mini-reports of what God was doing in different parts of the world. The response was very encouraging, and undoubtedly the increased volume of prayer led to a strengthening of the work.

In all our travels we carried another burden.

Over the years we had seen missionaries of many societies working without adequate "tools" to help them get the task done more efficiently. I remember well the time in India when the missionary with whom I was staying took me in his car. It was an old vintage in more ways than one. He told me that he always parked on an incline—so he could be sure of getting the motor started! Fortunately it was hilly country, though that presented a problem at night. That is another ride I will never forget. Every time we came to a bend and the brakes were applied, the lights went out!

I have visited a number of print shops and have been troubled to see the old, inefficient equipment being used. Hours have to be spent repairing or replacing parts—hours which could be used producing pages of print.

I visited a Bible School in Africa. The missionaries were perplexed, for the generator producing electricity kept breaking down. They had two options. They could send to America for parts while doing their best to keep things going. If the parts were air-freighted it would be at least a month before things could be operating properly again. It would be much longer if the parts were delayed in customs—anything up to three months! The other solution would make things operative within days. The electric company was bringing its power down the street where the Bible School is located, and they could have the school hooked in for $2,000. How I wish I could have written out a check for them on the spot, or knew of an organization or individual with whom the need could be shared by telephone—and the check put in the mail that same day.

In 1967 Bessie and I invited a few missionary-hearted friends to our home. We just wanted to share our burden. We had some ideas but no serious conviction that anything could be done. This meeting was *ordered of the Lord,* because God had His man prepared and ready to put substance to the burden. Within a matter of weeks Frank Clifford had shared his vision with a number of close friends. The result? Mission Projects Fellowship was born. Its slogan, *Modern Equipment Makes a More Efficient Missionary,* spells out the purpose of the organization. Without high-pressure promotion, its ministry of service to missions has grown steadily. At their annual banquet in November 1980, they reported seventy-seven projects completed, with total giving over their thirteen-year history amounting to $327,826. Nearly fifty missions, including CLC, have been helped by this dedicated fellowship, which takes nothing out of it for salaries and uses less than 2 per cent of the annual income for operating expenses. It is just another thrilling story of what can be done when God's people, concerned about getting the gospel to the ends of the earth, are ready to become personally involved.

After approximately two years of ministry in North America, Bessie and I were off again—this time to Europe and Africa.

We flew from New York to Paris, then took the train south to the main CLC base in the village of La Begude de Mazenc, about four miles from Montelimar. Here we met in conference with workers from our seven European countries and from Britain— twenty-six of us altogether. What a refreshing time it was! We fellowshipped around the Word, prayed often during the sessions, and shared informally with each other at the meal tables. All spoke convincingly of the goodness and faithfulness of God, both personally and in the ministry throughout each country.

One of the outstanding evidences of the Lord's working was the new headquarters where the conference was held. It came about through the generous gift of a three-acre piece of land by twin brothers—hard-working French farmers with large families and a deep love for the Lord.

There wasn't much money in the building fund at that time, but this gift of land clearly indicated that the time had come to act. The first building was completed in the summer of 1967, consisting of stock room, packing room, offices, and a meeting room. Now at this conference the second building, although not completely finished, was in use. It contained the central heating plant for all buildings, a garage, laundry, linen room, two bathrooms, a three-room apartment, four rooms for single ladies, a kitchen, a dining room and a general living room. These two buildings had cost $45,000 and were debt free, much of the money coming from the Lord's people in France and other European countries. A third building has since been completed, again without incurring any debt. It has two apartments and several rooms for single men.

As we have recorded earlier, the ministry of CLC France is reaching far across the land and across the French-reading world. Even during our five-day visit orders had come from the island of Martinique in the West Indies, from Viet Nam, and elsewhere.

Yes, our hearts were full as we listened to the reports from each center in France and from the other six countries, telling of vital contacts made and steady expansion in all phases of the ministry. There was a new climate of genuine spiritual inquiry everywhere. Priests and nuns are frequent visitors to our book-centers and they talk openly of spiritual things, ask pointed questions, and buy study and devotional books. The Bible is being read gladly by the people in these countries and, thank God, many are finding Christ and are boldly testifying to their new-found faith.

We moved on to Britain for almost three weeks, where deputation meetings had been arranged in England, Ireland and Scotland. Then we went on to The Netherlands. We were intrigued to see the keen interest being taken in the presidential election in the U.S.A. A large blackboard at the airport gave the latest returns, showing Nixon slightly ahead! Ineka Stuiver met us and she, too, was politically minded. She carried her portable radio, and as reception wasn't good while we were on the move, she would pull to the side every so often to get the latest count! Of course, it was all on the pretense that we would be interested! And we were!

This was my second visit to Holland, Bessie's first. The steady growth of the work in Amsterdam was impressive. The publishing program was also developing, and this included some of Corrie ten Boom's earlier titles. Now we were able to share in the expansion nationwide, for just a few weeks earlier, on September 21, a second store had been opened in Almelo. We were so happy to fellowship with the Verkouter family who were in charge of this new center. CLC is still in Almelo, though in a more central location.

By 1979 two more centers had been added—Winschoten and Flushing (Vlissingen). Then in 1980 the largest advance was undertaken when facilities in a large conference center in the town of Ede were offered to CLC. The field leaders, Volkert and Wobke Spanjer, are residing there. Now the publishing arm and, of course, the general administration of the work are based in Ede. Some further building will still be necessary to house the larger staff which will be needed.

After twenty years of steady growth we look forward to further development which, we trust, will include Holland becoming a sending base, with a stream of Dutch literature missionaries going to many parts of the world.

Next we were off to Germany, fellowshipping with Helmut and Waltraut Grosspietsch and their lovely family. It was good to see the steady work being done at the Hamburg bookshop. In 1978 they moved to a much bigger store in a better location and, as a result, distribution increased significantly. Those who have seen this center report glowingly of its attractive appearance and beautiful displays.

A German edition of the *Floodtide* magazine, called *Wort Unterwegs,* is produced by Reinhilde Helmreich, who once served with CLC in Chile, South America. This is helping to make the worldwide work of CLC better known and will, we believe, bring more German workers into our fellowship, both for the overseas program and to make possible further expansion within the country.

We had a delightful few days in Switzerland. The WEC have graciously served CLC's interests for years, representing the literature ministry in deputation and handling support funds for the several Swiss workers serving in the ranks of CLC in France, Italy and the Ivory Coast. They also channel funds to non-Swiss workers in other countries and to some of CLC's projects worldwide. We are indeed grateful for this bond of living fellowship.

Then we made our promised visit to Austria. We traveled from Zurich to Graz by train, and it is a journey we will ever remember. What majestic scenery—another breath-taking example of the Creator's skill!

The bookshop in Graz is CLC's closest center to the Iron Curtain areas of Europe. It is not wise to report about our contact with the living church behind this curtain, but we can say emphatically that there is a living church on the other side. I do not mean that it merely exists. Indeed, not. I only wish I could share with you in detail some of the fascinating things we were privileged to hear during our visit with Elizabeth and Helga.

Many of the Christians are by no means "secret disciples." Many are young, and yet they gladly "count not their lives dear unto themselves." They distribute Bibles and Christian literature, knowing that in so doing they are taking great risks. It is a privilege to help this "hidden church" in its hours of need.

Our final country in Europe was Italy.

Because of limited time we visited just the newest of the three bookshops. It is located in Milan, Italy's second largest city, and the heart of the industrial North. It had only opened earlier that year, but it was already making an impact for God. The mezzanine floor included a counseling corner, and we were blessed as we listened to reports of some of the contacts they had made.

It continues like this today. Troubled people find their way there, not realizing that it is a "religious" shop. Just recently a middle-aged man wandered in. When he realized he was in a Christian bookshop, he told Ruth Sutter that he was fast becoming an atheist. Ruth shared from the Word and from her own knowledge of God, then she recommended a book about the Lord's great power and love. He bought it and Ruth, reporting this incident, said, "We are praying that God will reveal Himself to this man, and that he will find forgiveness and true peace." To this we add our Amen.

To make the outreach from this center more effective, a bookmobile was provided soon after our visit. This ministry has proved tremendously effective in getting books to the local Milan market and, further afield, to some of the annual Trade Fairs.

The two other centers—Florence, and Messina, Sicily—were also seeing real fruit. During the seventies three more centers were added—Naples and Perugia on the mainland, and a second center on Sicily, in Palermo. From all six centers a similar outreach is now carried on. In Naples the small publishing program also keeps vital books coming.

We had hoped to visit the center in Messina, but flights could not be coordinated so we had to content ourselves with just a brief telephone conversation with Ernesto Schmitt. We also had to miss Spain on this trip, but we had met the workers at the conference in France.

The Spanish work had begun in 1966 when a Spanish couple opened a bookroom on the seventh floor of an office building in Madrid. The main ministry then was bookstalls at various markets, and at national and international Trade Fairs. Then in 1975 we came down to street level and opened our central bookshop in Madrid. A second center operates in Valencia, Spain's third largest city, and at the end of April, 1980 a warehouse was opened in Madrid. Again, this is one of those miracle stories. Our search for suitable premises had been very discouraging. Then a phone call came. A Christian businessman had property to rent, but a lot of work would be needed to put the building in shape for our purposes. Young people rallied around to help. A construction company working near the warehouse supplied cement for a new floor—without charge! Two missionaries gave valuable help—one, a qualified electrician, did the wiring and installed the florescent fixtures; the other, with carpentry experience, gave guidance regarding installation and construction procedures. Again, earmarked gifts for this project came from various sources, so that by opening day all expenses for this new venture had been met.

Spain is just one more country with new and far-reaching opportunities. Its new constitution, signed by King Juan Carlos on December 27, 1978, guarantees human rights, free enterprise, and religious liberty. A new day indeed! One noticeable consequence is that the demand for Christian literature has increased dramatically. Once again, it is a case of more personnel needed to enable us to buy up the increasing opportunities.

30

OUR FIRST VISIT TO AFRICA

Our six weeks in Britain and Europe had left us with thankful hearts. The CLC work was becoming stronger and the expectation of all of our workers was that God had great things ahead. Now that we have updated the story, we can see some of the results of their expectant faith which have developed over the past twelve years since our visit, and the vision continues to enlarge. This decade will see some big strides in our present countries and in those yet to be added. A start has already been made with the addition of Finland on January 1, 1981.

It was now mid-November and Bessie and I were headed for Africa.

Our first stop was Tunisia. Eric and Gladys Hepburn were now living in Tunis, and it was so good to once again meet up with our immediate family. As in Algiers so in Tunis, we could "feel" the darkness and see the bondage of Islam wherever we traveled. Some literature work was being done, and we visited a small Christian bookshop in the city. Unfortunately it is not operating today, but there are indications that the younger generation in many of the Muslim countries is searching for something better than their religion offers. We must continue to keep a keen eye on just how this need can be met.

We flew across the great Sahara Desert, refueled in Nigeria, and then went on to Ghana. Thankfully there is an active literature ministry in this country. We were visiting Accra because of several invitations CLC had received to begin our ministry there, but again we were not convinced that our presence was needed. We are still not convinced, though always open to any fresh light our Captain may shed on the situation. In a sense the same is true of neighboring Nigeria.

We were particularly glad to fellowship with the workers of the Africa Christian Press, a group from Britain with a commission to get more African-written Christian literature on the markets of English-speaking Africa. They are doing an excellent job, and the number of titles is increasing each year—with very encouraging results.

The next stop was Abidjan, capital of the Ivory Coast.

The ministry began here in 1962. Again it was simple: book tables at strategic street corners and in the market places, and a small book depot in a church compound. The following year the bookshop was opened and we are in the same premises today. It has a multi-purpose ministry. First, of course, selling the books over the counter. Then, there are the bookmobile trips made several times a year into the interior. There are day trips to neighboring towns and schools. During the ten-day Trade Fair each July, CLC moves a selection of stock into the street. This gives greater opportunity for face-to-face discussions, and thousands of tracts and Scripture portions are distributed.

The shop premises are also used for a Bible study each Friday evening, attended by people of different nationalities and denominations. This helps to present a true one-in-Christ picture for, unfortunately, there is much individualism and constant doctrinal battling by evangelicals, which hinders an effective testimony. Consequently, African syncretistic cults are on the increase. Rosicrucianism is very popular among the African upper class. Islam is on the increase. There are indeed many bidders for the minds and souls of men in the Ivory Coast today.

Another interesting function of the bookshop is training. Several African young people from neighboring countries have been trained in literature evangelism at CLC Abidjan, including those who now serve in Cameroon as an associate literature ministry. This began in 1973, a few years after our visit. The work continues to go well, and there are now five bookcenters in different parts of the country. The main base is in Douala, the country's largest city. In 1979 a new building was erected. Now larger stocks of literature in both French and English are carried, and undoubtedly things will continue to move forward during this decade.

We also had a link with another inter-mission group, Centre de Publications Evangeliques, based in Abidjan. Two CLC workers, Davyd and Leona Hepburn, were on loan to them for about nine years. Their mission is to produce Christian literature in easy-to-read French, for all of French-reading Africa, both the young and old. It is fulfilling a vital role.

So the overall CLC ministry and influence in Abidjan is meaningful. It is helping to build fellowship with all God's people, acting as a "bridge" between various churches, enabling them to appreciate one another.

Our week in the Ivory Coast went all too quickly, and on December 2 we flew on to Liberia, our first visit to one of CLC's oldest countries, where the work began twenty years earlier in 1948.

A new experience awaited us here.

We were thrilled to become personally involved in the bookmobile ministry. On one occasion at the Firestone Rubber Plantation, we were delighted to see literature in several of Liberia's vernaculars, as well as in English, changing hands. We held impromptu meetings there, too. Another time we visited the Bomi Hills Mines, where there is constant digging for another of Liberia's major exports—iron ore. No sooner had the bookmobile arrived than some of the fellows, in their work clothes and hard hats, were there to look over what was available and make their purchases. Some of them were obviously keen Christians.

Schools are open to Christian instruction. For years our own Bonnie Hilton and other missionaries have been free to teach the Bible during school time. And there are some good youth groups. On one occasion we shared in a sort of Youth for Christ rally in Monrovia.

However, low literacy (about 20 per cent) hampers overall development, both in Christian service and in the country's need for skilled workers, technicians and managers. Although English is the official language, the majority of Liberia's less than two million population speak at least one of some fifteen tribal tongues, and only a smattering of English. However, the demand for Christian literature has increased significantly during the seventies, with many customers buying commentaries and study books as well as devotional titles. The overall picture had been encouraging but slow, and we were hoping to see some significant advances, including a new store,... when things were changed abruptly on April 12, 1980, as twenty-eight-year-old Master Sergeant Samuel Doe led a coup in which President Tolbert and twenty-seven other political leaders were killed.

Things are still far from normal, but we press on. Our small team of Liberian workers, under the good leadership of Isaac George, who has been with CLC seven years, is doing an excellent job. In spite of the troubles, the 1980 sales increased by 33 per cent. This was a remarkable achievement, especially since the mobile unit, which could account for up to 20 per cent of distribution, was not in service after the coup.

We believe there is still a real future for the literature ministry in Liberia. With the combined consecrated efforts of our Liberian personnel and at least one dedicated, determined couple from overseas, *we shall overcome!*

The CLC ministry in Sierra Leone, which we visited from December 9 to 18, began just five months earlier, when on July 8, 1968 the nation's first evangelical bookshop was opened, signalling another advance for the kingdom of God. Actually, this was the culmination of two years of preparation. The need for an aggressive literature ministry had been brought to our attention in 1966, and Ron Evans went over from Portuguese Guinea to survey the situation and appraise what would be needed to get things going. His report was fuel for prayer and faith.

After furlough in America, the Evanses arrived in Freetown, Sierra Leone, in March 1968 to begin to put the pieces together. With the new bookshop opening in July, the first goal was reached. The second objective followed quickly, when a Volkswagen Kombi bookmobile was provided through the generosity of Mission Projects Fellowship. A third objective was reached when Ken and Bunty MacLennan arrived in the country from Britain, just about a week before we did. Yes, indeed, 1968 was a great year. For a change our beginning in a new country was more imposing—a first-rate bookcenter, a brand new bookmobile, and four missionaries on the job who could get going immediately because English is the national language.

Yet, in spite of that, the work has been uphill. The political unrest of the seventies and the sagging economy have contributed to this. Literacy nationwide is estimated at 20 per cent, though it is close to 40 per cent in the capital city of Freetown, where the bookstore is located. Difficulties in importing books have often kept stock in short supply, and handling all the "red tape" induces frustration and almost despair at times.

But the tide is now turning. The 1981 picture is much brighter than we dared to expect, especially since our missionaries, Phil and Sylvia Cheale, were on furlough. Congratulations to our Sierra Leone colleagues!

We believe the day of resurrection for both Sierra Leone and Liberia is at hand. A new strategy for the eighties is being developed. Because both countries are English-reading, we are linking them together as one field. All supplies from overseas will be brought into Monrovia and then redistributed by road. We are, in one sense, following the lead given by the two governments, for in 1973 the Mano River Union was formed for mutual economic cooperation. The first undertaking of the new organization was the construction of the bridge over the Mano River. This bridge is now completed and in regular use.

With the maturing of our national teams, with our international workers (currently we need two more couples or singles), with the easing of political tensions, and with improving educational opportunities, we have high hopes for significant advances during this decade.

Our last stop in Africa was Dakar, Senegal. CLC had operated a small literature program in this country back in 1953 in the town of Ziguinchor. This is another of the countries where our roots did not go down, and after a few years of faithful endeavor by Vera Duke from Britain the work was closed. The need in this country is still there, and several years ago Jean Treboux of CLC France visited Senegal. His conviction was that another attempt should be made as soon as workers become available. We still await them! When Vera was there, the population of Senegal was two million. In 1981 it approaches six million. All of the added four million would be under thirty years of age. How many have found out about Jesus? Or do they still wait?

There was one other country we were not able to visit— Mozambique, just north of South Africa. CLC began a ministry there in 1966, with Edward and Alice Cain and Hazel Marsh. That in itself was an outstanding accomplishment. Being linked at the time with Portugal as an overseas province, there was strong opposition in the country to evangelical missionary work. However, a year after our arrival CLC was given official recognition by the government, becoming the first missionary society in years to enjoy unconditional approval and freedom in the country. That was a triumph of God's ordering, and it was clear that once again the Crusade had "come...for such a time as this." But times have changed. For the present no fresh chapter in the Mozambique story can be written although faith knows that sooner or later it will be!

On December 22 we flew back to the winter blasts of Pennsylvania. Our knowledge and burden for the great African continent had greatly increased.

31

SOUTH AMERICA AND THE CARIBBEAN

In less than two months we began our third major tour, this time to South America and the West Indies. First, there were a few meetings in Maryland, South Carolina and Florida, and then a couple of days in Jamaica to be with our daughter, Margaret, husband Bill, and our first grandchild, David. Then on to Venezuela.

Here, we were on a survey visit. The WEC had a small book department attached to their headquarters in Barquisimeto. But they had made a major decision and had shared the news with me as International Secretary of CLC. Because of increasing involvement in church development, the staff had reluctantly agreed that they should pull out of literature work; would CLC be interested in taking over their stock? If so, the Crusade would be more than welcome to develop a full-fledged literature ministry in the city. This was the main subject of discussion during our two-day visit at the end of February, 1969.

The young man who had been responsible for the bookroom, Robin Little, was on furlough with his family, and apparently they did not plan to return. Yet, as we listened to reports of what God was doing in Venezuela and could project what the future might hold, we felt quite strongly that literature should be making an increasing contribution to that growth, for without books, no church or individual Christian grows to maturity. We also visited the TEAM bookstore in Maracaibo. It was a good active ministry, but apparently the mission did not have any plans for nationwide expansion. If CLC was to become involved in Venezuela it was now my responsibiltiy to share our findings with our worldwide fellowship, particularly with Britain, Australia, New Zealand and North America. Within the year the Captain's strategy began to unfold.

The rest of the journey would be in CLC countries, so after a night in Panama we flew to Chile, arriving on March 1. Our ten days there were encouraging. First, there was the Annual Conference in a pleasant location outside Santiago. Of course, in non-English-speaking countries we were always limited in person-to-person rapport, and although one and another did their best to whisper interpretation, we missed much of the general discussion. Still, we were encouraged to see another demonstration of our democratic fellowship way of operating. It has stood up well over the years in country after country.

After the conference we visited our second bookstore, in Concepcion, stopping along the way to leave books with various agents. How glad we were to see the printed word getting around and to have fellowship with those who worked with us in this growing enterprise. At one stop we were given several bunches of delicious grapes, fresh from the vine in their patio! That was fellowship with an added dimension!

We flew across the Andes, awed by another majestic wonder of creation, including the loftiest peak in the western hemisphere, and landed safely in Buenos Aires. It is now a sprawling metropolis of nearly 10 million people. Those were days of precious fellowship with Raul and Rosa Roldan and their three fine boys. On the Sunday we visited two of the growing churches and rejoiced to see many evidences of how the work of the Lord was expanding. We met many who spoke appreciatively of the Roldans and the literature ministry.

Next, we made the short flight to Montevideo.

This brought back memories of my first visit in 1955. How things had changed, but not for the better! There was a time when Uruguay was considered the most outstanding example of political democracy in South America, but strikes, general political unrest, and guerilla activities had brought an economic slowdown. By 1973 Uruguay's forty years of democracy came to an end. Thankfully, things seem to be improving and the government has serious plans for a new beginning, continued stability, and progress in the eighties. CLC also has weathered these storms and is experiencing brighter times.

It was so refreshing to spend our three days with Jake and Dena Prins and their lovely family. With the Lord's help and their dogged Dutch frugality, ingenuity, and perserverance, they and our other workers had kept the literature ministry on target in spite of prevailing adversities.

Although we only had two stores in Brazil—Porto Alegre and Recife—we spent over three weeks in this facinating country.

At the time of our visit Tom and Lily McClelland were heading up the work, and things were moving along encouragingly. Tom had planned for us to visit most of the main cities where different groups were busy in literature ministry. Indeed, he had arranged for us to stay with literature workers, who in turn did a great job introducing us to others.

In Sao Paulo, Peter and Bobbie Cunliff were our hosts. His group was busy publishing books and had just produced a Portuguese edition of the Chicago/Wheaton-based *Christian Life* magazine. Our time was fully occupied, for Sao Paulo is the publishing hub of Brazil. While we were keenly interested in all phases of the Christian literature program, our main interest was distribution, and many of our questions were directed to this subject. I was asked to speak on distribution at a literature conference in the city held under the sponsorship of CLEB, the Christian Literature Fellowship of Brazil. That conference gave us a great opportunity to find out more of what was being done throughout Brazil.

Our next stop was Rio de Janeiro, where we were hosted by the Carl Hultgrens, missionaries with the Assemblies of God of Springfield, Missouri. They were most gracious and Carl was an enthusiastic literature worker. The basement of their home was overflowing with books, and from this center Christian literature was mailed all across the country. We were intrigued by the businesslike way things were done, and the good systems Carl had developed to keep their extensive mailing list up-to-date. Later the operation was moved to larger premises and when, in the late seventies, the Hultgrens left Brazil, CLC was privileged to carry on this program into which they had put many years of faithful service.

We again met up with David Glass. He was as enthusiastic as ever about Christian literature, very gracious in his appreciation of CLC's efforts, and encouraged us to press on.

He also had a great story to tell about his own work. The large building in which his bookstore was located had recently come into his hands. His hope was to turn it into an evangelical center, and his faith was reaching for the $100,000 which he estimated would be needed to bring the vision to reality. In 1981 that goal is nearing completion. Congratulations, David!

However, the literature work was also in need of a financial injection at that time. After our return to the States I was able to channel $10,000 to David to help meet this need, through the generosity of the Back to the Bible literature fund. Apparently it arrived right on time to meet the specific problem.

On we went to Belo Horizonte, where the Bethany Fellowship of Minneapolis had their main base. They have majored on publishing and printing, and it was thrilling to see the presses producing very attractive literature. This group continues to make a big contribution to the overall literature needs of Brazil.

Our next stop was Brazil's new capital, Brasilia. A dozen years earlier this area was part of a vast wilderness, but it had been chosen by the government to encourage development in the interior. At the time we were there it was still very much in the making, with a population of perhaps 25,000. By 1980 its population was well over three-quarters of a million—and still growing! The Mennonites had an attractive bookstore in an excellent location. It was good to see that someone was already there with Christian literature, right at the beginning of this great and enterprising venture.

And so to Recife, CLC's other city, where Tom and Lily McClelland were now located. The bookstore was in its fourth year of operation. Right from the start the response had been beyond all our expectations. The demand for literature, both by Christians and non-Christians, was constantly increasing. Much of this spiritual awareness was undoubtedly the fruit of the many years of Presbyterian missionary endeavors in this part of the country as well as of other groups who were newer on the scene.

One personal note. On arrival at the McClelland's home we were given a telegram which had arrived a day or two earlier. It was from Jamaica announcing the safe arrival of James Kenneth Almack, our second grandchild—on April 1, of all days!

With thankful hearts we headed for Belem, where we took the Pan Am flight for the next leg of our journey. We arrived at the Belem airport somewhere around midnight and were off the next morning by ten o'clock, so we had no time to make any contacts.

Again, what a transformation! What progress! I had been here fourteen years earlier. Then it was just a small town with less than one mile of paved road and a population of just a few thousand. Now it boasted a modern airport, miles of paved streets, business skyscrapers, several modern hotels, and a population of perhaps ten times what it was. A busy, flourishing city of the far North, just a degree south of the equator.

We left Brazil deeply impressed. In size it is the fifth-largest in area (greater than the continental U.S.A.), occupying almost half the South American continent. It is the seventh largest in population (in 1981 it will pass 125 million). It has an industrialized economy with tremendous untapped potential. Most of all, it has a new spiritual vitality. Growth is evident everywhere—from small house groups to the great 25,000 seat Pentecostal church in Sao Paulo. When we were there the church was still being built and had a seating capacity of about ten thousand. At the evening service we attended there must have been eight thousand people present!

We also left deeply committed...to pray, and to work towards a much greater involvement in the literature thrust all across this "Awakening Giant." As reported in a previous chapter, these past twelve years have seen some big strides taken towards reaching some of our objectives.

There was one more stop in South America—Guyana, where CLC had been operating since 1953. Our plane had made two stops before reaching Georgetown: in French Guiana and in Dutch Guiana. We did not know it at the time, but in French Guiana plans were already underway for CLC France to establish a small literature base in Cayenne, the capital of this French outpost on the northeastern coast of South America. It is now another of the associate ministries of CLC's world coverage, and this living testimony continues to this day under the guidance of a Swiss couple—Daniel and Rachel Cretegny. In 1980 they reported that, on the average, they had sold one Bible and two Testaments every day of the year! Along with a market stall every Saturday, they had enjoyed many opportunities for witness and counseling and had seen a 41 per cent increase in distribution.

The next six weeks we were back in English-speaking territory—Guyana, Trinidad, Antigua, Dominica, St. Lucia, and Barbados. Approximately one week was given to each. Our workers had arranged a fairly full speaking ministry at local churches along with an interdenominational gathering where both the local and worldwide outreach of CLC was presented. They were great days of mutual fellowship and refreshing.

Our last stop was unscheduled—back to Jamaica. Yes, you guessed it—to see our new grandson and, of course, mother, dad, and brother David. Bill was helping in the print shop and Marge was giving whatever time she could to *Caribbean Challenge* correspondence. This was the Almacks' first term of service and, as all first terms, it was a learning experience which contributed to their further terms of service in Trinidad and now Barbados, with oversight of the work in the Eastern Caribbean.

Back in the States we stopped in Columbia, South Carolina, to share the happy occasion of our younger daughter, Janet's, graduation from Columbia Bible College. Finally we arrived back in Fort Washington on June 3.

It had been a great tour. We had seen much, we had learned much, and we knew that we would be sharing in greater measure in the ongoing work in these countries to the south in the years ahead. And so it has proved, as we shall see.

32

MONEY MATTERS

These three extensive journeys gave us much food for thought. We had seen and heard so much. How thankful we were for all that had been accomplished in spite of the occasional failure or setback. The pros far outstripped the cons. That very fact encouraged us, for the second emotion which our travels had aroused was concern because there was so much remaining to be done. In every country and in all our discussions the possibilities for the future loomed large.

Invariably it had touched on two fundamentals—manpower and money supply. I must admit that occasionally I fantasized about a God-fearing, totally dedicated millionaire, who wanted every penny of his wealth to be used in the work of the kingdom through CLC! Then I would settle back to realities, admitting that such an idea was not totally impossible but very improbable.

Then, we would find ourselves meditating—and quietly recounting how faithful the Lord has been as our Provider and Sustainer over the years, both for us personally and for the CLC ministry.

We had built both our lives and the Crusade on the foundational kingdom principle: "Seek ye first the kingdom of God and His righteousness, and all these things shall be added unto you." Or as J.B. Phillips puts it: "...and all these things will come to you as a matter of course" (Matt. 6:33). Phillips goes on to exhort: "Don't worry at all, then, about tomorrow!" Good advice, but it is not always carried out!

Actually this kingdom principle is discussed beginning from verse nineteen. Only one master can be served. Once that has been settled—and acted upon—the rest falls readily into place.

For me it had meant giving my planned business career to my Captain. He was free, then, to use the business acumen (which was of His implanting anyway!) in the work of His Father's kingdom. We do not have to give up or downplay our abilities, as though they were unspiritual intrusions. Quite the contrary. They are the talents which He has given us and which He expects to be used in His kingdom program. For "we are His workmanship, created in Christ Jesus to do those good deeds which God planned for us to do" (Phillips).

In essence Bessie did the same thing, gladly getting out of business—one that was prospering because of her talent of a pleasing personality, which attracted customers and their money only to pad her boss's pocket. She saw that her talent could be used in the service of the King, who had promised very rewarding compensation—"all...things will come to you as a matter of course"!

He is not promising prosperity, just adequate provision according to the need. This is what we have proven over the nearly fifty years since we "stepped out in faith," living on and enjoying His *all things* from whichever source they have (and do) come.

Only in the last few years, since banks started giving interest on checking accounts, have we had a personal bank account! We own no car, no house, no property, no insurance. Yet, the occasional doctor's bills have been paid. We have never gone without a meal and have always been adequately clothed. Our two daughters finished college with all their bills paid. We have no regrets (and no worries!) and if we had to do it all over again we would—gladly.

Yet, in one sense you could say we have prospered. The CLC has grown unbelievably. From just the two of us and one small bookroom, with first year's sales not much over $5,000, our 1980 World Report shows 594 full-time workers, with perhaps another 100 volunteer and part-time helpers, operating out of 150 book-centers in 46 countries, with total sales amounting to over 15 million dollars. Add to that the gifts of God's people toward support of personnel and projects, and you have a sizeable income for just one year of operation. As we have mentioned in an earlier chapter, I had said to Bessie that I believed the Lord was going to allow a lot of money to pass through our hands, but not for us personally. This has been proven on both counts, for out of the millions which "passed through our hands" in 1980, about $4,000 came to us personally. It is a joy and privilege to live simply so that multitudes around the world can be nourished with the Bread of Life.

That is another reason why CLC has prospered. All our personnel choose to live simply and take only a minimum allowance, which means that all our workers the world over are indirectly making a personal contribution to the cause of the gospel through literature week by week. To my knowledge no one in our ranks has ever made a survey of the personal income of our 594 workers, but I would dare to say that it probably averages somewhere between a $1 and $1.25 per hour per adult worker. (A family would add approximately 50 per cent per child.)

There is yet another reason—the revolving aspect of our ministry. Simply put, we sell our merchandise. Of course we do give some away, using funds specifically earmarked for such programs or a percentage of our own earnings. The current need for literature in China would be a case in point.

When a book is sold, we will say for $4, approximately $3 is used to buy another copy, so that one is available for the next customer who needs it. In other words, there is a constant turnover of money and of stock.

You ask, "What about the other dollar? You received four, and you need only three to replenish." True, but there are other bills to pay, for rent and utilities and the like. Also, in some developing countries the allowance for workers must be supplemented; so as long as a balance is kept between operating expenses and replenishing the stock, all is well. That is what has to be watched carefully month by month. Otherwise the only way to keep the work going is to subsidize it, and the more subsidy needed the less money there will be for growth and advance.

This is exactly the way the work started back in Colchester. This time it was not even an outright gift, but what you might call an internal loan of $500. Because we were not taking anything out of "the business" for salary or allowance, the total $500 could go to work. Consider what it did. It purchased the original stock, it replenished it, and because only a portion of the "profit" was used for overheads, and none was needed for wages, the stock steadily increased. Still a little was kept in hand, so that in less than two years the $500 loan was paid and the stock was probably three times larger.

Then the following year when the call came for a CLC bookshop in Leicester, we were ready to take on the challenge. True, we did not have to pay rent, which was tantamount to an outright gift and sincerely appreciated, but we did have to pay for all the fixtures and fittings as well as stock for the shelves. That original $500 had kept revolving and produced enough to keep the Colchester bills paid and open the shop in Leicester.

This was simply the Law of Use in operation. Our "$500 talent" had been put to work and was producing. It is still working today after forty years! Don't ask me where it is! It may be in Finland helping to get this first addition of 1981 established!

A few Crusade friends have caught this vision. I think of one couple. They had been missionaries in Africa, and after returning to the States they kept busy in deputation for their mission. It was during this period they came to know about CLC, and having been in business for themselves, they were intrigued by the way CLC operated. When they reached retirement they decided to take action about their personal possessions and agreed to put their assets into the Lord's work.

They could have put their wishes in a will, but why let the government get a share and consequently much less be available for the Lord's work, was their reasoning. Why not get the money working for the Lord now? Consequently, they sold their house and some other assets and put more than $40,000 into CLC—to revolve! We had agreed to put 5 per cent interest into their account every six months, but they never used it. Indeed, they even added a little from time to time, so when finally they went to heaven, their investment in CLC had grown to nearly $62,000. This couple truly knew the secret of *laying up treasure in heaven.*

What happened to that money? At the time, we were in the midst of our third building project in Fort Washington. Did the money get lost in buildings rather than producing books? Not exactly. Remember, all money in CLC "revolves"; it never dies. The building program produced, among other things, living quarters for some of the staff. The total present living area at Fort Washington now gives us fifteen single or efficiency rooms, and fifteen family apartments. We started our first modest building project in 1956. This latest one was finished in 1965. Averaged out, we could say that we have had the living quarters for eighteen years. Imagine how much non-revolving money would have been spent if we had been paying rent on these thirty living spaces!

Well, back to the couple's $40,000 investment. Less than ten years after it was used in the building project, it was back as liquid cash in the Revolving Fund and has been at work elsewhere ever since!

It is because of this Revolving Fund, plus designated gifts, and money from other sources such as the generous help CLC has received from a similar fund Back to the Bible Broadcast has (used solely for literature projects), that we have been able to buy property in many of our countries. The latest example would be Korea.

They bought their headquarters building in Seoul in early 1981, but after using funds from within Korea and earmarked gifts which had been sent from several countries, they still needed $17,000. This money was made available to them from the Revolving Fund, interest free, and will be fully repaid by mid-1984. Instead of having to pay rent to a landlord they repay the Fund and own the building!

The greatest advantage of this practice in our type of ministry is that when we own the property—a good center-city store, for instance—we cannot be moved at the whim of a landlord, which has been our problem on a number of occasions.

Does all this add up to the fact that CLC doesn't need money, and there is now no place for faith? Far from it. We are only scratching the surface of what needs to be done across our world. When I say "we" I mean the combined efforts of all of us in Christian literature work, from the great Bible Societies down to the smallest bookroom in some remote area of the world. With literacy constantly on the rise, will we ever catch up? Some suggest that there are newly literate young people slipping back into illiteracy because there is so little to read in their language.

The fact is that what CLC has been able to do thus far has been because of the combined efforts of God's people: the churches and individuals who support literature workers and literature projects; the revolving aspect of the literature program itself; and the consecrated, sacrificial efforts of the personnel making their "hidden" financial contribution by their simple living standard which they accept as unto the Lord. Still, we need to go faster. Time is short, and multitudes out there await the "books which radiate light"—and produce life in their readers!

This is the concern which gripped us during our journeys overseas.

Thank God we have never had to get involved in fund raising. Frankly, we wouldn't know how to do it; and we have no intention of doing it now, because we believe that the kingdom principle of Matthew 6:33 includes His supply for people and projects, without our trying to find it or "raise" it. So, "we don't worry at all about tomorrow!" Our policy is simply to share the information of what we believe God is leading us to do, and then leave the Holy Spirit to prompt the reader to act in the way He directs.

On the other hand, we do thank God for every missionary-hearted church which does have the ministry of Christian literature in its missionary budget. We do thank God for every reader of books from which spiritual help has been received, who then shares in a tangible way with those for whom so little is available. We do thank God for His people who "lay up treasure in heaven," following the kingdom principle of "hilarious giving."

We realize that we are stewards of His money, much of it given very sacrificially. Therefore, we do our best to assure that all financial matters are handled carefully. Our books are audited each year by Certified Public Accountants. We're privileged to have some wonderful people working with us in this area. A friend in Toronto does a great job keeping a watchful eye on things in Canada and the Detweiler organization does the same for CLC in the States. Harold Detweiler wrote to me recently and I thought you might be interested—and reassured—by what he had to say:

I have a strong conviction that the only way CLC could have grown to its present worldwide outreach is by the guiding hand of the Lord upon you and your organization. From a business standpoint, it seems impossible that one man could start with only a vision of helping people through Christian literature in England and end up having Christian bookstores all over the world! It has been a real thrill in my Christian life to watch you and your organization be led by God.

Every organization (commercial or nonprofit) will grow and develop only if the goals of top management are understood and followed by the personnel at all levels in the organization. I sense, after talking with various CLC personnel at different levels of responsibility, that there are, in fact, common goals shared by everyone. This is something that I've seen not often enough in my exposure to the business community. It is, however, very important.

Another area of observation that I made is that everyone has a burden for their fellow workers—even in other countries throughout the world. It is not a situation where each bookstore is a separate entity unto itself where the people do not care what happens to their fellow workers. Rather, it is an environment of love and concern for each other and a sharing of a common goal to spread the gospel throughout the world.

As you know, our accounting firm has had the privilege of performing various accounting services for CLC for many years....

In all these years, the staff at CLC has always impressed us with their concern regarding the importance of proper accounting methods—even to the point that their own personal lifestyles were frugal in order to give the greatest priority possible to the distribution of Christian literature.

Ken, my heart is full of appreciation for the relationship that we have shared over the years....

(Signed) Harold F. Detweiler, C.P.A.

SECTION V

I WILL CAUSE THE BRANCH OF

RIGHTEOUSNESS TO GROW
Jeremiah 33:15

In those days, and at that time, will I cause the Branch of righteousness to grow up unto David; and he shall execute justice and righteousness in the land.

Jeremiah 33:15

33

INTERNATIONAL DEVELOPMENTS

In the fourth decade of Crusade history, several significant developments and changes in our international affairs began to unfold.

The first took place in May, 1970. The International Council, which had become an official function following the two previous international gatherings (London in 1961 and Bangkok in 1965), met as a duly appointed Council for the first time at the Missionary Retreat Fellowship in the Pocono Mountains, about one hundred miles north of Philadelphia. Two full weeks were given to reviewing the past and planning for the future. When the Council sessions were over we summarized our findings under four headings: Nationalization, Evangelism, Expansion, and Co-ordination.

Nationalization referred to two matters: incorporating the work as a national enterprise and not as a branch of an overseas organization; and seeing God raise up qualified, high-calibre, spiritually like-minded national personnel in each country.

Under the topic of Evangelism we discussed such things as: planning for special events like the Olympic Games, National Fairs, and Expositions; organizing door-to-door and mass distribution programs; greater use of bookmobiles; and developing a cassette ministry, such as those in Thailand and Indonesia.

The subject of Expansion brought us another concept. During the course of the discussion twelve new areas of opportunity had been brought to our attention and were carefully reviewed. The Council agreed that such potential growth indicated a need for careful research, perhaps followed by on-the-spot surveys and consultations. Subsequently, four immediate surveys were authorized.

As a result of this conviction, the most significant, far-reaching, long-range development was the creation of a new department to be known as the International Research and Information Service, or IRIS for short. Bob and Ada Hiley of CLC Britain were asked to develop this. It was slow going at first, but today it is a very important department. Among other things it has produced a very thorough and comprehensive coverage of all Christian literature work being done by all groups or individuals within any given country. Again it is a service agency for all, and many missions make good use of the IRIS office in London. Currently a branch of this service is being set up in Fort Washington.

The final heading, Coordination, was mainly concerned with financial matters. It clarified our policies regarding the use of our funds for the distribution programs, for printing and publishing, for rents and/or purchase of property, and for support of both national and international workers. Also one new category was added to meet a growing need—children's education.

Of course there were many other subjects discussed, but as the two-week gathering ended all agreed that although we may not have found all the answers, we would go into the seventies with undiminished effort and renewed devotion to the cause of the gospel around the world through the medium of the printed page. We realized that we were living in a changing world, but we reaffirmed, in what we called a Declaration of Conviction, that "whatever the changes may appear to dictate, the Crusade will never deviate from the basic principle of complete and utter dependence upon the Lord for the constant supply of men and women and the means and spiritual fortitude to meet every situation."

The following year I made another visit to the Eastern Caribbean. The main purpose was to help change the location of the bookshop in St. Lucia, but it also included visits to Trinidad and Barbados. Such visits always allowed time for discussing the work in the islands of the Eastern Caribbean.

In 1972, Bessie and I made another visit to Britain, and this time our daughter Janet joined us. We were able to visit many of the British centers in England, Wales and Scotland. Some of them we had never seen; others were in new locations, such as the excellent shop right in the heart of Birmingham. One development of particular significance was the new warehouse, shipping room and administrative offices located in Alresford, on one of the main routes between London and Southampton. These premises had been dedicated to the Lord in October, 1969 and have since become the hub of the distribution program throughout the nation. From the warehouse literature goes to the majority of Christian bookstores in Britain, and sometimes to as many as 150 other countries during the year. The work continues to expand, so that with the increasing world demand for living print, these 10,000 square feet may prove inadequate before the end of the 1980's. There just seems to be no end in sight.

Another busy year of travel faced us in 1973. In early January we went to Scotland where the second International Council had been convened in beautiful Kilcreggan, nestled on the side of the busy Clyde River. This kept us occupied until the middle of the month, after which Bessie and I spent another two weeks in Cornwall. Bob Hiley from the new IRIS department joined us, and we had the full use of a lovely, modern bungalow generously made available to us by a niece of Bessie's. It was in these quiet and delightful surroundings that Bob and I worked on the official report of the Kilcreggan Council gathering.

One outcome of the Council was another trip for me. The destination was New Zealand. The purpose was to discuss the matter of leadership because of Maurice Thomas's resignation due to increasingly poor health. The Council had asked Donald David to pray about this possibility. He and Ida agreed, and although not committing themselves, expressed a willingness to go if it was confirmed by unanimous agreement of our New Zealand Council. It was, and by the end of the year the David family took up residence in New Zealand, where the Lord used Donald to move the work forward into the bookshop ministry. It was so good to renew fellowship with the Thomases with whom I stayed, and with Alec Thorne who had been God's instrument to get the CLC established there back in 1960, as well as a number of other friends of the Crusade.

On my homeward journey I stopped for a few days in Australia. How encouraging it was to see the excellent facilities of the new headquarters in Pennant Hills, Sydney, which had been dedicated on August 2, 1969. I shared a session with a number of new candidates who were there for the Orientation Courses before being assigned to a particular task. They and many others were certainly needed, for Australia was on the threshold of rapid growth. By 1980 nine new outposts had been added, giving them a total of fourteen literature centers from north to south and as far west as Perth. They did not know all that was ahead of them when I was there in 1973.

I flew on to South Africa. This was, I believe, the longest night I have ever experienced! Flying west for almost twelve hours, it seemed as though daylight would never come! It did, though, during our refueling stop on the island of Mauritius in the Indian Ocean!

Finally I reached Johannesburg, and the next morning I flew on to Mozambique.

What a thrill to see that living lighthouse in the heart of the country's thriving capital, Lourenco Marques (now Maputo). CLC had begun its ministry here seven years earlier. It had been an uphill climb, but now it was flourishing in spite of the political unrest. Literature was available in Portuguese, the official language, and also in several vernaculars, with the demand for what was available steadily increasing. CLC was busy publishing in two or three languages and was running out of storage space!

I had the privilege of speaking at a newly formed church. There were almost one hundred in the congregation—many fine young people, some of them seriously "letting their light shine" in bold witness. News from the northern part of the country was also most encouraging. Response to the gospel was increasing, and CLC saw the possibility of opening a center in Beira to serve the coastal region even further north. However, when independence came in June, 1975, the new Marxist leadership began a vigorous attack on all religious activities. Many missionaries were forced to leave the country. Some were imprisoned. National Christian leaders faced persecution, some paying the supreme price and receiving the martyr's crown.

Eddie Cain, a South African, was heading up the CLC ministry, but things became increasingly difficult for him and his family. After one visit back to his home, he was not allowed to return. Actually he had missed being taken prisoner by hours. In spite of this the bookstore continued to operate with the help of local Christians, and as far as we can ascertain the store is still operating, although on a limited scale. We still look for the "resurrection" of this work, hopefully in the not-too-distant future.

I took the early morning flight back to Johannesburg and was met at the airport by Len Buck from Pennsylvania, who, with his wife Nina, was serving in the literature ministry of TEAM. Len gave me his undivided attention, and I was greatly impressed by the excellent and efficient job being done. The outreach was nationwide—and growing. Indeed they were, at that time, in the throes of putting up a two-story literature building in the outskirts of the city. I did not have time to see this because of my evening flight to London, but it was a refreshing visit, and I rejoiced in all I had seen of this vigorous literature enterprise.

The 747 flight to London was on time, though later we did have to make an unscheduled stop at the Rome airport because strong headwinds had put a strain on the fuel supply. That flight along the Italian coastline was another unforgettable experience. At one time we could see nothing below because of the dense clouds, but above the clouds the snow-covered peaks of the mighty Alps rose in sheer majesty. Breath-taking! Awe-inspiring! I found myself agreeing with the hymn writer, "This is my Father's world! I rest me in the thought of rocks and trees, of skies and seas—His hand the wonders wrought." Then I began to hum another masterpiece, "Great God of Wonders! All Thy ways display the attributes Divine, but countless acts of pardoning grace beyond Thy other wonders shine. Who is a pardoning God like Thee? Or who has grace so rich and free?" How good to be in touch and in union with such a God!

A two-day stop in London gave me the opportunity to share the highlights of my journey, and especially the situation in New Zealand. Donald and Ida David were in London at the time, and the positive word I had to report came as a confirmation to them. They were ready for service with the Crusade in New Zealand.

On Good Friday I completed the last lap of my journey across the Atlantic to Philadelphia. When I arrived home I had a surprise for the family—six genuine, English hot cross buns! British Airways had served buns at mealtime, and when I commented to the steward about how good they were and how my family would have enjoyed them, he gave me six—compliments of the airline! So ended the longest three-week flight I have ever made. In actual miles I had been around the world once and was on the second lap...something close to 28,000 miles. I felt like an astronaut!

It had been a rewarding journey, and I was thrilled with all I had seen and heard, particularly the part which CLC was being privileged to have.

Following this latest journey I found myself reviewing the past and wondering about the future. I had been serving the Crusade as International Secretary for eighteen years, from 1955 to 1965 in a part-time capacity along with my duties as Director of the work in North America, and for the last eight years full time. Now, as I entered my ninth year, I had a growing conviction that this could be the year of fresh direction. I was beginning to feel that I had carried the International affairs of the Crusade as far as I could. Perhaps a new International Secretary was needed to take things further.

Slowly the conviction grew, and was shared with the other members of the Council by mail and later with a small group of the members who met in Fort Washington. As a result a change was agreed upon, and Bob Gerry was appointed as interim

Secretary. He did, however, continue as Director of the CLC work in Japan, and I assisted him in every possible way during the transfer of responsibilities. This included another journey to the Eastern Caribbean including Guyana.

The "fresh direction" which we anticipated came toward the end of the year. The North American staff asked us to take up leadership again, which we did in December, 1973. This I knew would include more overseas travel, for the North American base was still responsible for much of the expanding ministry in many parts of the world.

34

A NEW SPIRITUAL CLIMATE

Although the pace of overseas development slowed slightly, the seventies saw very significant growth within many of our countries—Brazil, Chile, Japan, Korea, Australia, New Zealand, Britain, Canada, and the U.S.A., just to name a few.

Of the new countries, three were in South America.

After our visit to Venezuela in 1969 and the conviction that God had a place for CLC in this country, things began to happen. We made contact with the Robin Littles on furlough in New Zealand and shared our conviction with them. They saw God in this for themselves and agreed to spend part of their furlough in Fort Washington, learning more about CLC and particularly about our hopes for Venezuela. By Easter of 1970 they were back in Venezuela, ready to give themselves fully to the literature ministry.

It seemed right to continue in Barquisimeto, the country's fourth largest city, and it wasn't long before a good store was opened in center city. In addition, Robin had a vision for the whole country and particularly for the growing church in the plains of Apure state, four hundred miles south and east of the city. It had all started there with literature about thirty years earlier.

One man on muleback had traveled hundreds of miles selling Bibles. Through his efforts another man named Diaz was reached, and he in turn traveled hundreds of miles carrying the gospel to the peasants of this huge area, where rivers are the roads and canoes the cars. Today the state of Apure is dotted with almost one hundred congregations, each with its own pastor, meeting in its own mud-walled, tin-roofed chapel. At the time Robin began making literature visits, this brother, Diaz, testified to having baptized over 6,000 people who were now members of these churches. Truly God has been at work in His Diaz "temple."

Now visits to this area are made every Easter, when a minimum of 6,000 people gather for a united convention and spiritual retreat. The bookmobile arrives loaded with literature, and more than $5,000 worth changes hands in a matter of days. Graded Sunday School materials and literature for Daily Vacation Bible Schools are in use by most of the churches in the area.

Other outreach developed. Bookshelves for churches were provided and by 1980 about thirty of these were being serviced regularly. Contact with other bookshops throughout the country led to developing a wholesale division. Churches all across the land were introduced to Sunday School material and the demand grew steadily. Then the opportunity came to take over a bookstore in Caracas, Venezuela's sprawling metropolis of over two and a half million people.

I visited Venezuela again in 1973 and was thrilled to see the progress which had been made. By that time demand for Sunday School materials was increasing rapidly—and I got caught in the middle of it! For the day after I arrived, a consignment of 130 sacks of mail had reached the post office. Each sack weighed approximately sixty pounds. Robin is no respecter of persons, so he roped me into helping transport all these sacks over to the bookcenter about a couple of blocks away. It was great fun! The only vehicle available at that time was a small car, so Robin and a couple of others packed as much into the car as they dared and drove over to the CLC, while the rest of us dragged the sacks several hundred feet from the back of the post office to the street. By that time Robin was back for another load. So it went until about ten o'clock that evening! We had rented extra rooms above the shop to take care of the task of packing and mailing all of this to the various churches.

By 1980 things had really grown. We now carried publications from about a dozen publishers, which included several bindings of the Scriptures, so instead of sacks through the mail we bring the merchandise in by ship in container loads. Each shipment means receiving approximately fourteen tons of living, Christ-centered literature approximately every two months!

All this is handled in our large warehouse about ten miles from Barquisimeto, where we also have adequate living facilities for the staff. What a decade of progress it has been for CLC Venezuela.

On that same journey I was in Bogota, Colombia, on a survey mission. Once again it was to consider continuing the literature work which WEC had been doing since the 1930's. This time it was a two-fold thrust: distribution and printing, both in the same building on the south side of the city. Subsequently agreement was reached to transfer the whole operation, including the building, to CLC and to continue the work under the leadership of Dave and Bonnie Peacock. However, to help all missions and church groups realize CLC's basic premise as an international service agency, it was mutually agreed to register the work with the Colombian government under a different name. This was accomplished, but some unforeseen complications arose, so later the work was registered under the name of Christian Literature Centers.

Later that year a second bookstore was added, much nearer the center of Bogota. It had been opened by an independent missionary who was now returning to Canada; CLC purchased his stock. However, the location was just a block or two outside the central commercial and shopping area. But in 1978 we were able to buy a fine store in an excellent location right in the heart of the city. As a result we have seen a considerable increase in sales. Many more unsaved people come in to ask questions and to purchase books and Bibles. That same year the bookstore in the south of the city was remodeled. The print shop has also seen a number of changes, being remodeled and enlarged to make room for a considerable input of updated equipment, which has enabled us to print more books and increase our own publishing program.

There is also outreach through the twenty-six literature deposits for which CLC is responsible. These are located in different parts of Bogota, and in small cities within four hours travel time from the city. The books we publish are also available to all the other bookstores throughout the country.

All this is so exciting because it clearly indicates the new spiritual climate among the people of Colombia. Today's new religious freedom is allowing both Catholic and Protestant to find personal "freedom" through their encounter with Jesus Christ. It is all so different from my first visit in 1955. The living church is growing and maturing in Colombia today.

So, in both Venezuela and Colombia CLC has been privileged to keep alive and develop several literature ministries which were already in existence. That is what happened also in Panama.

Word had reached us that the bookstore in Panama City, which for many years had been operated under the Latin America Mission but had recently changed hands, was experiencing difficulties. Apart from expressing concern, we took no action. Then a second time and from a different source we heard that there were problems and the ministry might even have to close. So serious was it that a concerned party paid my airfare to go and look the matter over. It was a quick thirty-six hour visit in November, 1975. Not until I had returned to Fort Washington did some of our staff know that I had gone!

The information I gleaned confirmed that things were not good. At first glance it was fairly certain that the store had been running with a deficit of $10,000 for each of the last two or three years. Later this proved to be an underestimate.

Yet as I talked with the Board Members and others, the unanimous appeal was that the store not be closed down. I agreed. Returning to Fort Washington, I told our staff that this was a challenge CLC should accept, although I warned that the necessary turn-around would not happen overnight, and we would have to expect a deficit for at least the next couple of years.

The Crusade took the work over on January 1, 1976 and slowly began to make the necessary adjustments. By the end of 1979 it was once again operating in the black, but it had been a long pull and there were some casualties along the way.

In actual fact there were really two distinct functions: the ministry of the city bookstore in both English and Spanish, and serving the Americans in the Canal Zone. I think some of our friends in the Zone were disappointed in CLC's service, but the Crusade policy has always been that our priority as a missionary society must be to serve all the people of the country.

The change has proven effective in more ways than one. When we took the work over, the sales ratio was 60 per cent English and 40 per cent Spanish. Now it could be as high as 70 per cent Spanish and 30 per cent English. One of the new things we did was to begin taking books to country churches with the bookmobile. A second store, on the other side of the Isthmus, in Colon, is now functioning as a CLC outpost. Thought has been given to the possibility of another store in the town of David, close to the Costa Rica border.

All this has been made possible by the small team of dedicated workers. The senior member of the staff is Ramon Helleby. He has served in this same bookstore almost since its beginning, nearly twenty-five years ago, so he is well known and well appreciated. Truly he is a man with a heart, and his bilingual ability enables him to serve and counsel in both languages. In 1979 the shop was remodeled and an area set aside as a Counseling Corner, much to Ramon's delight. Many are being helped in that little corner and many more are being counseled over the telephone.

The future of the work in Panama looks bright, and as the Lord adds more dedicated personnel to our ranks we expect to reach further afield, until the whole country is "filled with the knowledge of the Lord as the waters cover the sea."

There was one further advance in this part of the world—the island of St. Vincent in the Eastern Caribbean. Once more it was a take-over! For some years a bookstore had been operated by a keen Christian couple, who had concentrated on supplying school materials to help improve the educational standard in the island: A small selection of Christian literature was included in the stock. But advancing years caused a change and CLC was asked to take over the work. This we did in 1977 with the understanding that we would phase out the secular, educational stock and concentrate on Christian merchandise. However, the transition in this little island has not been easy.

Early in 1979 the island's tallest volcano, 4,048 foot Soufriere, erupted and caused twenty thousand people to be evacuated from their homes. Although sales during this time were very slow, our workers had opportunities to witness to many people who were fearful. In spite of these setbacks the year-end figures showed a 28 per cent increase.

In April 1981 a small bookmobile was given to the work, and it is anticipated that this will add appreciably to distribution throughout the island. All in all, things do look quite encouraging. Hopefully, time will be found to penetrate the cluster of islands to the south, called The Grenadines. They form part of this small country which became a nation on October 27, 1979.

35

STRATEGY CHANGE CONSIDERED

The first significant happening in 1974 was the Annual Conference of North American workers, which gathered in Fort Washington, April 14-19. Some of the results of that conference were to prove far-reaching.

First, there was Canada. The only link we now had was our bookstore in Montreal, which was considered an outreach from Fort Washington. The finances went through the U.S. books and were included in the annual audit. At this conference we felt the time had come for a change. Canada should be operating as a separate country. In one sense it was, having been separately incorporated in 1965, although administratively it was still under Fort Washington's wing.

Back in 1973 when I met John Davey in Australia we had discussed his future. After thirty-three years of service in the West Indies, the Daveys felt the time had come for a change. Should this be in Australia, John's home country, or in Canada, Ethel's homeland? I had asked John, should the Lord indicate Canada, would they be ready to take on the leadership for CLC there? Now at this conference they were ready to give an affirmative answer—for a four-year term of service. However, they had previously agreed to do furlough relief in Barbados, so they would not be ready to take up the Canadian challenge until the following year. At least, we could now work toward Canada's "independence."

Then there was the United States. Had our Captain any fresh word regarding future strategy here? There were indications that He did. For some years CLC had considered the possibility of returning to a bookstore ministry in the States and had been making some investigations. The Conference agreed that this idea should be pursued more vigorously, but that we would need some very clear word from the Lord if we were to move forward in this direction.

There were also several overseas developments discussed. Dave Peacock from Colombia had come to the States hoping to purchase more equipment for the print shop in Bogota. The Conference agreed that we would help him in this. His report of what God was doing in that country was most stimulating.

An official farewell was given to two workers soon to be on their way—Betty Wendland to Liberia and Roger Perry to Barbados and the Eastern Caribbean. That kind of function always puts added enthusiasm into any Annual Conference! We are always thrilled to see workers moving on to their respective assignments.

Another overseas development involved financial help for Korea, as we have recorded in an earlier chapter. As well as this help for Korea we had been able during the year under review to assist several other projects, such as the new bookmobile in India, further help for the work in the Philippines, providing the funds for a bookstore in Colombia, and for bookmobiles in Venezuela and Pakistan.

The following month Dave Shaver and I were personally involved in the opening of Brazil's fifth bookstore. For two years Victor Cardoo had been working in Salvador with a bookmobile, visiting the churches and assessing the possibilities of a bookstore in that city. Out of this the conviction grew that a store was needed.

A good location was chosen and premises purchased with help from North America and other countries. After several delays opening day was set for May 11, 1974. They do things in a big way in Brazil! The Salvation Army Band played hymns outside the store before the opening to attract attention. Then came the time for the actual ceremonies and dedication. Dr. Cleriston Andrade, Lord Mayor of Salvador, gave a gracious word of welcome and good wishes. He saw the bookstore as a further contribution to the good will and spiritual progress of the city. Then he and I cut the tape. The doors swung open and the crowds poured in until there was no room to move! A prayer of dedication was given by a local pastor and CLC Salvador was under way.

We knew God's blessing was upon this enterprise for even before this official opening a life had been touched. An open Bible in a special display case had been in place for several days, and a young man had paused to read the Scriptures. One verse so convicted him that he went inside to seek counsel. A missionary pointed him to Jesus and he left the premises that day "a new creature in Christ." Thank God, since then many others have been helped in their spiritual search.

Dave and I were able to see our four other stores, in Recife, Joao Pessoa, Natal, and Porto Alegre. Some of the travel was by long-distance bus, some by car. and the rest by air. Everywhere we went there were signs of progress, not only in the affairs of commerce and industry but, more importantly, in the work of God.

Other things were happening elsewhere. On July 7, 1974, over sixty delegates representing eight countries of the Caribbean, plus Venezuela and Guyana in South America, gathered just outside of Port-of-Spain, Trinidad, for a Christian Writers Seminar sponsored by CLC. Bonnie Hanson, then editor of CLC's *Flood-tide* magazine, was there as part of the team of lecturers. Some years earlier a similar writers seminar under CLC's sponsorship had been held in Jamaica, guided by Robert Walker, Editor of *Christian Life* magazine based in Wheaton. These represent just some of the other ways CLC has been able to help in strengthening the ministry of Christian literature in different countries. Being a service agency brings a variety of exciting opportunities across our path.

The efforts of our new research department showed up again this year. Through information being gathered by the IRIS office, a need in Gibraltar came to our attention. A small bookshop on the Rock had been opened in 1970 by two ladies formerly with the North Africa Mission. Later this shop was managed by an ex-CLCer, Ruth Barkey, who was currently serving with NAM. CLC was approached about assuming responsibility for this literature center. We did so in 1974, having worked out an agreement with the NAM that Ruth could continue as manager.

The shop serves not only the local residents but also people from the south of Spain and from Morocco. There is also continual contact with those serving in the British forces, especially with the constant coming and going of their ships. Literature is available in English, Spanish and Arabic. Roy and Beth Anson from Britain became responsible for the work in 1979 when Ruth Barkey retired, and they too are encouraged by the many opportunities which this small bookshop brings.

In the fall of 1974 a personal need unexpectedly brought significant developments in our own spiritual growth and, consequently, affected the ongoing CLC ministry. The two are always intertwined.

36

GOING DEEPER WITH GOD

Along with our worldwide missionary outreach the Crusade has become known as a publisher and distributor of "deeper life" books. This is particularly true in North America, where we are the sole distributor for a growing number of titles from British publishers. These appear in the States, and in some cases in Canada, under the CLC imprint. For many years the books were printed in Britain and shipped to Philadelphia, but more titles are now being printed in the States, thus saving ocean freight.

The very fact that we produce these books on "the deep things of God" brings its own challenge. We are a company of full-time Christian workers—literature missionaries. How well do we practice what we publish? How well do the words of our lips and the ways of our lives compare with the literature which we produce and energetically distribute? Do we really have a workable and demonstrable answer?

If we had no other book, the Bible gives us all the answers we need. That is, if we use it as a textbook for living, and practice what it says. We are in danger, I fear, of using The Book to study its theology, from which we formulate our doctrine, which in turn produces our denomination. Then we spend our energies defending these convictions! Whereas our Bible, particularly the Gospels and the letters of our Testament of the New Covenant, essentially instructs us on how to "stand fast in the liberty where-with Christ has made us free." It tells us of Christ dwelling in His temple and of the day-by-day operation of the Holy Spirit—"the power that worketh in us"—enabling us to work out our own salvation doing His good pleasure with a will.

This is good news indeed, but often we fail to acknowledge that it is the same Christ and the same Holy Spirit dwelling in all His children. We are all blood relations of one Family by virtue of our new birth made possible by "the blood of His cross." We are all cells, as it were, in one Body of which Christ is the Head, directing every moment-by-moment function of that Body.

To grasp this fact is to discover the solution—the answer—to the disastrous problem of the personality-clash syndrome which plagues our missionary endeavors and our church activities. I have just looked up the dictionary definition of the word *syndrome*. It is enlightening—"an aggregate or set of current symptoms indicating the presence and nature of a disease." The Greek from which the word originates simply means "to run together"—perhaps to clash!? A disease, if you please.

To understand this truth is, I believe, to discover the joyful possibility of walking with each other in "the liberty wherewith Christ has made us"—all of us—"free." Has, note you. Present tense. Christ in us—all of us—the glorious hope! Yet, how slow we are to live in the reality of this.

By the autumn of 1974 Bessie was showing signs of tiring physically. Her blood pressure was high, and the more I watched her the more I knew that a complete rest was necessary. So on January 2, 1975, we flew to London and headed for Cornwall, Bessie's home area in the West of England. The weather was unbelievably mild. Roses were still blooming in London and by the end of the month daffodils were in full bloom in Cornwall.

A daughter of Bessie's oldest sister put a lovely little cottage at our disposal. With mild weather, this cottage in delightful surroundings, and the constant outpouring of love from the various families (Bessie is one of twelve), what more could we ask? We looked forward to our complete rest—all six weeks of it. It was the longest and most relaxed vacation we have ever experienced.

No meetings had been planned, so we had plenty of time for country walks, an occasional drive, an abundance of home-cooked country food, our books, and rest whenever we wished.

All was set for the physical renewing which Bessie needed, and I too settled down to enjoy these quiet weeks. I brought no work with me across the ocean! However, you can't be quiet and alone with each other like that without something happening. We had time to talk and to reflect, not so much about the thirty-seven years of service together, though we were constantly thinking and praying for our fellow workers around the world, but just about our thirty-seven years of being together. We were a happily married couple. We had two daughters whom we loved dearly and who were in the Lord's service. We had seen His hand of blessing upon the CLC ministry—and so on.

As we reflected on the brighter side, we also took a look at the other side of the coin, for there was another side—a darker side. There were casualties, failures, distressing situations to which we had contributed, and personality clashes which had resulted in coming to the parting of the ways. Even deeper, there were misunderstandings between ourselves, fears, short tempers, wrong attitudes, and misjudgings. The list got longer. We were not being deliberately introspective, no, but as we shared and prayed together tensions relaxed and we began to discover, as someone has aptly noted, that *the real truth sets you free.*

Yes, we had read our CLC books like *The Calvary Road, Continuous Revival, Show Me Thy Way, The Liberating Secret,* and many others. All our years we had read our Bibles together. We had prayed together. We had worked together. So why should such things be?

The Pascoes, whose cottage we were using, had a weekly Bible study and sharing time at their farmhouse just down the road, and after a couple of weeks rest I was asked to share from the Word. I agreed. Ephesians was the Epistle we looked into, and I enjoyed digging out some of the rich truths in this letter and sharing them at the Wednesday night gatherings.

We finished our third evening by reading the last few verses of chapter 4, "Grieve not the Holy Spirit,...be kind one to another, tenderhearted...." Then His voice whispered, privately, right into the ear of my heart, "That's right, son, kind, tenderhearted." I knew what He meant. But why had it taken me more than forty years of Christian living to "know" something which I had known for years—through reading my Bible, through reading this particular Epistle many times, through reading CLC books?

Well, we don't need to spend time looking back. One thing I do know, in that moment I stepped into a new dimension of life and our happy marriage has been better yet these past six years or so. Our love for one another has matured. Our love for our children and their families is deeper. Our love for our fellow workers has been refreshingly enriched. This new freedom—this new dimension of tenderness and love—has touched our public ministry, too. People seem to be aware of an authority of the Spirit which is contagious!

Now we just keep taking one step after another in the process of spiritual maturing: moving forward, as Weymouth puts it, "from one degree of radiant holiness to another." We live expectantly—by the "faith of the Son of God" operating in us moment by moment in every circumstance of every day.

Yes, in every circumstance. Like having arthritis. For while Bessie quickly grew stronger, so that the doctor on a recent check-up told me, "You have a very healthy woman," I began to experience osteo-arthritis. It still persists. Some will tell you this ought not to be, for "He healeth all our diseases."

True, He heals the "disease" of unlove, of disunity, of personality clashes, of bitterness, and of an unforgiving spirit. But not necessarily the physical diseases, as Paul, Timothy, Gaius and scores of others knew. On the other hand, our physical body often experiences a surge of release after His healing touches the diseases of the spirit.

Neither do we have to limp along enduring our physical limitations. We do not live in our disabilities. We live in His ability. Remember, we live in union with Christ. He indwells us. Our body is His temple. So when we have a headache, it is His headache as well! My arthritis is His arthritis! We handle it together, living in the reality—and triumph—of His indwelling moment by moment. It's a great life!

In the early days of CLC we saw this in operation. Miss Flatt lived in the small village of Diss, in Norfolk, and whenever we were in the area we made a point of visiting her and getting a spiritual uplift. What a woman of prayer and intercession she was. Pictures of missionaries were everywhere. Maps of various countries adorned the walls of her bedroom, the living room, the kitchen and the bathroom! She knew, in detail, what each missionary was doing, where they were going, the latest project, the newest arrival. She spent her days reading prayer letters, reading the avalanche of personal mail which came to her continuously, and reading missionary biographies and magazines so that she understood each country and its customs. All this made her an intelligent intercessor as she carried each person and each need to the Throne.

Here was a woman who walked the highways and byways of the world, and yet her own legs had never carried her one step. She had been born a cripple, lived a cripple, and died a cripple. Physically, that is. In mind and heart she was a woman of great stature. She didn't live in her infirmity. She triumphed over it!

So whether in life or in death, whether in sickness or in health, whether in poverty or in wealth, we can know consciously the day-by-day reality of Christ in me and Christ in my brother and my sister. We are all members of one Body, drawing from one supply, motivated by the same heartbeat. The love of Christ constraineth me.

Even while this manuscript has been taking shape CLC has published another book, entitled *Love Covers,* by Paul Billheimer. I believe it has a message for these times. It speaks right to this very matter: letting God's *agape* love solve the problem of disunity within the Body of Christ, member by member, mission by mission, church by church, denomination by denomination. When this day comes it will be a climactic answer to our Lord's passionate prayer, "That they may be one,...that the world may know,...that the world may believe."

This is just one more CLC publication which CLCers must face up to. I believe we will!

37

THE NEW STRATEGY CONFIRMED

We returned from England on February 16, 1975, refreshed in body, mind, and spirit. The Easter Annual Conference was the next subject to occupy our thinking and it proved to be another encouraging time. But I will refer to just one matter of special significance.

At the previous conference we had discussed returning to the bookstore ministry in the States. Nothing had happened during the year, and yet we were reluctant to close the issue. There is a Bible verse which says, "Command ye Me concerning the work of My hands," so we took the Lord up on His word. We said, "Lord, You give us an unmistakable word during this coming year; otherwise, by next conference the matter will be closed permanently!" Well, we didn't have long to wait.

News of possible bookstores began to come in. One was in Texas, close to the Mexican border. Alan Harris was on furlough from Venezuela so we sent him to look over the situation. Several other things came to our attention, and we began to sense that the Lord was saying something to us. Was it the green light? We were still not certain, until a letter arrived from Connecticut.

A friend of the work had contributed from time to time but always earmarked the gift for our Spanish program in South America. This time she wrote in a different strain—"Isn't it time you folks began to meet the need of the heathen in America, and open a bookstore in, say, New York City?! Please use the enclosed toward a bookstore in North America." The "enclosed" was a check for $5,000! Mark you, this good friend knew nothing about what the Captain was saying to us, but she was obviously in touch with the Master and obedient to His promptings. That letter sealed it for us. Thank you, Lord. Now, You show us where.

One of the places we had looked at some years earlier was Scranton, Pennsylvania. We decided to look at it again more closely. Then, who should come into my office but a couple from Scranton! It was what they had come to talk about which almost floored me. They started with the comment, "We understand CLC does not open bookstores in the States." Then they continued, "We feel Scranton needs an evangelical bookstore and we are considering opening one! Can you give us some advice?" So I told them our story and how the Lord seemed to be leading us back into the bookstore ministry—and that we had planned to look again at Scranton! They were delighted with the news. They encouraged us to proceed and assured us of their interest and readiness to help in any possible way, which they did.

The following year, when we were ready to look for property, it was this good brother who contacted the real estate agents for us. Finally we made an offer on a building right in the heart of the city; but the day before we signed, a fire ended negotiations—or so we thought. A couple of months later, the owners offered us the building at half the figure we had offered them! We had intended to completely remodel the store, so the fire, which was quite minimal and had caused no structural damage, presented no problem.

By the end of February, 1977 a lovely new store was opened to the public. Several have found the Lord within its walls. Others come for prayer and fellowship. And, of course, vital Christian literature blesses lives.

That same year a second store was opened, this time in the greater Philadelphia area. Actually it replaced the bookroom at Fort Washington, just five miles away, and opened the door to a much wider clientele. From the beginning people expressed their interest with enthusiasm. Its lovely, large windows attract attention, especially the flags. On the inside window-ledge there are over forty of them, each small flag representing a country where

CLC has a similar bookcenter. It is interesting to see customers spotting "their" flag, especially if they are just visiting the United States. And for a few of these international customers we even have some literature in their language. How glad they are to find it.

This multi-language service has just begun to take shape. It has tremendous potential and is already beginning to meet a very real need throughout the country. CLC Britain has had a multi-language program for some years, but this one in the States started when one of our newer workers expressed interest in an overseas ministry but was not able to go in person. We shared this idea with her and she seized at the opportunity to begin developing the program.

But it was not until 1980 that things really began to move. Now that the news is spreading, response is increasing rapidly. In a right sense, it could almost get out of hand! It won't, although we will certainly have to see personnel with a working knowledge of some of these languages called into our ranks.

Take Spanish as an example. It is the fastest growing minority language in the States, with close to twelve million people of Hispanic descent. There are also more than three-quarters of a million people of Indian background, over half a million Japanese, close to half a million Chinese, well over a quarter of a million Filipinos, and so it goes. Probably several hundred languages are spoken on the North American continent at any given time.

Surely the best way to reach them, whether they are neighbors on the same street or fellow students in a university, is to give them something to read in their own language. This is the whole idea of the multi-language program: putting the "tool" of print into the hands of concerned Christians, and they in turn passing the word along to those who need to know the good news of Christ here and in other countries as well.

In March 1981 a supply of Arabic materials was mailed to a businessman in New Jersey. He in turn took the books on his business trip to Saudi Arabia! In January $50 worth of books were mailed to national pastors in Zaire at the request of retired missionaries living in Florida.

Then, there is the monthly booktable at the Tenth Presbyterian Church in Philadelphia serviced by CLC. It is just for international students—90 per cent of whom are non-Christians. What a joy to see someone buying an Arabic New Testament for an Egyptian student studying at the University of Pennsylvania.

Here is what some who use this multi-language service have to say: "Thanks for the tapes and literature which you sent. The Holy Spirit has convicted a Laotian family of their sins and they have accepted Jesus into their hearts. We are looking for more tapes to help them grow. Have you any books about the Holy Spirit and how to pray? They are witnessing to their Laotian friends. How we thank God for the seed that has been planted in their lives."

Another wrote: "Thank you for your extra kindness and personal attention to my letter for Japanese books. I really appreciate your research and Christian help in this. My wife is Japanese and prefers reading Japanese to English—also she has quite a ministry to unsaved Japanese ladies who are married to military husbands. Some have been saved through her ministry." He had ordered $50 worth of Japanese books.

Spanish is the top seller at the moment but Chinese is next! A pastor of a Chinese church in Philadelphia bought $150 worth of Chinese books. They celebrated March 22 as a special "Wang Ming Tao Sunday" at their church.

So far, stock in thirty-nine languages is carried at Fort Washington, and the Scripture booklets entitled *Help From Above* and *God's Simple Plan of Salvation* are available in at least fifteen other languages. Just where the stopping point will be, who knows!? As Virginia Steffel rightly says: "Making the program known, and the personnel to keep updated order sheets and stock on hand, are the two essentials to expansion of this vital and exciting ministry." Christine Morris, a faithful overtimer in the multi-language department, adds this plea: "Use these foreign language books from CLC and you may have an opportunity to save a life for eternity."

Surely the *mission field* is at our own doorstep. If through our combined efforts just one of these international people finds Christ, and then returns to his homeland to share the good news with his countrymen, it will have been a rewarding accomplishment. But the potential is far greater than that.

One more ministry, also multi-language, is in Honolulu— where our fourth U.S. bookcenter was opened in 1978. This was done jointly by CLC Tokyo and CLC Fort Washington, though the vision for it came from Japan. Four languages are currently handled—Japanese, Chinese, Korean and English. Others will be added as the need arises. Eiko Soronaka has been doing a great job almost single-handedly but, consequently, has not been free to handle outreach, such as booktables or book parties. This year things should improve when Phyllis Trim, with CLC in the Eastern Caribbean for twenty years, joins forces with Eiko.

So we have seen steady expansion of the work in the United States over the last six years. Just what the future holds is not clear at the moment, but one thing is certain. As new workers continue to join us for the home front or for overseas, there will always be a task awaiting them, either filling an existing gap, strengthening a present operation, or advancing to new opportunities.

Nineteen seventy-five was also an exciting year for Canada. The John Daveys were back from their assignment in the West Indies and ready to begin their leadership in Canada. They would work toward an autonomous operation of the ministry as agreed by the previous Annual Conference. Now, where to begin? Our only bookstore was in Montreal. However, a link had been retained in Toronto. This is where the mission side of the work had been maintained. Through the kind help of several, and more recently of Percy and Joyce Page (who later assumed leadership), the mission books had been kept, receipts issued, support funds sent to Canadian workers, and general correspondence handled. Because the Daveys expected to spend most of their time developing public relations, sharing about the work, and ministering from the Word in churches, it seemed best that they make Toronto their base. That was the right decision, for something more than they had anticipated was soon to unfold.

John later called it "another glorious example of God working on both sides and from both ends." Through two members of the newly enlarged Advisory Committee, he was introduced to Mrs. Betty Smith. Seven years earlier she and her husband, Victor, had opened a Christian bookstore on Avenue Road, and because of his recent heart attack they agreed that others should carry on this ministry. In God's ordering CLC was to assume this responsibility. The Lord sealed this decision a few days later while John and Ethel were visiting a friend whose interest in CLC went back to the mid-forties. Indeed, his wife had given many hours of voluntary service to the bookstore for several years. She was now with the Lord and her husband wanted CLC to have a check for $1,000 in her memory. At the committee meeting the next day the chairman summed it up this way: "We can only second what God has already moved!"

So on August 1, 1975, CLC officially took over the Christian Book Center at 1757 Avenue Road, Toronto. By 1981 this store had become multi-language, for today there must be at least twenty languages spoken in cosmopolitan Toronto.

Commenting about this return to the city John had said, "We expect to see Him do this increasingly—both here and in other parts of Canada—for the extension of this ministry." That was almost prophetic, for by the summer of 1976 a small mail-order and wholesale department had developed. Ethel began introducing book parties. John was getting increasing opportunities in the churches. Yes, indeed, the ministry was expanding, but there was more to come.

In 1978 a fifty-acre parcel of land in Elgin, midway between Kingston and Ottawa, had been given to CLC. Was this the Lord's answer for a central administrative headquarters for Canada? That could be, but as a first step it became clear that this land should be used for the wholesale program; not only for English books, but for many of the other languages now being used throughout the Dominion. This would be especially true of French, which is now the first language of Quebec and is steadily reaching all across the country. For the present this is being handled in Montreal.

So a building program was launched, and by late summer of 1979 the first building was completed: a house for the Purdy family, with a full basement for warehouse and offices. This area was planned so that as soon as the next building is completed it can become another complete apartment for staff. This year, 1981, has seen the beginning of that next building, which will include an office block, warehouse and shipping room. Another long-range possibility for this Elgin property is development of a bookmobile ministry to operate in the rural areas of Ontario and Quebec. Some ambitious friends in western Canada have talked about donating a couple of Greyhound buses for this purpose!

Then it was Montreal's turn. Something had to be done because the lease on the shop was to expire in May, 1980. We were not seriously interested in renewing the lease because there was not sufficient room. The work had grown so, especially during the last few years. Well, the Lord had His answer on Guy Street just one block away.

Two brand new shops had stood empty for almost three years. Perhaps they were reserved for CLC. They were certainly attractive and on a main two-way thoroughfare in the city. The conviction grew that this was God's place for us. More than that, one of them could be for French literature and the other for English, urged Rose Burrowes, who for many years was with CLC in Guyana, her home country, but was now part of the Montreal team. Was that too wild a dream? No. The conviction grew with the staff that this "dream" was *His will* also.

Negotiations were completed, the owner giving us permission to remove part of the dividing wall, thus making one store and yet creating a two-shop atmosphere. By early April the move from Mackay Street to Guy Street took place. Roger Perry, assisted by Tim Harris and others, had done a fantastic job installing all the fixtures and fittings. Inside and out the place looked so attractive and inviting. As planned, the store on the left was English and the store on the right was French, each with its own counter and cash register—and yet one CLC center. The official dedication was held on May 24, 1980. Pastor Pierre Bergeron of Montreal and Dr. Paul Smith of the People's Church, Toronto, both spoke, passing on encouraging words.

The day after opening a young man from Hull came into the store and was so excited at finding so much French literature that he shared the good news with his pastor that evening. The next day both were in the store. The pastor exclaimed with delight, "Now at last we have our own French bookstore." Between them they bought over $500 worth of French material!

The fact is that the demand for French literature is growing so fast we can hardly keep enough stock on hand. There is a genuine hunger for God in Quebec. Now three possibilities face us: to open more bookstores throughout the province; to put a French-literature bookmobile on the roads; or to develop a full retail mail-order program. We are thankful for Davyd and Leona Hepburn who are heading up the French side of the work in Montreal. Their nine years in the Ivory Coast, West Africa, and their bilingual abilities are proving most valuable in this developing literature ministry in Quebec, but to do all that must be done we look forward to more workers sharing with us in this exciting adventure.

The same is true of the English side of the work. Clara Bort is doing a Trojan job, but reinforcements are needed. A new challenge is before us, too. People of other ethnic backgrounds are asking for literature in their language, so in 1981 we have begun to meet this need with limited stocks of Spanish, Portuguese, German, Italian and Arabic. Other languages will be added as the need becomes apparent.

What a difference being in the right location makes—even if it is only one or two blocks away. The 1980 figures for Montreal show a 50 per cent increase over the previous year in the old location. My, how I wish there was room to tell of the fruit which is being seen. Needy hearts are being ministered to. Lives are being touched and transformed. The beam of that lighthouse on Guy Street, through its "books which radiate light," is penetrating far and showing many a searcher the way.

The John Daveys, after handing over the leadership to Percy and Joyce Page, now reside in Edmonton, Alberta. They are back to their public relations ministry which they thought was to be their main task back in 1975! Undoubtedly, their big contribution to the work now will be to inspire younger people to "come over and help us" with the exciting adventures still ahead for Canada—and from Canada, to the world.

38

SPRINGBOARD TO CHINA

There was one more significant journey in 1975. CLC Japan planned to celebrate their twenty-fifth year and had kindly invited me to share in this anniversary. Travel plans were made to include visits to the Philippines, Hong Kong and Korea first. While it was refreshing to again fellowship with our workers and see the progress being made in our three CLC countries, the focus of this journey zeroed in on Hong Kong.

Bessie and I had been there in 1966 and we had promised David Adeney that the Crusade would keep an open mind about helping the literature work in the Colony. Signs of possible involvement began to develop when Bob Sjoblom paid occasional visits to Hong Kong in connection with his Living Books for Asia program, which was then based in Manila. Here he met Mrs. Yuan and the Bellman House Publishers, or to use its Chinese derivation, "The Morning Star Publishers."

Mr. and Mrs. Yuan had started their literature ministry in 1948. The flood of refugees from mainland China following World War II had pressed them into this decision. Surely, here was a golden opportunity to put the message of hope into their hands. For twenty-three years this devoted couple labored tirelessly to publish original Chinese manuscripts and to translate books from the West into Chinese. In 1971 Mr. Yuan went to be with the Lord, but his wife bravely carried on the vital ministry of the Morning Star Publishers. Now in 1975 Mrs. Yuan was looking to the future. She knew others would have to take over from her. But who?

Through Bob Sjoblom's visits she had learned about CLC, its

missionary literature commission, and how it was reaching out to the ends of the earth. Surely this would include the Chinese people around the world. If so, would CLC be the group to carry on the Bellman House ministry, making its influence even more far-reaching than she and her husband had been able to do? The conviction grew with her. Even though others had indicated an interest in continuing the ministry, she knew that CLC was the group God wanted to assume this responsibility. Therefore, she persisted in her approach to CLC whenever Bob was in Hong Kong.

Of course Bob had shared all of this with me and with Bob Gerry, CLC's International Secretary. When I was graciously invited to share in Japan's twenty-fifth anniversary celebration, this seemed to be a God-appointed opportunity to take a closer look at the Hong Kong situation and CLC's possible involvement. Thus it was that on October 9, Bob Sjoblom and I traveled to Hong Kong from the Philippines. Bob Gerry joined us there, and for six days the three of us unhurriedly reviewed the complete situation. We made many valuable contacts and, of course, discussed all the details with Mrs. Yuan (who understood English) and her close advisor, Mr. John Wang.

By early November I was back in Fort Washington and our findings were shared with the staff. Once again the Captain was in charge, and He clearly indicated that this was His time and His way for CLC's involvement in Hong Kong. He impressed something else on us: this was to be a steppingstone to help meet the ever-pressing need for Christian literature in the mainland.

Officially CLC took over the Bellman House ministry on January 1, 1976, but it was several months before everything was finalized. The Bob Sjobloms took up residence in Hong Kong and began to gather a team of workers around them, for there was much to be done.

During the twenty-eight years of Bellman House history almost one hundred titles in Chinese and some in English had been published. Altogether, with books they were carrying of other publishers, their catalog listed 150 titles. At least three-quarters of their publications were of Chinese authorship—original writings, not translations—and this is the direction CLC is now continuing: to encourage Chinese writers.

In our first full year, sixteen Chinese titles and twelve English titles were printed. Some of these were reprints (with improved full-color covers) and some were new titles, but the pace was quickening. New manuscripts had been approved, awaiting time and funds to get them through the presses and onto the world markets. Then things began to happen on the mainland.

Opportunities to get books across the Hong Kong-China border increased, and by 1979 there seemed to be a new climate developing on the part of the government. Tourists were welcomed. Business with the West was being encouraged and, more significantly, churches long since closed were being allowed to open—approximately eighty of them by 1981. An edition of the Scriptures—50,000 Bibles and 85,000 New Testaments—was printed on government presses in China in 1980.

With this new freedom new opportunities of fellowship with believers became possible. Earlier estimates had given the figure of Christians in China at two million. This has now been increased to ten million—and this is still only an estimate. The actual number could be much higher. By all observations this number includes many young people, especially in the numerous "house churches" scattered throughout the land.

One thing is clear. Whatever the future holds, the church in China will continue to grow. It does not appear that the Western missionary will have a place there in the foreseeable future. The urgent need of the hour is to see the present believers grounded in the faith, and this will be done almost entirely through the radio and the printed page. This is clearly the request—almost the demand—of the church within China: "Send us Bibles; send us books." Along with others, CLC is trying to respond. It is a big undertaking.

What we are doing could almost be called "Operation Raindrop," but every drop—every piece of literature—counts. Of that we are certain.

292 / The Foolishness of God

One of the books CLC publishes is *Streams in the Desert* by Mrs. Charles Cowman. It was always a favorite among the Chinese but now is in ever-increasing demand. Three years ago a three thousand printing was adequate for a year's supply. In 1980 a seven thousand printing lasted less than six months. A second printing that year was increased to ten thousand and more recently to twenty thousand!

Thankfully we have a big God, for this is a BIG challenge calling for dedicated manpower and a constant flow of finances to meet what is undoubtedly the biggest opportunity CLC has ever faced.

I am tempted to write in more detail but that would be unwise. Suffice it to say that things are happening. The word is getting around in China today. Indeed, many believe this is China's hour for which she has long waited. The fruit of the faithful is now being seen. During the thirty years of silence occasional lone voices were heard, but we were never sure how many Watchman Nees and Wang Ming Taos there were behind the Bamboo Curtain. Now we know there was a veritable army of the redeemed! A quiet but resolute testimony was being maintained. The church was far from dead or dying; it was actually growing. This is the church which is now meeting the new opportunity of the eighties. Its people are now gathering in the harvest which their expectant faith has made possible. The seed they had "sown in dishonor" is now being "raised in glory." Another blessed resurrection day is operative to the eye of faith.

There was one other interesting development in 1975.

I had met Hugh and Christine Canagasabey when I was in New Zealand two years earlier. They were studying at the Auckland Bible Institute and asked to meet me following my talk to the students. Their homeland, Sri Lanka, needed Christian literature and they felt that God might have a place for them to help meet this need. The Lord confirmed this to them, so after graduation they went to CLC Australia for training before returning to their own country.

Sri Lanka, the Resplendent Land, formerly known as Ceylon, is a literate country second only to Japan in Asia. There is freedom to publish and distribute Christian literature, but until recently no Christian books could be imported. Therefore, when the Canagasabeys returned to their homeland, they began a lending library along with some limited publishing of tracts.

A bookstore seemed to be out of the question—except to faith! This faith was quickened when the government lifted the ban on imports in 1979. Quickly, orders for literature were placed. A search for premises was made in Colombo, but without success. Perhaps the best way to get the books to the people would be through a mobile ministry, Hugh reasoned. Vehicles in Sri Lanka were hard to come by—but not to faith, always alive and expectant. When International Secretary Bob Gerry learned of this thought of mobile outreach he shared the need with his colleagues in Japan. They gladly agreed to send a bookmobile to Sri Lanka as a gift—part of their annual appropriations to overseas ministries.

This arrived in 1979 and was quickly put to work. Still the thought of a bookcenter persisted. Then light came. Try the town of Kandy—an important crossroads almost in the center of the nation. In a remarkable way a fine new shop was made available and was ready to open for business just before Christmas 1980. Kandy's central location may well prove to make the mobile ministry more productive as it reaches out north, south, east and west.

Once again it would seem that the Lord has allowed CLC to be on hand just when new opportunities are emerging. We have been right on Divine schedule—"for such a time as this."

39

TRANSITION

The following year, 1976, proved to be exceptionally full. It almost takes my breath away as I think of it now. Yet God was totally adequate, keeping us both in good health and expectant in spirit. The year was rewarding in every way.

There were four journeys overseas. First, in January I went to Panama, for fellowship and discussion regarding plans for this new CLC responsibility. The next stops were in Colombia and Venezuela, again for discussion and decision making. In Trinidad we joined forces, for Bessie had flown from New York for meetings in both Trinidad and Barbados.

In May I made a fifteen-day trip to Brazil. Once again, I was refreshed in spirit to see the continual growth in the work. The new multi-language center in Sao Paulo was a delight to behold.

On May 31 Bessie and I returned to England where a series of meetings had been arranged. One which had been agreed to almost two years earlier was a particular joy. We shared in the Jubilee weekend of Bethel Chapel in Chignal, which is now a suburb of Chelmsford, Essex. Years before Fred and Rose Whybrow joined CLC, the Lord had used them, particularly Mrs. Whybrow, to bring this chapel into being. People in the village had been systematically visited and witnessed to. Some had found the Lord and this had resulted in this wider ministry, with regular Sunday and mid-week services. It is just another example of the Law of Use in operation.

Altogether some fifteen meetings had been arranged, which included my being the missionary speaker at the first Southern Keswick Convention (an outgrowth of the famous Keswick Convention in the Lake District of Northumberland), on the Isle of Wright, just across the Southampton Channel.

We returned to the States on July 9, just in time to share in the third International Council, again held at the Missionary Retreat Fellowship in Pennsylvania. Then on August 6 there was a wedding—our younger daughter, Janet's! That was a day we will never forget as we welcomed Tom Courtney into the family.

Finally, I spent a month in South America from October 22 to November 17. Ten stops were made along the way, which included all the CLC countries of the continent, plus Trinidad and Barbados. Tucked in between these journeys was the "daily care" of the work in North America as well as constant correspondence with other countries overseas.

In close fellowship with Bob Hiley, this correspondence included CLC's possible involvement in one of the countries of the Middle East. This culminated when an American couple, who had had previous experience working among Muslims in Africa, went to a Middle Eastern stronghold of Mohammedanism during 1976. A quiet, unpretentious, but effective ministry continues there to this day.

This ended one of the busiest years we have ever experienced. It was one that again left us full of praise, rejoicing in all that we had witnessed of the constant growth of the work, and the ever-increasing flow of life-giving literature to the ends of the earth.

The following year we concentrated on developments in the States and Canada, which saw new doors opening as we have recorded in a previous chapter. Then in early 1978 we were overseas once more, again to Panama, Colombia, Venezuela and Trinidad. This proved to be the last journey we would make as leaders of the ministry in North America. After thirty-seven years of continuous leadership, first in Britain and then in North America, as well as in the International Office, we stepped out of administrative responsibilities, as required by our International Constitution. Bob and Dorothy Gerry, who had served so effectively in Japan for twenty-eight years, took over from Bessie and me on July 1, 1979. Bob also continues his responsibilities as International Secretary, which means he carries a very full load.

What would now be ahead for us –rocking chairs, fishing rods, retirement? Hardly!

To allow the Gerrys a free hand in their leadership, we felt it right that we should not continue to live in Fort Washington. Much to our delight, for we were both brought up with beaches and sea gulls as a way of life, the staff graciously made a lovely apartment in Ocean City, New Jersey, available to us. Well, it's more than an apartment, for they saw the possibility of other uses for a house at a seaside resort. The house in which we have our apartment also serves as a place for furloughing overseas workers, and for CLC personnel in the States and Canada, where they can get away for vacation, or even for just a quiet weekend of retreat and renewal.

The Adamses, still functioning as full members of the Fort Washington team, have been assigned to deputation and public relations. This is keeping us busy as doors of opportunity continue to open here in North America and overseas.

Perhaps it was significant that in the very first month of the eighties we were back in "the old country." It was a four-day visit to share in "Ma Why's" Victory March, for a few days earlier she had completed her earthly assignment and crossed over to "the other side." What a welcome she must have received. She had run well and she had given nearly thirty-nine of her eighty-six years to the ministry of Christian literature in CLC. Her name lives on, for her husband, "Pa Why," is still on course at eighty-eight! Also their daughter, Doris, who first served with CLC in Uruguay, continues, now with her husband, Allan Race, to make an important contribution to the CLC ministry in the United Kingdom.

Three months later we were back in Britain for a stay of three months. After ten days with our relations in Cornwall we began an extensive deputation program, covering approximately five thousand miles, and speaking seventy-two times in England, Scotland, and Northern Ireland. We left Britain encouraged by the evident interest in the CLC ministry and an overall sense that there is a new climate of spiritual awareness throughout the country.

We returned to the States in time for another International Council. These are held every four years, and it is amazing how quickly four years seem to slip by! At the previous gathering we had set some four-year goals, and it was encouraging to see the progress which had been made toward reaching them. Evidence, once again, that this is an ongoing ministry within each country and to the ends of the earth.

After a busy autumn of meetings, we returned again to the Caribbean and spent three wonderful weeks over Christmas and the New Year with the Almack family in Barbados. Bill's mother was also able to come, so this made it a special get-together for all of us. Bessie and I had several opportunities for ministry. On Christmas Sunday morning I gave the message at a local church to a congregation of more than five hundred. This assembly had only begun earlier in the year.

It was in this Caribbean area that the forty-fifth country was added to the worldwide CLC family: the French island of Martinique. The work here had been started some years earlier by Erwin Buchmann from Switzerland. Discussions about the possibility of CLC taking over this ministry had been going on for several months, and by early 1980 all was settled. In mid-February the bookstore in Fort-de-France and its related ministries passed into CLC hands. Mary Lovett, who formerly served with CLC in the Ivory Coast, had arrived in the island the previous October. She felt at home immediately, quickly adjusting to daily routines, so when the transfer took place she was ready to assume charge of the work.

It has gone forward steadily. Recently, regular visits have been made to market stalls, and a bookmobile outreach has been added. Book tables in churches are also getting the work more widely known, so the future of this ministry in the French Caribbean looks very promising. This decade will see some significant advances as more personnel, locally and from overseas, join the present team.

Country number forty-six was added on January 1, 1981: Finland. CLC's contact with Finland goes back twenty years, when Christian Finnish students were in London to learn English and found fellowship at CLC headquarters in the city. Through them the news spread quickly to others in Finland. Every year friends of those first students came to England and purchased books. More links were forged, and CLC discovered that numbers of young Finns desired to serve the Lord, but they were aware only of limited opportunities for missionary work.

The links between the two countries kept growing. The CLC catalog, mailed directly to contacts in Finland, produced orders, and ever-increasing quantities of English books were shipped out by the mail-order department in Alresford. At the 1975 British Annual Conference, the staff agreed that the time had come for a closer study of the situation in Finland, so Bob Hiley of the IRIS Department got busy.

Bob made contact with a Christian bookstore in Helsinki. The directors of this bookstore agreed to greatly increase the stock of English books and, accordingly, to increase floor space to accommodate this new development. The Free Church of Finland, under whose auspices the Kirja Paiva Bookshop was operating, made 1978 a special year for Literature and Mission. The program included a workshop for church bookstall workers, and Bob Hiley was invited to help arrange the schedule and take part in the training course. That same year visits were made to many of the Free Church congregations. A large bus was fitted with shelves and filled with books—English along one side and Finnish along the other. Bob Hiley and Alasdair Cameron, Overseas Secretary of the British CLC, joined the Finnish workers for the month of November. Together they visited twenty-six towns, sold close to twenty thousand dollars worth of literature, and spoke to enthusiastic congregations, often drawn from miles around.

In 1980 the Free Church of Finland indicated that they planned to dispose of their Helsinki bookstore, and CLC expressed interest. Details were worked out and an agreement was reached. CLC would take over the ministry as of January 1, 1981.

The Lord had His prepared instrument. Mrs. Kaija Roinila, the manager, applied to CLC and became the Crusade's first full-time Finnish worker. Kaija was greatly encouraged when, upon sharing her leading with her church, they agreed to recognize her as a home missionary and to support her financially.

We expect to see other Finnish people joining CLC ranks: to strengthen the work in Helsinki; to enable further outreach within the country; and to serve as overseas missionaries with CLC.

So already two more countries have been added in the eighties—and there are still eight and a half years left in the decade! Where will CLC be as it draws to a close? How many new countries? How many new bookcenters and bookmobiles will there be within the borders of our present forty-six countries? Will our personnel have reached the one thousand mark?

We live expectantly. Faith says a confident "Yes." Perhaps some who have read this book will be part of the answer! Rise up, O men and women of God, the King is coming and we must "occupy until He comes."

SECTION VI

PURGED...TO BRING FORTH MORE FRUIT
John 15:2

Every branch in me that beareth not fruit he taketh away; and every branch that beareth fruit, he purgeth it, that it may bring forth more fruit.
John 15:2

40

ANOTHER DECADE DAWNS

Our story is finished. Well, no, not finished; this is just a convenient stopping place. On November 1, 1981, we will have completed forty years of CLC history.

Twenty years ago, Norman Grubb graciously prepared his *Leap of Faith,* which covered the first twenty years. He had been very much a part of the Crusade's beginning and early growth. He neither served in one of our bookcenters nor operated a bookmobile, but as the man of faith that he is, Mr. Grubb saw the potential of literature. He knew of the steadily growing literacy around the world, and consequently he gave Bessie and me his unqualified approval as we began to develop a Christian literature program to help meet the need. He urged us on constantly by his enthusiasm, putting confidence in us as a young, untried couple. He could well have found grounds for a much more cautious approach, taking a try-them-out-first attitude. Instead he preferred to believe that the Holy Spirit within us should be given unrestricted liberty to bring into being the ministry of Christian literature which He had planned.

We do not wish to single out Norman Grubb or Ken and Bessie Adams, for without doubt the Founder of this Crusade is none other than God Himself. He only needed channels through which to do His specific work.

That is how it has been all along. With the vision more clearly defined, other "channels" were needed. Thankfully, many people have responded over these forty years.

We have mentioned earlier that our complement of full-time personnel numbers 594 as of December 31, 1980. A truer picture would be that the full complement has reached at least a thousand over these past forty years. Every person who has stepped across the CLC threshhold, whether as a short-termer for just a matter of months, or one who has been with us for several years before moving on, has had a share in bringing the Crusade to its present dimensions. All will share in the "spiritual dividends" when the records are opened and the Judge of all will *do right*.

Then there is the band of faithful pray-ers, who have believed with us and whose personal faith has made us strong. The givers, both individuals and churches, have made possible the advances we have recorded, by their generous support. All have laid up treasure in heaven with their investment of time in prayer or finances.

What can we say of those "helps" who have made such a vital contribution to the work? Some gave just a few hours a week in the print shop. Others gave their fingers to walk over typewriters. Still others assisted in the shipping departments, getting the books out to the readers. Many others have given one, two, three days a week or more to the bookstores, meeting customers, guiding them in their choice of helpful books, and offering spiritual counsel. The work worldwide just would not be where it is today without the help of those who have volunteered their time and talent to the Lord for use in producing and promoting His literature crusade. They, too, will share the "dividends" of their time investment.

We have deliberately woven this story around our own lives. We wanted our readers to see that God is no respecter of persons. He doesn't first demand a good education or adequate academic qualifications before He will use us. We do not downplay education; I have often wished I had a better one. I have had to fight an inferiority complex many times—and in one sense still do—because of my educational limitations; both of us have.

What we have learned, however, is that both limited education and advanced education have to go to the Cross. They must be sanctified. They must be totally surrendered to Him. "Surrender"—perhaps that is the wrong word. Too often we bemoan that to be a true disciple we must give up this and give up that. What a battle this has often proven to be! I can almost hear the Captain saying, "O fools to believe that!" Why do we struggle, when surrender is the highest honor and the happiest privilege—and the simplest solution!

That is what we have proven over the years. Life has been so full and exciting! Not that it has all been a "bed of roses"; there must be travail if there is to be birth, and travail there has been— even to the point of considering giving up, quitting, resigning; the grass looked so much greener elsewhere. It is a sort of paradox. In one breath we say giving all to Jesus is the simplest solution, and then in the next breath we talk about being tempted to quit, to change course, or to change missions!

From observation, we have seen that a change of course is not necessarily the answer, especially if we have not faced up to the real issue and submitted to the refining work of the Holy Spirit in the place where He has put us. It will still have to be faced somewhere down the road. Very humbly we can say that by His grace we have kept on course. We have been tempted, yes, but never actually turned aside.

Now what of the future?

The CLC story is certainly not finished. There is more, much more, ahead. New countries must be entered, or re-entered. Several are being researched even now and perhaps before we have actually reached our fortieth birthday on November 1, another country will have been entered. Within our present countries, new advances will have taken place. Even while writing this story, which has taken more than six months, changes have taken place, so that a paragraph or two had to be rewritten to keep the facts correct!

The word "Crusade" in our name is full of meaning. We are an army, and an advancing army. World conquest for Jesus is our goal because that is what He commissioned His disciples to do. One of our hymns keynotes it: "The whole wide world for Jesus, this shall our watchword be!"

He gave us a platform from which to carry out the mandate

to "evangelize through literature." C.T. Studd, who wrote those stirring words on his way to Africa, "If Jesus Christ be God and died for me, then no sacrifice can be too great for me to make for Him," also talked about "five smooth stones" to be used in the battle against the giants in our path and the enemy of our cause. Well, CLC has "five smooth stones": Faith, Sacrifice, Fellowship, Holiness and Love. May our Captain help us to use them well in the years ahead. We dare not deviate from these well-tried and well-proven standards.

It will not be easy to stay true. We must vigilantly guard against the desire to budget carefully before taking action and against the encroachments of affluency. Some would advise that we be "less mystical" about our walk in the Spirit along the Highway of Holiness. Others would tell us not to "go overboard" in our love and thereby fail to discern the subtle dangers of spiritual ecumenicity.

Guard, we will. Go on, we will, turning not to the right nor to the left. Jesus told us clearly that this gospel must be published as a witness to all nations, after which He would return.

We are nearly there. Even so, come, Lord Jesus.

INDEX